Privatization, Deregulation and the Macroeconomy

Aan de marktmaffia

Privatization, Deregulation and the Macroeconomy

Measurement, Modelling and Policy

Peter A.G. van Bergeijk
Robert C.G. Haffner

Edward Elgar
Cheltenham, UK ● Brookfield, US

Published by
Edward Elgar Publishing Limited
8 Lansdown Place
Cheltenham
Glos GL50 2HU
UK

Edward Elgar Publishing Company
Old Post Road
Brookfield
Vermont 05036
US

British Library Cataloguing in Publication Data
Bergeijk, Peter van, 1959–
    Privatization, deregulation and the macroeconomy :
    measurement, modelling and policy
    1. Privatization 2. Economic policy 3. Macroeconomics
    I. Title II. Haffner, Robert C.G.
    338.6'1

Library of Congress Cataloguing in Publication Data
Bergeijk, Peter A.G. van, 1959–
    Privatization, deregulation, and the macroeconomy : measurement,
    modelling, and policy / Peter A.G. van Bergeijk, Robert C.G.
    Haffner
    Includes bibliographical references and indexes.
    1. Economic policy. 2. Economic policy—Mathematical models.
    3. Privatization. 4. Deregulation. 5. Microeconomics.
    6. Macroeconomics. I. Haffner, Robert C.G., 1970–   . II. Title.
    HD87.B463 1995
    338.9—dc20
                                                                96–6433
                                                                CIP

ISBN 1 85898 347 9

Printed in Great Britain at the University Press, Cambridge

Contents

v

PART IV POLICY

Figures and Tables

Preface and Acknowledgements

This book reports on a sustained research programme on the macroeconomic consequences of microeconomic rigidity and its reform. The aim of the book is to provide a unifying framework for relevant material on privatization, deregulation and competition policy. These topics constitute an interrelated set of microeconomic policies that combat product market inertia and aim at structural reform of the economy through greater reliance on the market mechanism. The material on these issues is presently scattered in time, books, journals and the so-called grey literature (conference and working papers, pamphlets, etc.).

The project started in 1992 at the Ministry of Economic Affairs in the Research Unit of the Economic Policy Directorate. As privatization, deregulation and competition policy are still evolving, this book reports the results of an ongoing effort in applied policy analysis. The usual caveat applies: the book does not necessarily reflect the views of the government of the Netherlands.

Obviously such a project can only become a success with the (critical) support of employers and colleagues. Jarig van Sinderen stimulated this undertaking at the Ministry of Economic Affairs and supervised Robert Haffner's (1993) master's thesis on the measurement of the speed of price and profit adjustments.

Useful comments on parts of the manuscript were given by Harry van Dalen, Mathijs van Dijk, George Gelauff, Cees van Gent, Raymond Gradus, Gilbert van Hagen, Christiaan Hiddink, Alexander Italianer, Dick Kabel, Aad Kleijweg, Ernst van Koesveld, Simon Kuipers, Ruud de Mooij and Jelle Wijnstok, while numerous fellow economists at universities, international organizations, national ministries and central banks helped us by providing us with documents and work in progress.

We also benefited a lot from the comments of participants of the Tinbergen Institute's workshop on Industrial Organization (Rotterdam

1992), the International Joseph A. Schumpeter Society's congress on Economic Dynamism and Policy (Münster 1994) and a workshop on deregulation organized by the Research Center for Economic Policy (OCFEB) (Rotterdam 1993). Mathijs van Dijk and Gijs van Donselaar provided valuable research assistance. Bert Greve helped us in the preparation of the figures.

Material from the following sources is either edited, updated or partially reprinted and appears by kind permission of the editors of *Economisch-Statistische Berichten*, *De Economist* and *Kyklos*:

P.A.G. van Bergeijk and R.C.G. Haffner (1993), 'Op zoek naar dynamiek', *Economisch-Statistische Berichten* **78** (3894), pp. 52—6.

P.A.G. van Bergeijk, R.C.G. Haffner and P.M. Waasdorp (1993), 'Measuring the Speed of the Invisible Hand: The Macroeconomic Costs of Price Rigidity', *Kyklos* **44** (4), pp. 529—44.

D.I. Bos and P.A.G. van Bergeijk (1994), 'Structurele hervorming: ervaringen in Nieuw-Zeeland', *Economisch-Statistische Berichten* **79** (3989), pp. 1134—8.

R.C.G. Haffner and P.A.G. van Bergeijk (1994), 'The Economic Consequences of Dutch Politics', *De Economist* **142** (4), pp. 497—505.

J. van Sinderen, P.A.G. van Bergeijk, R.C.G. Haffner and P.M. Waasdorp (1994), 'De kosten van economische verstarring op macro-niveau', *Economisch-Statistische Berichten* **79** (3954), pp. 274—9.

Peter A.G. van Bergeijk and Robert C.G. Haffner
Nieuw Vennep and Den Haag

PART I
STRUCTURAL CHANGE

1. On the Macroeconomic Consequences of Microeconomic Reform

Since 1960 employment in the United States has increased by about 80 per cent; employment in Europe grew by only some 10 per cent. American jobs by and large were created in the private sector; Europe essentially relied on public sector jobs.[1] The labour market is not the only place where Europe is underperforming.[2] The comparative analysis of production, productivity, technology and international competitiveness often revealed the inflexibility and absence of economic dynamism which stood at the basis of the Eurosclerosis syndrome that was diagnosed by many in the early 1980s.[3] The European twin deficit with respect to economic dynamism and market flexibility is generally speaking not taken into consideration when discussing economic policy options (a welcome exception is the 1994 EU *White Paper on Unemployment*). As a consequence, the challenges to domestic policy making are often underestimated.[4]

It is increasingly being recognized that competition and dynamic entrepreneurship are the driving forces for cost minimization, innovation and adaptation to changes on the (world) market. Accordingly, privatization, deregulation and competition policy have been proposed as important elements of any strategy that aims at restoring or creating economic dynamism.

In this book we deal with the questions of, on the one hand, how market structure, (lax) competition policy, (over-)regulation, collusive behaviour, etc. may influence macroeconomic performance through their impact on the adjustment process of the markets for goods and services and, on the other hand, how economic policies that aim at larger flexibility can be analysed. The literature already covers much of the ground especially where the focus is on the impact of such rigidities at the individual market or sectoral level.[5]

The macroeconomic consequences of these microeconomic phenomena have not yet been satisfactorily analysed, however. This is especially true from an empirical point of view. Indeed, empirical applications of the available theoretical approaches are scarce. This is a relevant gap in economic knowledge as the functioning of microeconomic markets is bound to have effects on macroeconomic variables such as employment, per capita income growth and price stability. These variables are also among the principal goals of economic policy, so policy analysts, policy makers and politicians should take the effects of microeconomic phenomena into account. Microeconomic rigidities may influence both intermediate policy goals, the policy instruments and the sequencing of policies of structural adjustment.

The insufficient knowledge about both the functioning of markets for goods and services and its impact on macroeconomic performance is remarkable. The economics profession has paid much attention to the concept of labour market (in)flexibility, has developed concepts and indicators in order to measure the extent of labour market (in)flexibility and has related labour market (in)flexibility to an economy's growth and ability to adjust to changing circumstances. It would seem to be quite useful if a comparable research strategy could be followed with respect to the functioning of product markets (goods and services).[6]

This book is intended to serve as a stepping-stone for such a research strategy. It deals both with the diagnosis (or measurement) of product market inertia at the mesoeconomic level and with its consequences on the macroeconomic level. We do not consider ideological motivations for structural reform policies (Wright 1994, pp. 13—15 and 16—18, McAuley 1993 and Valdés 1995 provide succinct reviews of such motives). Suffice it to say that structural adjustment is needed in order to meet the challenges posed by globalization, environmental degradation, etc., as will be explained in the following section. However, we do focus on one important argument for privatization, deregulation and a more vigorous competition policy, which is the cost imposed on the economy by a lack of flexibility on both the product market and the labour market.

This cost can arise in the form of a welfare loss, but can more easily be measured in terms of production and employment forgone.

1.1   Structural Change

Structural change is the reform of policies and institutions in order to promote economic growth. The need for reform and adjustment derives from both the private sector and the government. In the private sector, consumer preferences are rapidly changing (cultural developments, individualization, increased mobility, etc.) while firms are facing continuous changes in the business environment (globalization, technological change). Government concern with structural change emerged due to public concerns related to the mature welfare state (inactivity, disincentives) and environmental concerns related to the need to develop the economy in an ecologically sustainable direction.

Indeed, it is generally acknowledged that constant change is a fundamental characteristic of countries and firms that operate on world markets where globalization of both consumption and production is today's tune. Modern communication technologies, new modes of transportation and the liberalization of international capital flows have reduced transportation costs and have revolutionalized production and management processes. Products are increasingly being produced and distributed within corporate networks. Many products have become international composites. Hence international exchange pertains not only to products but also (and increasingly) to research, design, marketing, advertising, financing and routine components and other services as well. These changes in society underline the need for flexibility. International competition is a major driving force of this trend, as it has become an important incentive for firms to minimize costs and to innovate products and production techniques.

The need to adjust to an ever-changing economic climate has been accompanied by environmental concerns that the production structure needs to change in order to allow for 'sustainable development' both in developing countries, emerging economies and the industrialized world. The goal of sustainable development, as set out in the Brundtland report (WCED 1987), implies that environmental policy is

targeted at restructuring the economy in a direction that is
environmentally more sound in terms of production and consumption
patterns. This definitely does not mean that economic activity *per se*
has to be reduced, but rather that the economy, so to say, needs to be
rearranged. This requires a fundamental transition towards other
economic activities that are not (or less) polluting and a concomitant
reallocation of the factors of production. The challenge posed by
sustainable development is to let this adjustment process work as
flexibly as possible.

The need for structural adjustment has also been felt because of
the present crisis of the welfare state and the globalization of the
world economic system. The question is how to deal with
multinational corporations that optimize their production processes by
deciding on the location of their core operations according to the
specific characteristics of many jurisdictions. This optimization
problem considers various aspects such as tax structures, quality and
quantity of the labour force, technological and physical infrastructure,
etc. Multinational corporations have become more 'footloose', as they
are constantly weighing the costs and benefits of remaining or
investing in a particular location. At the domestic level, relatively
generous welfare state benefits, national institutional arrangements,
high collective burdens, over-regulation and complicated decision-
making procedures distort incentives. This has a negative impact on
economic dynamism (see, for example, Snower 1993). Once the
disincentives from government intervention become too strong and
economic activity is too much discouraged, public expenditures will
need to be curtailed. If this leads to a reduction of public investment
in infrastructure, technology and education or if taxes are increased
instead, the attractiveness of the economy as a location for
multinational activities will deteriorate. These processes, however,
traditionally have not played a major role in analyses of policy topics,
as the consequences are revealed only during the course of time.
Their impact on the ability of a nation to meet external and domestic
challenges is a medium-term and possibly long-term process:

> It is with a medium-term perspective that the problems of unemployment,
> inflation and slow growth in many OECD countries have come to be closely
> identified with structural features of the economy, particularly within labour

markets and the supply sector, rather than trend or cyclical developments in the macroeconomy (Turner et al. 1993, p. 90).

Structural adjustment focuses attention on the need for flexibility of the economy, because more flexibility lowers the macroeconomic costs of any transition process (Killick 1995). Structural change in the real world requires that employees do more different activities during their working life than traditionally. Often they need to change jobs. Taken together, this requires frequent retraining, the removal of barriers to mobility between occupations and flexibility of wages. Likewise, capital goods need either to be adjusted or to be debited more quickly as changes in the economic system also change the optimal allocation of capital over sectors. Flexibility of the factors of production must be complemented by flexibility of institutions to result in economy wide flexibility. Sufficiently flexible formal rules and informal constraints (for example, norms of behaviour and conventions) are necessary to allow the economy to adapt to new opportunities (North 1994).

1.2   Three Strategies to Tackle Product Market Inertia

We use the term product market inertia to indicate situations where an economy or a market is ill-structured to react to external shocks. Essentially, product market inertia is a lack of adaptability and flexibility of markets. This may be due to bureaucracy, governmental policies such as regulation which limit the flexibility of the companies on these markets, and the absence of any pressure of competition. Product market inertia may also be caused by collusive behaviour which weakens the functioning of the market mechanism. In this book, we will confine ourselves to the economics of structural change. Although structural change takes place in a wider policy context, it may pay to consider the three policy elements which constitute the basis for any strategy that aims at tackling product market inertia (Helm et al. 1991): privatization, deregulation and competition policy.

Privatization
Privatization is a policy that reduces the scope and functions of the public sector. This means that privatization goes beyond the sale of

physical assets. Some (for example, Kornai 1992, p. 154) simply equate privatization to a process that allows the share of the private sector to grow until the private sector has become the dominant sector of the economy. In our analysis, privatization comprises the set of policies that:

● sell (stock in) or recapitalize public firms to private investors;
● aim at substituting private for public services (among others by contracting out public service implementation); and
● encourage the application of the direct benefit principle and introduce private sector principles, management techniques and procedures into public sectors.

Deregulation
Often 'deregulation' is used as a very broad concept (admittedly a bit like in the title of this book). The term is ambiguous when it concerns areas such as government expenditure, taxation, and industrial policy (Fane 1995, p. 2). In order to provide clarity we confine ourselves to a stricter definition of deregulation, which in many cases is synonymous with liberalizing the economy. Deregulation in our approach is a strategy that aims at three goals simultaneously:

● less detailed rules, especially less competition-restricting rules;
● greater use of market forces; and
● a clearer division of responsibilities between the market and the public sector.

Deregulation can be attempted in a number of different gradations (Geelhoed 1993). First, deregulation can involve a repositioning of the respective roles of the public and the private sector. Such a repositioning can originate in a changed attitude towards the perceived necessity and ability of public policies to correct market failure. Technological developments and international economic integration have had a major impact on this changing role of the public sector. Second, in the case of a rearrangement of public policy, the position of the public sector *vis-à-vis* the private sector remains unchanged, but the goal and ambition of the intervention are altered. An example of a rearrangement is the streamlining of an establishment law. Many OECD countries regulate the entry to specific professions by demanding a certain level of professional skills and general commerce knowledge. Knowledge of basic accounting principles is an example of the latter. Although the number and strictness of the establishment obligations are reduced, governments continue to assume responsibility for a minimum quality of the services provided. Third, the least far-reaching form of deregulation simply involves a change in the instruments of government intervention in order to strengthen the market mechanism. This involves an evaluation of the (compliance) costs and benefits of the chosen form of intervention.

When we use the term deregulation, this refers to all three of the above forms of deregulation. A full deregulation is a repositioning of the role of government to such an extent that the policy field at stake is now 'completely' left to the private sector. In the case of a partial deregulation, the degree of government intervention is reduced, although not fully. Deregulation may also involve re-regulation. The above example of the streamlined establishment law is a case in point, as it requires the creation of new rules and regulations. Re-regulation may also occur because the private sector formulates its own rules when the government withdraws from the market. This 'self-regulation' may be just as restrictive in effect as the governmental rules which it replaced.[7]

Competition policy
Competition policy is the body of laws and regulations that govern horizontal and vertical agreements between firms, monopolization, mergers and acquisitions.[8] More competition and less regulation are not always two sides of the same coin. Indeed, the proper functioning of the market mechanism requires at least protection of property rights and the enforcement of contracts. Likewise, a shift towards a stricter competition policy regime requires rules and regulations to change the formal competences of the competition policy authorities. According to the OECD (1990, p. 10):

> In order to control the abuse of market power, the traditional area of competition policy, namely merger and anti-trust policy, has become all the more important after the move towards privatization and deregulation.

Privatization, deregulation and competition policy are interrelated and often mutually reinforcing phenomena. For example, technological change, deregulation and privatization in telecommunications have improved transparency of (world) product markets, reduced transportation costs and fostered both domestic and international competition. This has urged countries to modernize both the public supply side of their economies and to improve on regulatory frameworks. At the same time increased co-operation between firms and mergers have put competition policy authorities on the alert. Obviously, then, a strategy of structural reform will often consist of a balanced mix of privatization, deregulation and competition policy.

1.3   Focus on the OECD

Structural change and the problem of product market inertia are relevant to many countries in Central and Eastern Europe and the Third World, where policy changes are a necessary condition for getting the development process under way. Extensive privatization programmes are currently being implemented in Central and Eastern Europe, which is now moving away from central planning to deregulation and decentralization, while substantial programmes are also being considered in developing countries and in the so-called Newly Industrializing Economies (NIEs).

Moreover, these phenomena are increasingly being recognized as policy topics for OECD countries. In our discussion we will often focus on four OECD countries:

- New Zealand: Structural adjustment was implemented rigorously in the mid-1980s without any analysis of the costs and benefits of structural change or consideration of the question of sequencing.
- Germany: The need for structural change was analysed and the costs of market inertia were assessed by a team of IMF experts in 1989. At the same time, an independent committee was installed which evaluated a large number of fields of regulation in terms of their costs and benefits. However, changing policy has proved to be difficult, because of the emergence of pressure groups. The German unification in 1989 was another

factor which shifted the attention of policy makers away from issues of structural change (although not completely).[9]

● Australia: The costs and benefits have been analysed very rigorously by an independent committee but progress has so far occurred mainly in the field of liberalization of international trade.

● The Netherlands: The Netherlands is on the brink of a major change in its competition policy and the Dutch government is starting official investigations into the costs and benefits of deregulation and privatization. The available analytical tools, however, are still considered to be in their infancy. In 1994, a ministerial committee on 'Competition, deregulation and the quality of regulations' was formed which annually reviews a number of fields of regulation.

Our motives for considering structural change in the OECD (and of these four cases in particular) are both theoretical and pragmatic. Syrquin (1995) and Galal et al. (1994, p. 559) point out that the level of development may to a large extent determine an economy's performance and flexibility and warn that it is dangerous to generalize on the basis of the experience of a few case studies to a whole range of countries.

The availability and comparability of statistics is an additional reason to restrict our analysis to the relatively homogeneous group of OECD countries. Actually, as argued by Levine and Zervos (1993), conceptual and statistical problems may substantially undermine the relevance of including vastly different countries in a sample: a group of some hundred economies may have so little in common that one may question the merits of putting them in the same regression analysis. More pragmatically, excellent reviews of the macroeconomic consequences of structural reform are already available for the non-OECD countries (see, for example, Goldin et al. 1994) while it is to be expected that many emerging economies in the near future will either join the European Union (Poland, Hungary) and/or follow the example of Mexico and the Czech Republic and become new OECD member countries (South Korea, Israel). Hence our approach to focus on the OECD is parsimonious and relevant.

1.4   Modelling and Policy Making

Essentially, our book is an exercise in what Tinbergen (1952) labelled
qualitative policy when he referred to the changing of certain aspects
of economic structure. Two examples of qualitative policy (Tinbergen
1952, p. 71) are changes of the micro-structure such as changes in
competition policy and changes in business organization or property
rights. Tinbergen (1952, p. 72) pointed out that

> the scientific treatment of problems of qualitative policy meets with great
> difficulties [because] our empirical knowledge of human behaviour under
> different structural conditions is so restricted.

The policy maker who proposes qualitative policies often wants to
support his or her idea with quantitative and qualitative analyses. The
appropriate tools, however, are often lacking and this may delay
intended institutional changes. Pointing out that 'it is often difficult to
deregulate given that general efficiency considerations have to be
weighed against the interests of specific groups', Gradus (1995, p. 3)
stresses the importance of 'a clear-cut understanding of the economic
effects of different regulation options'. Admittedly, economic data
and predictions are only one facet of the political debate. For this
reason too, a caveat is in order against too detailed (ab)use of
economic analyses. It is, however, a fact of life that a proposal which
cannot be evaluated, may soon lose the attention of policy makers.

   It may pay to consider two extreme approaches that can be
followed with respect to the role of quantitative analysis in policy
making. First we will look at the case of New Zealand, where
structural change was radically implemented without *a priori* analysis
of the costs and benefits and where, as a consequence, large costs
were put upon the population. The second case is the Netherlands,
which presently runs the risk of being caught in a quantification trap,
i.e. where it is very difficult to initiate and implement structural
adjustment policies because quantitative evaluation techniques are not
sufficiently well developed. The Dutch case illustrates that the
difficulty of producing estimates of the costs and benefits of structural
change may impair economic policy if the policy formation process
(too) heavily relies on econometric analysis.

New Zealand[10]

Between 1984 and 1991, New Zealand implemented a radical economic liberalization programme. Major policy changes towards a greater use of market forces occurred in areas such as government spending and taxation, financial markets, monetary policy, the exchange rate, trade and foreign direct investment, privatization and deregulation. The deregulation programme involved the elimination of most market entry restrictions, price controls, regulatory monopolies and operating restrictions (Bollard 1994, pp. 75—81). In this period, New Zealand was transformed from a relatively closed, highly regulated economy into an economy with open markets for competition from both domestic sources and from abroad.

In formulating strategies for structural adjustment, policy makers in New Zealand shifted from a traditional macroeconomic point of view to an essentially microeconomic approach. The implication was that dynamic and general equilibrium implications were neglected as the implicit model was static and assumed that microeconomic improvements would naturally add up to a better macroeconomy. Three observations illustrate the supremacy of microeconomics in New Zealand policy analysis. The Treasury reduced employment in its macroeconomic divisions, it stopped publishing macroeconomic forecasts and Roger Douglas (at that time Minister of Finance and the key personality in the reform process), in detailing the expected results from policy proposals, never went beyond basic accounting principles which he based on a set of exogenous assumptions for economic growth, inflation and public finance.[11] This approach, according to Bollard (1994, p. 96):

> appears to have taken relatively little consideration of such transitional issues as the loss of output during the transition, the flexibility of adjustment mechanisms, the timing and sequencing of measures, and the hysteresis effects. It also paid little attention to distributional issues, such as the costs of adjustment and whether there should be compensation for the relative losers in the transition process in the longer term.

Actually, the case of New Zealand shows that regulatory reform is not a free lunch. Importantly, the adjustment process in New Zealand lasted at least from 1985 to 1992. Seven meagre years indeed. According to OECD (1993a) data, the economy stagnated,

unemployment increased from 4 per cent to 10 per cent and a quarter
of the jobs in industry were lost. At the sectoral level, the reform
programme led to a contraction of industry's share in GDP from 27
to 22 per cent and its share in total employment was reduced from 24
to 17 per cent. With the exception of the financial services industry,
the negative impact of structural adjustment superseded the beneficial
effects on employment and production in all sectors (Savage and
Bollard 1990).[12] One might argue that the adjustment process took
so long because the sequence of reform was not optimal. This may
have led to frictional macroeconomic costs. It is important to note
that growth was not restored until a new structural policy framework
was put into effect in 1990, aiming at wage flexibility through labour
market reform (see, for example, Ostry 1993, p. 18 and Lang 1993,
p. 28). Therefore, the most important practical policy lesson from the
experience of New Zealand is the need to consider the length of the
economic adjustment processes and the timing and sequence of doing
away with structural rigidities in both the product and the labour
markets.

The Netherlands
The Netherlands has a longstanding tradition of empirically supported
economic policy making. This tradition started when Tinbergen
(1936) built his first econometric model of the Dutch economy and
was institutionalized by the founding of the Central Planning Bureau
(CPB) in 1947. CPB calculations with large-scale econometric models
are the basis for forecasting, policy making and policy review. As the
models of the CPB provide the foundation for a rational and well-
documented discussion, the impact of econometric models on Dutch
policy makers is very substantial. This is especially true in
comparison with other countries. It is, moreover, not only Dutch
economic policy that relies heavily on the CPB. Since 1986 the larger
Dutch political parties have also sought the CPB's seal of approval
for the economic content of their electoral programmes (Haffner and
van Bergeijk 1994). One of the economic consequences of the present
role that large-scale econometric models play in Dutch politics and
policy making may be that economic policies related to structural
adjustment are rarely considered, because the CPB as yet finds it
difficult to quantify the economic impact of such measures.

In this way, policies aimed at structural change are severely hampered by the fact that the CPB does not take changes in institutional arrangements into account, although they may have economic consequences. Examples are the liberalization of the Shop Hours Act, the plans to improve the functioning of markets in regulated and sheltered sectors such as telecommunications and the reduction of administrative compliance costs that were proposed by the major political parties in 1994. The CPB repeatedly explained that it did not take such changes in the legal framework into account because it could not quantify the effects of institutional change: no modelling tools were available.[13]

Obviously, it is a wise policy to avoid the dangers that are inherent in the extreme strategies of the Netherlands and New Zealand. Hence one should investigate different methods for quantification, but at the same time one should avoid the quantification trap and allow for qualitative analysis as well. This book provides background information for such a two-tier approach.

1.5   Plan of the Book

The next chapter discusses some recent publications by international think-tanks, such as the Institute for International Economics, the OECD and the World Bank, which deal with structural change. The aims of this chapter are to provide a quick introduction into the economic literature on (the need for) structural change and to sketch the problems and prospects of a number of countries in a comprehensive way. This is much in line with the OECD's (1990, p. 15) assessment that it is useful to develop knowledge systematically about the policy stance in structural policy areas and to make qualitative and quantitative comparative assessments of the effects and prospects of structural reform.

The organization of the remainder of the book reflects the fact that industrial organization economists and macroeconomists have at least one interest in common: the interest in understanding how markets clear. As pointed out by Carlton (1989, p. 911),

When prices fail to clear markets, inefficiencies develop, resources are wasted and unemployment can arise. If industrial organization economists find that

certain prices are rigid, that fact should be of great interest ... Whether or not
one is a Keynesian, understanding how markets clear over time is valuable
information to a macroeconomist.

In this sense Part II (on industrial economics) provides an empirical
and very practical microfoundation for Part III on the macroeconomic
aspects of privatization, deregulation and competition policy.

Part II provides an overview of industrial organization methodologies
for measuring product market inertia. In addition, the extent of
product market inertia in the OECD is identified by means of a
comparative analysis of price and profit dynamics across countries.

Chapter 3 uses the industrial organization paradigm, which relates
market structure with conduct and performance, as a tool to classify
indicators which can help to assess the functioning of the market
mechanism. The structure—conduct—performance (SCP) paradigm
has been used before (and proved to be a quite fruitful approach) in
the context of the comparative analysis of national policies, for
example, by Porter (1990a) and Mayes and Hart (1994).

Chapter 4 offers both new results and a review of empirical
findings which are presently scattered in time and journals. Although
we use many methodologies to assess product market inertia, we will
often resort to the concept of hysteresis, which has been used by
labour market economists. The hysteresis concept can equally
fruitfully be applied to product markets, as has been shown by our
own work and recent applications of this concept by Dixit and
Pindyck (1994) to investment decisions.

Each section contains a discussion of the literature related to a
specific methodology (for example, hysteresis, price rigidity, etc.).
Next we deal with estimation issues and the empirical findings,
respectively. This allows us to make a preliminary assessment of
which countries are rigid and which countries are flexible, using a
number of different methodologies.

In Part III we relate empirical findings at the mesoeconomic level to
the macroeconomy.

Chapter 5 starts with a discussion of theoretical approaches that
may be followed in modelling the macroeconomic consequences of
microeconomic rigidities. Where possible we relate the theoretical

approaches to empirical findings. The focus is on potentially relevant mechanisms that shed some light on the macroeconomic consequences of structural change. In a way this chapter provides the groundwork for an analysis that makes the micro to macro translation. In doing so we distinguish two channels through which product market rigidities may influence the economy: the macroeconomic efficiency effect and the impact of rigidities on the instruments of economic policy. We discuss both static and dynamic efficiency and take a closer look at issues posed by stabilization policy, incomes policy and balance of payments considerations.

In Chapter 6 we review approaches that have been followed to analyse these questions empirically for practical policy purposes. We take a fresh look at applied general equilibrium analysis. So far this line of research has mainly considered issues such as taxation, social security and distortions of international trade (see, for example, Shoven and Whalley 1984). Still, for a number of OECD countries (Australia, Germany, and the Netherlands), studies related to structural (microeconomic) rigidities exist. We discuss the pros and cons of these methodologies that use a general equilibrium framework to arrive at estimates of the macroeconomic benefits of privatization, deregulation and a more vigorous competition policy.

Part IV focuses on strategic policy topics in the implementation of structural change.

In Chapter 7 we consider the issues of credibility, the appropriate speed of reforms and ascertain the need to follow a synergetic approach in which labour and goods markets are liberalized more or less simultaneously. We also deal with pressure groups, analyse their role in discouraging structural change and discuss some of the basic lessons from the political economy literature on implementing structural change. Finally, we take a look at some of the empirical evidence.

The final chapter summarizes some lessons from our discussion. The main lesson, however, is that both the quantitative and qualitative analysis of the potential macroeconomic costs and benefits of structural change are fruitful and highly relevant fields of research.

Notes

1. See OECD (1994d) for a detailed analysis.
2. See, for example, Porter (1990b).
3. A very readable account is Harrison (1995).
4. See, for example, Geelhoed (1994).
5. See for overviews of the literature for privatization, deregulation and competition policy: Vickers and Yarrow (1988), Winston (1993) and Kühn et al. (1992), respectively.
6. The same holds for the functioning of capital markets. The increasing international integration of capital markets has not prevented competition from being weak in some segments of the domestic market. Empirical investigations for the European banking industry show that banks have considerable market power both in household and in corporate markets. This market power is shown to cause high mark-ups of prices over funding costs in these market segments. See Gual and Neven (1992), Swank (1994), Neven and Röller (1995) and van Bergeijk et al. (1995).
7. A price-fixing cartel can also be seen as a form of self-regulation.
8. *OECD Interim Report on the Convergence of Competition Policy* No. 79, Paris 1994, p. 8.
9. The old, ongoing *Standort Deutschland* discussion on the business climate in Germany is evidence that structural issues are still on the policy agenda.
10. This section draws on Bos and van Bergeijk (1994).
11. See Bollard (1994) and Douglas (1993), especially pp. 264—305.
12. As always, it is difficult to disentangle the effects of the structural adjustment programme from all the other factors which were influencing the economy during that period.
13. During the process of editing this book, the CPB back-tracked on this opinion, as a study on a change in the institutional framework was published (the liberalization of the Shop Opening Hours Act, see Bernardt et al. (1995)).

2. Structural Change: The Policy Stance

Privatization, deregulation and competition policy have become increasingly important elements of the policy mix in the industrialized countries since the OECD initiated its structural reform programme in the 1980s.[1] Motivated by the structural character of the problems of stagflation in the mid-1970s, the deteriorating situation of public finance and the high and persistent level of unemployment in the 1980s, governments increasingly recognized that 'open and efficient markets for goods and services, exposed to domestic and international competition, provide the crucial underpinnings for dynamic, high income economies' (OECD 1994a, p. 7). Economists have made important contributions to the marketing of the policy prescription of liberalizing and integrating markets (Winston 1993). A well-known example is the European Union, where economic analysis played an important role in motivating the 1992 move to an internal market, which involves market integration and deregulation in addition to trade liberalization (Emerson et al. 1988).

Economists are trained to think in terms of overall long-term gains when they discuss these issues. Generally speaking, their arguments pay little attention to the costs of integration and liberalization. The general public, however, may consider these transition costs to be more important than the potential benefits of reform that may only emerge in the long run. This means that policy matters: whereas the costs of adjustment have to be borne anyhow, it takes sensible macroeconomic and microeconomic policies both to reap the full benefits of privatization, deregulation and competition policy and to keep the adjustment costs within reasonable limits.

The predicted net welfare gains of economic integration and trade liberalization that motivate policy makers to embark on a course of structural reform are only one side of the coin, however. Reality is often much more complex than economists assume because of non-optimizing behaviour, imperfect information and other variables which affect the political viability of structural reforms. Clarkson (1993, p. 63), for example, observes that:

> a problem arises when theoretical economists put on their policymakers' hat without changing assumptions and offer advice based on unsupportable assumptions about human behaviour and societal institutions.

Hence, the domain of economic analysis, which is the main thrust of this book, needs to be supplemented by a more political analysis that deals with the opportunity and feasibility of privatization, deregulation and competition policy. Indeed, it is important to be aware of pressure groups, asymmetries of power and the rhetorical and political use that neo-conservatives have made of the need of global competitiveness to achieve a capitalist restructuring of the economy. According to Wilkinson (1993), the neo-conservative ideology is driving the economic system, both in Europe and in North America, where (trade) liberalization and structural change are now high on the political agenda. For the time being, we postpone the detailed discussion of these and related questions of policy prescription and policy implementation until Chapter 7.

Three further caveats are in order before we start our review of the policy stance for privatization, deregulation and competition policy.

First, policies aimed at combating product market inertia are only a subset of a broader policy initiative aimed at structural reform. Our focus in this book on product markets (goods and services) is dictated by the need to specialize and to improve on our knowledge of the reform of product markets. This means that we cannot do justice to important developments in adjacent fields. Discussing microeconomic policies at the start of the 1990s, the OECD (1990) observes that deregulation and liberalization have been particularly fierce in areas where policies are interdependent in the sense that each country's policies impinge on other countries. Accordingly, in the 1990s, structural reforms were implemented in financial markets, taxation, foreign direct investment and international trade. (Incidentally, in these areas substantial economic research was available or in the pipeline and actually guided policy making in many OECD countries.) Moreover, ample scope for improvement exists in the labour market, in agriculture and in industrial policy. It should be emphasized that we consider complementary structural change outside the product markets (especially of the labour market) crucial for the ultimate success of privatization, deregulation and a more vigorous competition policy.

Second, our focus in this book on the OECD does not mean that we consider structural change outside the industrialized world of minor importance. On the contrary, structural reform in the OECD is part of a wider (if not global) movement. Important evidence about the problems and prospects of reform programmes can be derived from a large sample of countries, as shown by our discussion in Section 2.2. Structural adjustment programmes of the International Monetary Fund (IMF) influence many developing countries as the Fund urges microeconomic and macroeconomic reforms which are aimed at external equilibrium (balance of payments, foreign debt, etc.). Comprehensive steps towards a market economy in Central and Eastern Europe involve economy-wide deregulation and privatization at an unprecedented scale and speed. The experience of these countries may help to put the prospects and problems of OECD countries into perspective.

The third caveat concerns the fact that privatization, deregulation and competition policy are often interrelated problems. For example, the international integration of markets due to a reduction of non-tariff trade barriers (aiming at more transparent and non-discriminatory public procurement practices) will influence the effectiveness of the competition policy regime. Indeed, in empirical investigations of structural reforms it will often be very difficult to distinguish between the effects on efficiency of changes in ownership, competition policy and regulation (Vickers and Yarrow 1988, p. 39, Cottarelli and Kourelis 1994). So while it is analytically convenient to discuss privatization, deregulation and competition policy as if these policies were implemented in isolation, one should in practice be aware of the need to develop a comprehensive view on such structural reforms.

2.1   Structural Reform in the OECD

Many industrialized countries are making progress in combating
product market inertia through privatization, deregulation and a more
vigorous competition policy. New instruments are being developed,
existing ones are sharpened. This process is illustrated in Table 2.1,
which summarizes the OECD's (1994a) findings with respect to
policy measures related to privatization, deregulation and competition
policy in the years 1990—93. To some extent, national economic
policies in the early 1990s appear to converge in the direction of a
greater reliance on market forces.

Table 2.1 also illustrates that deregulation and competition policy
often appear to go hand in hand, for example, when licensing
arrangements are opened up, when price and entry controls are ended
or when private firms are allowed to enter markets that were
previously the exclusive domain of government monopolies. In the
wake of the completion of the internal market in 1992, European
economies are all moving in the direction of more vigorous
competition policies, aligning their national Competition Laws to the
standard set by the European Union. One possible explanation for the
apparent pattern of convergence with respect to deregulation and
competition policy is that countries have to 'join the process of
reform in order to avoid compromising their competitiveness' (OECD
1990, p. 7). Button and Keeler (1993, pp. 1018—19) list
demonstration effects, theoretical innovations (such as the
development of the Chicago School model for deregulation and the
theory of contestable markets[2]), the growing political power of
consumer groups and widespread taxpayer dissatisfaction as the main
long-run forces that provide momentum towards structural reform.

Table 2.1 also illustrates that privatization of banking, insurance,
telecommunications, postal services, shipping, shipbuilding and
railroads is under way in many countries. Large differences between
countries, however, continue to exist, as the public sector appears to
be an area where domestic policies are more self-contained (OECD
1990, p. 7). Even here, however, progress often is impressive.

Table 2.1 Selected structural policies in OECD countries (1990—93)

	Public sector	Deregulation	Competition policy
Australia	Corporization and privatization	Deregulation of telecommunications, transport and electricity sectors	Competition Law amended, new merger test
Austria	Corporization at federal level	Reform of Price Law, new Cartel Law	
Belgium	Privatization initiative for period 1993—96		New Competition Act, creation of independent Competition Council
Canada	Corporization and privatization	Deregulation of telecommunications, transport and financial services	
Denmark	Introduction of user charges and voucher systems in education sector	Deregulation of selected postal, telecommunication, and transportation services	New Competition Law (abuse principle)
France		Improved transparency of public procurement, improved access to professions	Competition Law aligned with EU
Germany	Privatization by Treuhandanstalt (Eastern Germany)		
Greece	Privatization	Shop-opening hours completely freed	Most price controls lifted

(continued)

Table 2.1 (continued)

	Public sector	Deregulation	Competition policy
Ireland	Emphasis on improving performance	Deregulation of air transport	New Competition Law (aligned with EU)
Italy	Corporization and privatization, suppression of Ministry of State Participation		Introduction of Competition Law, establishment of independent Anti-trust Authority
Japan	Increasing foreign access to public procurement	Administrative Procedure Law to ease burden of regulation	Anti-monopoly Act enforcement, increased penalties, monitoring of Keiretsu firms
The Netherlands	Privatization, contracting out		Prohibition of horizontal price agreements, alignment to EU competition laws
New Zealand	Divestiture of public shares in port facilities and airports, end to government ownership in telecom, transport, insurance and banking sectors	Deregulation of telecommunications, transport and energy sectors	
Norway		Deregulation of air transport and energy sectors	New Competition Law

(continued)

Table 2.1 (continued)

	Public sector	Deregulation	Competition policy
Portugal	Privatization	Administrative price controls lifted, private entry in air transport, telecom and broadcasting	
Spain	Abolishment of state monopolies in value added telecom services and oil sector		General Secretariat on International Economy and Competition, a more active Competition Court
Sweden	Privatization	Deregulation of inter-regional transportation, taxis and entry of supermarkets	New Competition Act in line with EU
Switzerland			Dismantling of cartels in banking, insurance and sanitary equipment
Turkey	Privatization and revision of Privatization Law	Deregulation of insurance industry	
United Kingdom	Privatization of electricity and telecommunications		Competition and Service (Utilities) Act
United States			New Horizontal Merger Guidelines, increased penalties

Source:　Based on OECD (1994a), pp. 23—114, subject to the usual reservations.

Indeed, the message conveyed by Table 2.1 is that structural policy instruments are energetically being constructed and implemented in many OECD countries. Qualitative economic policy is in a state of great flux. Privatization, deregulation and sharpening of competition policy are widespread and potentially far-reaching instruments of structural reform. One obvious implication of the policy stance that is evident from Table 2.1 is the need to consider the consequences for macroeconomic performance and the scope of the more traditional instruments of economic policy (especially of demand management and supply-side policies) in this changing economic environment.

Table 2.1 provides a snapshot only: a static image that does not reflect the dynamism that presently characterizes the development and implementation of qualitative economic policy. In many countries further privatization, deregulation and plans related to competition policy are in the pipeline. Moreover, in a number of cases new legislation was only relatively recently drafted, so that learning effects in the implementation are to be expected.

In addition, new challenges arise with respect to public infrastructure management as technological developments make natural monopolies increasingly less 'natural'. An example is telecommunications, where the provision of services now can actually be separated from the ownership of the network infrastructure so that competition among providers of services can be introduced. In a number of cases, the implementation of initial reforms uncovered structural rigidities of which policy analysts and policy makers were unaware, thus pointing out the need and scope for further complementary reforms.

However, it should also be clear that large differences between countries continue to exist even where the OECD economies appear to be moving more or less in the same direction. Table 2.2 summarizes the existing differences for the area of competition policy with respect to three factors:

- independence of the competition agency,
- the principle of competition law enforcement; and
- the legal mode of competition law enforcement.

Table 2.2 Competition policy regimes (selected OECD countries)

Country	Competition agency	Independent	Principle	Enforcement
Australia	Trade Practices Commission	Yes	Prohibition	Mixed
Belgium	Dienst van de Mededinging	No	Prohibition	Administrative
Canada	Director of Investigation and Research	Yes	Mixed	Mixed
Denmark	Koncurrenceradet	Yes	Abuse	Administrative
France	Conseil de la Concurrence	Yes	Prohibition	Administrative
Germany	Bundeskartelamt	Yes	Mixed	Administrative
Greece	Market Research Directorate	No	Prohibition	Administrative
Ireland	Competition Authority	Yes	Prohibition	Criminal
Italy	Autorità garanta della concerrenza e del mercato	Yes	Prohibition	Administrative
Japan	Fair Trade Commission	Yes	Prohibition	Administrative
Netherlands	Directie Marktwerking	No	Abuse	Criminal
Portugal	Competition Council	Yes	Prohibition	Administrative
Spain	Servicio de Defensa de la Competencia	Yes	Prohibition	Administrative
Sweden	Konkurrentverket	Yes	Prohibition	Administrative
UK	Office of Fair Trade	No	Abuse	Administrative
US	Federal Trade Commission and Department of Justice	Yes	Prohibition	Mixed

Sources: World Bank (1991a), Gradus (1994) and Ministry of Economic Affairs (1994).

The independence of the competition agency is an important feature as political influence on the decision whether or not to prosecute a cartel may give rise to pressure group activity that undermines the policy stance. Principles of competition law enforcement range from selective control of abuse to the general prohibition of anti-competitive practices. Enforcement of a competition law that is based on the 'abuse principle' is much more difficult as it puts the burden of proof on the competition agency. Finally, Table 2.2 illustrates the different modes of enforcement: either by administrative law (which is the easier route from the point of view of the competition agency) or by criminal law. Note, however, that Table 2.2 does not reflect some national differences that may be very important for the effectiveness of competition policy enforcement, such as the number and quality of the staff of the competition agency, the level of the fine that can be imposed and, most importantly, the actual policy stance followed in implementation (given the available instruments). One of the reasons why policy convergence in the OECD is not complete and why countries seem to move at different speeds (as is suggested by Table 2.1), is that initial conditions at the outset of the 1990s differed substantially. An obvious point is that in some countries (the United States comes directly to mind) traditionally only limited scope existed for state-owned enterprises. In addition, the timing of privatization differs between countries, some countries starting earlier than others. Hence, the potential for privatization can also differ considerably. Consequently, large differences in privatization proceeds are observed even between the European countries where government interference traditionally has been relatively important (Table 2.3).

Table 2.3 Accumulated privatization proceeds (selected OECD countries, per cent of average annual GDP over privatization period)

Country	Period	Proceeds
Spain	1986—90	0.5
Germany (West)	1984—90	0.5
Austria	1987—90	0.9
The Netherlands	1987—91	1.0
Sweden	1987—90	1.2
France	1983—91	1.5
Portugal	1989—91	4.3
United Kingdom	1979—91	11.9

Source: Stevens (1992) quoted in Bös (1993), p. 100.

The United Kingdom, for example, relatively early privatized substantial parts of its public sector (including water, gas and electricity), while other countries still have to develop or start a privatization programme. Hence the scope for many privatization options in the United Kingdom may already be exhausted.

Whereas the progress in privatization can be measured by its proceeds, evaluating major shifts in economic regulation is a much more difficult task. Simply counting the number of obliviated rules would obviously not be a solution. Since some regulations have a much more far-reaching influence than others on an economy, this would amount to comparing apples and oranges. Hence an applied welfare analysis that takes into account the impact of deregulation on consumer welfare, labour and firms becomes necessary.

Table 2.4 Welfare effects of deregulation in the United States (billions of 1990 dollars)

Industry	Total welfare	Additional benefits if (de)regulation is optimal
Airlines	14—20	5
Railroads	10—13	0
Trucking	11	0
Telecommunications	1—2	12
Cable television	0—1	0—1
Brokerage	0	0
Natural gas	n.a.	4
Total seven sectors	36—46	22

Note: n.a. = not available.
Source: Winston (1993), Table 6, p. 1284.

Table 2.4 summarizes the findings of *ex post* quantitative assessments of the actual effects of deregulation in seven sectors of the United States economy, primarily in the transportation industry. This was basically done by analysing the change in consumer and producer surplus that results when prices reach their post-deregulation level. The total welfare gain of deregulation amounts to a welfare improvement of 36—46 billion dollars and is equivalent to 7—9 per cent of the production in the sectors concerned (Winston 1993, p.

1284). The final column in Table 2.4 shows an estimate of the additional benefits that could materialize if pricing and service approach 'optimality'. This was calculated by comparing the actual result achieved with a benchmark assuming average-cost pricing (in the case of telecommunications) or marginal-cost pricing (all other cases). In airlines, railroads and trucking, deregulation seems to have been relatively successful. In these sectors, additional deregulation measures would not have a high pay-off as these markets are already close to the optimal situation. By contrast, in telecommunications deregulation has done relatively little to achieve optimal pricing behaviour as the larger part of the possible benefits have not yet materialized.

2.2 Eastern Europe, NIEs and Developing Countries

Well before most of the former communist countries in Europe in the 1990s started structural reforms, many developing countries especially in Latin America and South-East Asia had changed the orientation of their economic policies from import substitution to export-led growth in the 1980s. Structural reform in a number of countries was stimulated by IMF surveillance and the conditionality imposed on developing countries in the context of the Fund's balance of payments support programmes. Initially, these programmes concentrated on macroeconomic stabilization, prudential public finance and external equilibrium (debt, current account). However, the Fund increasingly recognized the need for structural microeconomic reforms, and structural issues such as the reform of the labour market became important elements of the Fund's policy advice.[3]

The evidence, however, on the relation between deregulation, privatization and liberalization, on the one hand, and economic growth, on the other hand, is ambiguous. This is clearly illustrated by the fact that the two success stories of economic development — Chile and South Korea — followed diametrically opposed strategies. These emerging economies liberalized trade, but differed in their choice between an interventionist model in which the government exercised a detailed influence on strategic sectors (South Korea), on the one hand, and a strategy in which deregulation, privatization and competition policy were considered essential ingredients of national recovery programmes (Chile), on the other hand. Many developing countries also differed in their choice of either a gradualist approach to structural change or an immediate 'big bang', leading to an economy-wide exposure of formerly sheltered economies to world market competition. Despite these differences, however, the 1990s appear to have become a decade in which structural reforms are implemented in a wide range of countries.

Table 2.5 *Infrastructure privatizations outside the OECD[a] and total of non-infrastructure privatizations (1988—92, billions of US dollars and number of countries)*

Sector	Total value	Number of countries
Telecommunications	12	14
Power generation	4	9
Power distribution	1	2
Gas distribution	2	2
Ports and (rail)road infrastructure	1	2
Total infrastructure privatizations	20	15
Airlines	3	14
Total all privatizations[b]	62	25

Notes: [a] Argentina, Barbados, Belize, Brazil, Chile, China, Colombia, Czechoslovakia, Estonia, Honduras, Hungary, Jamaica, South Korea, Malaysia, Mexico, Pakistan, Panama, Philippines, Peru, Poland, Sri Lanka, Thailand, Togo, Turkey and Venezuela.
[b] Including non-infrastructure privatizations.
Source: World Bank (1994), Table 3.2, p. 64.

The World Bank (1994, p. 105) estimates that out of the $62 billion of revenue that non-OECD countries (especially in Asia and Latin America) obtained from privatization, about one-third came from privatizing infrastructure entities. The Bank assesses that in many non-OECD countries, infrastructure stocks are generating neither the quantity nor the quality of services demanded. The bank discusses studies that estimate the impact of an increase in technical efficiency in roads, power generation, water provision and railways (World Bank 1994, p. 122). If privatization and deregulation could raise technical efficiency to best-practice levels, this would generate resource savings equivalent to one per cent of all developing countries' GDP. Accordingly, the Bank argues that performance should be improved through better incentives based on commercial management, more effective competition and shareholder involvement. Privatization is seen as a means to achieve this. Since the mid-1980s, considerable progress has been made in privatizing infrastructure, especially in telecommunications (Table 2.5).

The privatization and deregulation process in the formerly centrally planned economies in Central and Eastern Europe is especially impressive.[4] Until 1989, the vast bulk of productive capital in these countries was state owned. Substantial privatization not only of large conglomerate state enterprises, small businesses and shops but also of land and the housing stock was considered to be a pre-condition for the introduction of a market economy. In addition, anti-monopoly legislation was introduced in 1989—90 in Hungary and Poland, in Bulgaria in 1991 and in Czechoslovakia in 1992. Soon Rumania, Russia and the Commonwealth of Independent States will have anti-monopoly laws in place as well (UNECE 1993, pp. 173—4).

The evidence of structural reforms in Central and Eastern Europe to date is mixed. On the one hand, 'small' privatization and the creation of private (family) business appears to be rather successful. According to the United Nations (UNECE 1994, p. 9):

> In terms of total output and employment the share of the private sector is rather smaller than its share in the number of enterprises, but its growth is still impressive: from 29 per cent of GDP in Poland to 47 per cent in 1992; and from virtually zero in the Czech Republic to around 50 per cent in 1993.

On the other hand, it is questionable whether privatization and structural change are actually happening in the large conglomerate state enterprises. Borensztein and Ostry (1994) disaggregate industrial output data for former Czechoslovakia, East Germany, Hungary and Poland and conclude that by and large in these economies, the output cost associated with the reforms is a reflection of macroeconomic forces rather than structural adjustment. This puts discussions about the need for further structural adjustment and the required speed of transformation in a new perspective.[5]

The need for speedy reform is also indicated by the study by Hoekman and Pohl (1995). Hoekman and Pohl investigate trade data that reflect the extent to which firms in six Eastern European countries are reorientating their operations in order to create and exploit competitive advantages. Hoekman and Pohl (1995, p.1) find that:

> The data suggest that the country that pursued mass privatization the most actively and credibly — the Czech Republic — has done best in terms of restructuring its industries and reorienting them towards world markets. Those that pursued a gradualist approach — Hungary being the main example — have the weakest overall trade performance.

Galal et al. (1994) investigate the welfare effects of nine cases of privatization in emerging economies, comparing private operation of privatized firms to the counterfactual (hypothetical) scenario of continued government operation. Their *ex post* applied welfare analysis aggregates appropriately discounted changes in consumer surpluses, enterprise profits and welfare consequences for competitors and the providers of inputs.

Table 2.6 reports on aggregate welfare that takes these four categories simultaneously into account. With the one exception of the privatization of the Mexican airline (which was caused by wrong investment decisions by the airline management), the net benefits appear to be overwhelmingly positive, although certain groups may lose from privatization. The findings illustrate the need to consider privatization from a macroeconomic viewpoint, because, according to Galal et al. (1994, p. 534):

> The bulk of the welfare gains followed from divestiture-induced changes that were external to the enterprise ... Roughly three-quarters of the welfare improvements came from three sources: revised output prices, increased flexibility of hiring and in investment decisions.

Table 2.6 Total welfare gains of privatization as a percentage of annual sales in Chile, Malaysia and Mexico

	Net welfare change Domestic	World
Chile		
CHILGENER (energy generation)	1	2
ENERSIS (energy distribution)	5	5
CTC (telecommunications)	145	155
Malaysia		
Malaysian Airline	5	22
Kelang Container Terminal	50	53
Sports Toto (lottery)	11	11
Mexico		
Télefonos de México	28	50
Aeroméxico (airline)	53	49
Mexicana de Aviación (airline)	—2	—7

Note: All figures are the annual component of the perpetuity equivalent to welfare change, expressed as a percentage of annual sales in the last pre-privatization year.

Source: Galal et al. (1994), Table 23—1, p. 528.

2.3   Common Characteristics

It is a truism that the policy problems facing developing countries, emerging economies and the industrialized world cannot be solved with one universal recipe and that policy advisers should always consider the specific characteristics of the nation that they want to help. The level of education, the strength of the private sector, social security arrangements, the level and distribution of income, the functioning and depth of the capital market, the administrative skills of the government sector and of the political set-up are important determinants for any strategy that aims at structural change. Countries (and often even regions within countries) in many cases differ widely with respect to these characteristics. Consequently, any policy problem in the area of structural reform needs to be analysed on a case-by-case base.

Nevertheless it seems possible to identify common characteristics and common issues that are shared by many countries. Actually, as Vickers and Yarrow (1991) illustrate with their discussion of privatization in the United Kingdom, Chile and Poland, it is quite possible to apply a relatively small set of economic principles to various cases in countries that differ substantially with respect to culture, level of economic development and sociopolitical history. Benefiting from the experiences in many socioeconomic contexts, we will look in the remainder of this chapter at the question of what the widely differing cases in North, East and South have in common, in order to formulate relevant questions for further research.

Economics

In many countries, structural reforms were motivated by both macroeconomic and microeconomic experiences. Disordered public finances and high and increasing government debts in combination with high inflation and retarded economic growth are each to a different extent common characteristics of both the developing countries and the OECD countries at the start of the 1980s and of the former centrally planned economies in Central and Eastern Europe at the start of the 1990s. Traditional macroeconomic planning policies (both of the Western Keynesian stabilization type and the Eastern socialist variant) turned out to be ineffective to cure the economic downturn. Moreover, the need for fiscal consolidation implied that demand management could no longer be considered as an instrument variable, the value of which can be chosen freely. As a result, macroeconomic policy lost a degree of freedom.

At the microeconomic level, these countries share their dissatisfaction with the efficiency and accountability of government enterprises, while the growing interdependence of markets and the increased openness of economies means that flexibility and competitiveness had to become and eventually became substantial goals of economic policy.

Consequently, the functioning and role of markets became increasingly important ingredients of the development strategies that were followed by a wide range of countries; generally speaking without a resort to plain *laissez-faire* policies. Indeed, as the World Bank (1991b, p. 1) pointed out in its influential report on the challenge of development:

> Competitive markets are the best way yet found for efficiently organizing the production and distribution of goods and services. Domestic and external competition provides the incentives that unleash entrepreneurship and technological progress. But markets cannot operate in a vacuum — they require a legal and regulatory framework that only governments can provide. And, at many other tasks, markets fail altogether. That is why governments must, for example, invest in infrastructure and provide essential services to the poor. It is not a question of state or market: each has a large and irreplaceable role.

Obviously, these lessons are equally valid for developing countries, emerging markets in Asia and Latin America, economies in transition in Eastern Europe and the industrialized world.

Politics
Structural reform strongly influences the primary income distribution. Microeconomic reforms make an end to quasi-monopoly rents and privatization spreads formal shareholding across the population, thus creating or expanding the capitalist class, which has an interest in maintaining a good investment and business climate (and in re-electing right-wing governments, of course).[6] Consequently, structural reform is an inherently political process, both in industrialized countries and in developing countries. Jacquemin (1995) distinguishes the market economy (the 'invisible hand' adjusting supply and demand schedules), on the one hand, and capitalism (that is, the accumulated knowledge of past outcomes which can be used to control markets), on the other hand. In this sense, 'capitalism' is in the realm of politics.

New governments have often used structural policies to tackle socialist characteristics that were implanted by their predecessors and privatization has provided clear examples of attempts to make the steps towards a market-orientated economy irreversible. Cases in point are Chile (where the Pinochet military dictatorship used denationalization to reverse the attempt by the democratically elected Allende government to socialize the Chilean economy) and Eastern Europe (where democratically elected governments made irreversible steps away from socialist dictatorship towards a market-orientated democratic multi-party system).[7] This relationship, however, between an anti-socialist orientation and a preference for privatization, deregulation and competition policy is ambiguous — at least in the industrialized world — as illustrated by New Zealand's structural reforms that were implemented by the Lange Labour government in the 1980s and by the 1994 Dutch deregulation initiative of the Kok government which was based on a coalition of social democrats, liberals and conservatives.

2.4 Common Problems

Governments have encountered a number of similar problems during the implementation of structural reform. These problems relate, first, to the severity of transformation costs (the costs of reallocation, retraining, re-engineering and regrouping) and the period over which these costs are experienced and, second, to the complexity of structural reform, especially the relationship with existing distortions in other markets and sectors.

In a sense, these problems derive from the fact that most people, as Winston (1993, p. 1285) puts it, are 'not in the habit of thinking in terms of counterfactuals'. Consequently, politicians (like the general public) appear to be unable, first, to properly evaluate the benefits of crises that are averted or mitigated because the economy has become more flexible due to structural change and, second, to understand how the adverse consequences of external shocks may influence overall economic performance negatively although the impact of structural reform itself is positive.

In contrast, the actual course of the economy is often identified with the results of structural reform programmes. This may become a problem if an external and exogenous shock such as a slowdown of world trade coincides with the implementation of microeconomic reforms. The coincidence of macroeconomic hardship and the need for reallocation in the light of structural reform may have been incidental (as in the case of Europe 1992, see Harrison 1995, pp. 61—2) or a result of complementary economic reforms such as the tight-money policy due to the creation of an independent Central Bank in New Zealand (Bollard 1994).

It is important to investigate whether policy errors have been made in designing and implementing structural change which could have been avoided. An example is the Canadian policy failure to implement a strong-currency—high-interest policy in the wake of a major (trade) liberalization effort. This combination significantly increased the adjustment costs which came on top of a severe recession and in fact shifted the burden of adjustment to the export sector. Campbell (1993) presents evidence related to the period 1989—92 showing that employment for *all* Canadian manufacturing sectors persistently decreased, thus contradicting the belief (shared by many international trade analysts) that the losses of some sectors will be compensated by the gains of other sectors. The policy error to implement wide-scale privatization while the economic environment is very turbulent due to microeconomic reforms and macroeconomic stabilization efforts was also made in developing countries, most notably in Chile in the mid-1970s and early 1980s. The World Bank (1988) points out that the liberalization policies should preferably have been implemented before privatization was started.

This suggests that the sequencing and orchestration of reform measures are very important determinants of the outcome of any policy that aims at structural change. Generally speaking, agreement exists among economists that priority should be given to macroeconomic stabilization policies, including monetary and fiscal reform. In addition, it is hardly disputed within the economic profession that the beneficial effects of reform in one sector or market may depend on complementary reforms in other sectors or markets. Indeed, as will become evident later on, the lack of labour market reform may constitute an important bottleneck for flexibility of the product market and, likewise, product market inertia may hinder any substantial reduction of structural unemployment.

Opinions, however, differ substantially on many policy questions that would seem to fit into an overall framework for structural change. Should priority be given to reform of domestic markets in order to reduce the adjustment costs of subsequent liberalization of trade and capital flows? Alternatively: should international trade and finance be liberalized first so as to assure sufficient international competition in order to propose and enforce structural change? And as to national policy: should labour markets and product markets be liberalized simultaneously? Is it really necessary to deregulate labour markets, capital markets or product markets? We will encounter these questions and, if possible, try to answer them in the subsequent chapters.

Notes

1. Some of the groundwork was laid in OECD (1983). Structural reform became an international policy topic with the publication of the influential study *Structural Adjustment and Economic Performance* (OECD 1987a and 1987b). Structural reforms in the OECD have been monitored by the OECD's EDRC (Economic Development Review Committee) which annually reviews its members' economic developments, prospects and policies, see for example OECD (1993a, 1993b, 1994b and 1994c). Comprehensive reviews which summarize the policy stance with respect to structural reform in the industrialized world are: OECD (1990), OECD (1992) and OECD (1994a).
2. See Peltzman (1989) for an overview and assessment of the Chicago School model of deregulation and Baumol et al. (1982) on the theory of contestable markets.
3. See IMF (1995) for an evaluation of 45 IMF-supported adjustment programmes.
4. See Kornai (1992), McAuley (1993), Somogyi and Török (1993) and Neuber (1995) for insightful discussions of privatization, deregulation and competition policy in relation to the transformation process in Central and Eastern Europe.
5. See also van Bergeijk and Lensink (1993) who show in an applied neoclassical simulation model that there is little room for gradualism and that vigorous liberalization, even though it entails substantial destruction of obsolete capital, offers a viable transition for Bulgaria, Czechoslovakia, Hungary, Poland and Romania.
6. See, for example, Hettich and Winer (1993).
7. See Valdés (1995) on the case of Chile.

PART II
INDUSTRIAL ECONOMICS

3. Economic Dynamism, Competition and the Structure—Conduct—Performance Paradigm

The functioning of the market mechanism and the strength of competitive forces can be measured using a number of different methodologies. In this chapter we provide an overview of the methodologies for measuring the speed of product market adjustment processes and economic dynamism in OECD countries. This should allow us to assess empirically which countries are relatively rigid and which countries are relatively flexible in terms of market dynamism. So our ultimate goal is to illustrate how indicators of economic dynamism can be used to aid competition policy. Policy makers are in need of a framework to evaluate current policies and to assess the effects of changes in policies.[1] Such a framework could consist of a set of consistent indicators for the degree of competition on specific markets. These indicators could then be used to analyse changes in economic dynamism through time by relating them to changes in institutions such as deregulation, privatization and the competition policy regime. In this chapter we attempt to evaluate such indicators on the basis of the industrial organization literature that links market structure, conduct and performance.

Our aim is modest. We do not intend to give a complete overview of the literature. Rather we give a first impression of potentially useful indicators that can be used to assess certain characteristics related to economic dynamism. (In Chapter 4 we will discuss four of these indicators that have been applied in international comparisons.) Nor can the structure—conduct—performance indicators that we discuss in this chapter cover all aspects of economic dynamism. All that we can do, is to clarify the conceptual background and discuss both the advantages and the disadvantages of each indicator.

A complication of our analysis is that we can only consider single product firms which operate on one market. This is because the available national statistics and classifications of firms do not allow us to detect the diversification of firms which causes them to compete with each other on several international markets at once. This multimarket contact between firms allows for greater implicit co-ordination and tacit collusion and may have far-reaching implications for competition on these markets (see, for example, Scott 1993 and van Wegberg et al. 1994).

A second complication derives from the aggregation of observations at the level of individual firms or sectors into one macroeconomic or mesoeconomic figure. Although this is essentially a practical point that does not influence our theoretical discussion within the structure—conduct—performance paradigm, it is good to be aware of these problems from the start. Comparing aggregated data complicates the analysis. Static cross-section comparisons of aggregated observations may to a large extent be influenced by the structure of an economy rather than by the relative characteristics of the observations. In comparisons over time, the index number problem (i.e. the impact of the economic structure in the base year) may exert an arbitrary influence on the analysis. For obvious reasons, these factors may be especially relevant if structural change is occurring.

We start by explaining what we mean by 'economic dynamism', 'competition' and 'the functioning of markets'. In Section 3.2 we introduce the structure—conduct—performance paradigm, as this will provide a useful approach to classify the indicators of economic dynamism. Next we examine how the strength of competitive forces may be measured and finally we discuss indicators relating to market structure, firm conduct and firm or market performance.

3.1   The Invisible Hand

For a long time, Adam Smith's metaphor of the invisible hand has been synonymous with the co-ordinating role that prices and markets play as an allocation mechanism (Marris and Mueller 1980). The idea is that allocation is optimal in a competitive market, where suppliers compete for the favour of buyers and buyers are well informed about the prices and qualities of the products offered to them. Although each buyer and seller pursues his or her own self-interest, allocation cannot be improved upon from the point of view of society as a whole. This is because suppliers are in competition with each other to minimize costs and to maximize quality, and buyers can fulfil their needs against as low a price as possible.[2]

This story considers efficiency in production given current technologies. The term 'economic dynamism' can, however, be used in many different ways. On the labour market the term often designates situations in which supply and demand are matched in a flexible way, for example, by a high labour mobility and strong income incentives which encourage each worker to make optimal use of his or her capacities. In addition, wages adjust to changes in the relative availability and demand for different kinds of labour so that unemployment can only exist temporarily when the labour market is 'dynamic'. On the product market, economic dynamism indicates the degree to which firms are able to enter and exit markets, to grow or to contract, to innovate or imitate new products and to discover and implement new production processes. For the market as a whole, prices adjust in a flexible way to changes in the relative scarcity of products so that production is allocated between different suppliers. A dynamic market in general refers to a competitive and rapidly changing environment in which suppliers are uncertain about their position in the market in the near future. In such a market, suppliers compete for the exploitation of new, risky opportunities, the outcome of which is not determined and can neither be foreseen nor predicted (Giersch 1994).

All these characterizations of the term 'economic dynamism' focus attention on two factors:

● adaptiveness to change; and
● taking advantage of (new) opportunities.

Each factor is strongly connected to the intensity of competition. In order to survive in a competitive environment, market participants must respond adequately. That is why the promotion of competition is an important way by which policy makers in a mature economy can foster economic growth. This insight was, for example, formulated by the OECD in its influential 1987 report on structural adjustment:

> Ultimately, whether firms respond to the opportunities arising from technological advance, as well as to broader changes in economic circumstances depends largely on the intensity of competition — and on the incentives this creates for firms which successfully adjust, and the penalties for those which do not (OECD 1987b, p. 27).

Better competition often results in an expansion of the available supply of goods and services, more efficient production, and/or lower prices. If so, more potential buyers can be satisfied and welfare is improved.

One should, however, be careful not to equate rivalry and competition with dynamism. Indeed, more competition may not in all cases be welfare enhancing as co-ordination often helps to improve on the efficiency of the pure market solution. The classical motives for government intervention, such as external effects, information asymmetries and increasing returns to scope and scale, indicate situations in which this may be the case. Intellectual property rights, free-rider problems and public goods also provide examples where co-ordination is to be preferred to *laissez-faire*. Neither should one assume that the relationship between competition and dynamism is strictly positive. More competition may be welfare enhancing at a decreasing (and sometimes even negative) rate, for example, because incentives to invest are suboptimal if the number of firms is too large. The reason is that profits (and consequently investment in R&D) may be too low if there are (too) many firms (Scherer 1986). So in cases of market failure and in order to retain incentives to invest, it may be better to restrict competition rather than to let market forces work freely.

3.2   Economic Dynamism and the SCP Paradigm

In the economic literature a large number of indicators and methods can be found which can help to measure aspects of economic dynamism. Which methodology is to be used depends, first, on the purpose of the investigation and, second, on the available data. The analysis may in principle take place at any level of aggregation varying from the macroeconomic level to the in-depth case study of a specific market or firm. Generally speaking, the lower the level of aggregation and the more data are available, the larger the degrees of freedom in the choice of methodology and the more precise the measurement in principle can be. Here we focus on ways to measure the strength of competitive forces at the macroeconomic and mesoeconomic level.

All of the methodologies presented in this chapter in one way or another depend on the notion of market power. A natural point of departure is the hypothetical model of perfect competition, where market power is completely absent. The model of perfect competition rests on six crucial assumptions (Koutsoyiannis 1979, pp. 154—5):

- the number of sellers and buyers is large;
- products are homogeneous;
- entry and exit are completely free;
- all firms maximize profits, which means that no other goals are pursued;
- factors of production are free to move to the most attractive employment opportunities (perfect competition for factors of production); and
- all sellers and buyers have complete knowledge of the conditions in the market.

In addition, government intervention such as taxation, subsidization, and rationing of demand or supply is ruled out. Thus, when perfect competition prevails, each firm behaves as a price taker. The firms in the market are completely independent of each other: oligopolistic interactions between firms cannot take place. Prices are determined by matching total supply and demand and all firms earn a 'normal' profit to cover future investments.

Even though the conditions for perfect competition are too restrictive to be met in any market in real life and, moreover, the relationship between competition and dynamic efficiency is often ambiguous, much empirical research still uses the competitive norm as the best practicable basis (see, for example, Cubbin 1988, p. 7 and

Sexton 1995, p. 39). Given the assumptions of the model, an excess supply of production results in a price decline, and ultimately marginal firms will have to leave the market. In the case of an excess demand, the opposite happens.

This changes when a supplier has market power, for example, because he or she has a monopoly or because new entry is blocked. Now the supplier is able to raise his or her prices and earn an 'excess' profit. This excess profit could not have been reaped under fiercer competition, and consequently a consumer welfare loss results. This welfare loss arises because some of the potential buyers are not willing to buy the product at a higher price, and the rest of the buyers must reduce consumption of other products (now or in the future) to pay for the price increase. None of these sacrifices would have to be made if the product had been sold against marginal costs. Economic dynamism is low because market forces do not eliminate the excess profit by entry of new firms or by more competition between incumbent firms.

Before turning to the (firm-level and industry-level) indicators of economic dynamism, it is useful to present a framework of the market process. Here we use the structure—conduct—performance (SCP) paradigm well-known from industrial economics as a tool to group the different indicators of economic dynamism. This paradigm, first conceived by Mason (1939) and extended by Bain (1956), has dominated industrial economics since the Second World War (Martin 1993a, p. 5). Three key elements are to be distinguished (Scherer and Ross 1990, pp. 4—7):

●   *market structure*, that is, among others, the number and size distribution of sellers and buyers, the degree of product differentiation, and the extent to which entry and exit barriers exist;

●   *conduct*, which covers the pricing policies, policies in the area of product differentiation such as advertising and research and development, and strategic or collusive behaviour;

●   *performance*, which constitutes the productive and allocative efficiency, the dynamic efficiency in terms of economic growth and technological progress, and the profitability of the industry.

The SCP paradigm asserts that performance in a particular market depends on the conduct of buyers and sellers, which in turn is dependent on the structure of the relevant market. This is a two-way street: performance may also affect market structure, for example because high profits attract new competitors to the market, and firm conduct may influence the height of barriers to entry, which are a key element of market structure. Market structure is in turn influenced by certain basic conditions. On the supply side, these include the nature of the relevant technology, the location and ownership of raw materials, the durability of the product and the degree of unionization. On the demand side, the price elasticity of demand, the availability of substitutes and the cyclical or seasonal character of demand are basic conditions.[3]

In terms of our indicators for economic dynamism, 'market structure' indicates whether the pre-conditions to generate a dynamic competitive process are present. For example, the absence of barriers to entry or large dominant firms are pre-conditions which favour competition. When studying 'conduct', one tries to find out whether competition is actually taking place. This is done by looking at, among others, the pricing policies of firms and at company strategies in the fields of research and development and product differentiation. Finally, the 'performance' of firms or markets indicates whether the results of the competitive process are consistent with competition. For example, persistently high profits are generally not consistent with competition, as competition eliminates excess profits relatively quickly through entry of new firms.

Although an analysis based on one or more of these indicators can provide useful information on the state of competition in a particular market, a more comprehensive analysis of structure, conduct and performance is to be preferred as these characteristics of the business environment are highly interrelated phenomena. Resource constraints in terms of manpower and time, and inaccurate or unavailable data, however, often force researchers in the field of applied economics to resort to (combinations of) practical indicators such as the ones proposed in this chapter. These indicators should be seen as instruments for a first appraisal of the state of competition at the macroeconomic and mesoeconomic level. After potentially collusive sectors have been identified using these indicators, a further detailed analysis of these specific cases is required.

3.3 Market Structure Indicators

The pre-conditions for dynamic competition are reflected in market concentration, market contestability, entry and exit rates and other market structure indicators such as the export and import shares, the capital intensity and the composition of market demand.

Concentration
The most frequently used indicator to approximate market power is the degree of market concentration. It is a measure of the number and size distribution of sellers in a particular industry and has as a significant advantage that it can easily be estimated. Differences in market concentration are a key factor distinguishing the theoretical models of perfect competition, oligopoly, and monopoly. High levels of concentration improve the leverage sellers have *vis-à-vis* buyers, especially when the buyers are large in number. In addition, market concentration improves the opportunities for operating a cartel effectively, because members will find it easier to detect secret price cutting and because the costs of negotiating a cartel are lower if concentration is high.

Many indicators have been developed in this area.[4] Examples are the market share of the four largest firms (the four-firm concentration ratio $C4$), and the sum of the squared market shares of all firms in the industry (the so-called Herfindahl—Hirschman index of concentration).[5] Market concentration is high when the industry is dominated by a small number of large firms. Whether market power is also high depends among other things on the presence of substitutes for the product concerned, the openness of the market for potential entrants and on the concentration of buyers. If relatively close substitutes are available, incumbent firms can only raise prices to a limited degree, because otherwise buyers will switch to these products. When entry is costless, incumbent firms cannot raise prices either, because potential competitors would react quickly to the opportunities presented to them. The importance of buyer concentration as a countervailing power was pointed out by Galbraith as early as 1952. In fact, Galbraith (1952) identified the strength of buyers as the main force which disciplines sellers in their pricing policies. The best results for the consumer are achieved when

> upstream supply functions are highly elastic, when buyers can bring substantial power to bear on the pricing of monopolistic suppliers, and when those same buyers face substantial price competition in their end product markets (Scherer and Ross 1990, p. 528).[6]

Market concentration indicators therefore highlight the dominance of large firms. Indicators that focus on (changes in) the share of small- and medium-sized enterprises form the other side of the picture. As such, they are strongly correlated with concentration. Examples are the (growth in the) share of small enterprises in the total number of enterprises, and the (growth in the) share of small enterprises in employment (Thurik 1994).

Measures of concentration are often criticized for being static, especially by the neo-Austrian school of economic thought (Davies and Lyons 1988, pp. 10—16). If competition is seen as a process by which competitors strive to get 'one step ahead' of their rivals, measures of concentration may not give an adequate description of the strength of competitive forces. In these cases, measures of 'dynamic concentration' or market share stability may be helpful (Davies 1988a, p. 111). The basic idea is that because of the continuous thrust and counterthrust of competition, market shares will fluctuate accordingly. Indicators of market share stability measure the correlation of firms' market shares between time periods. For example, the index of market mobility of de Jong (1989, p. 23) is defined as follows:

$$M = \sum_{i=1}^{n} \left| a_{it} - a_{i(t-1)} \right| \qquad (3.1)$$

where M is the market mobility index and a_{it} is the market share of firm i at time t. If M has a value close to zero, then the market shares of the n firms in the market did not change much from one time period to the other, and economic dynamism is low. If, on the other hand, the market mobility index has a value close to two, then most suppliers were displaced by new entrants.[7] A problem with this measure of economic dynamism is that intensive rivalry need not always result in fluctuating market shares. For example, market leaders may be able to keep their market share stable through continuous improvements in efficiency. Competition in oligopoly may be on the razor's edge, even though each oligopolist is succeeding in retaining his or her market share.

Contestability

A concentrated market only becomes a problem when barriers to entry constrain potential competition. The so-called theory of contestable markets asserts that even in concentrated markets, firms will not (be able to) exercise market power as long as entry and exit are costless and can occur very quickly (Baumol et al. 1982). The reason is that in a perfectly contestable market, potential entrants can exploit all available profit opportunities by quickly entering the market, satisfying total demand and leaving the market again before the incumbent firm can react. This hit-and-run entry ensures that prices cannot exceed average costs in a contestable market.[8]

Perfect contestability depends on a number of crucial conditions (Paech 1995, p. 95). First, exit can only be costless when there are no sunk costs. This means that withdrawal from the market is without cost because the capital goods and all other investments can be leased, re-sold or transferred to other uses with no loss of value. Second, incumbent firms cannot change prices instantly, yet customers react without delay to price differences. This allows the entrant to undercut the established firms and (temporarily) serve all customers. Third, potential newcomers are available in sufficient numbers to present a credible threat to existing firms. Fourth, potential entrants evaluate the profitability of entry in terms of the incumbent firms' pre-entry prices. Finally, potential entrants must have access to the same technology and the same sources of finance as the incumbents. These conditions are quite restrictive; in practice not many markets will be perfectly contestable.[9]

Entry and exit rates

We can, however, assess the *degree* of contestability in three ways: direct comparison of entry and exit rates, comparison of the determinants of entry and exit rates and by looking at the impact of entry and exit rates on profitability.

First, entry and exit rates can be compared directly between industries or between countries.[10] A relatively high level of entry and exit would indicate that entry and exit barriers are apparently not a problem, so that economic dynamism is high. However, when entry and exit rates are relatively low, it is difficult to ascertain whether barriers to entry are high. The reason is that in theory, the threat of entry is sufficient to discipline incumbent firms so that entry need not actually take place. The direct comparison of firm dynamics in a cross-section of industries may also be complicated by differences in the stage of the product life-cycle. In the early stages of the life-cycle, firms compete for the best product design and best production techniques. Many firms enter competition and fail. Entry and exit rates are high. In the next stage of the cycle, only a small subset of products and processes has proven its superiority and is able to expand. The winners of this competition become the industry leaders whose product images and experience give them an advantage over potential competitors. The older the industry, the lower entry and exit rates become. A similar problem may occur when industries differ in the stage of the business cycle.

The second method relates entry and exit rates to variables which are expected to give incumbent firms an advantage over potential competitors such as product differentiation, economies of scale, excess capacity, absolute cost advantages or establishment regulations (see, for example, Lyons 1988, pp. 34—51). This enables the researcher to determine which factors actually act as barriers to entry. Product differentiation may help firms to attain monopoly power in the classical sense, by making their product unique due to differences in physical attributes, ancillary service or image. As a result, buyers may even be willing to pay a much higher price to obtain the 'unique' attributes of the differentiated product. Examples of monopolistic competition are the markets for clothing or personal computers, where large differences in prices exist which are not (fully) justified by differences in quality.

Economies of scale become important as a barrier to entry when a large part of the fixed costs are 'sunk' in the market. The greater the share of fixed costs in total costs and the larger the proportion that is non-recoverable on exit, the more difficult it becomes to enter the market.[11] Strategic investment in excess capacity can form an entry barrier because it can add credibility to the threat to expand production after entry or to start a price war. This is especially so if the excess capacity is a sunk cost to the incumbent, so that he or she is willing to sell against marginal costs (even when this incurs large losses: he or she has 'nothing to lose'). In addition, potential entrants may face more uncertainty about the industry demand curve than incumbents, which may cause them to interpret the excess capacity as a signal that no room is left for another producer.

Absolute cost advantages can occur when incumbents have access to cheaper or superior production factors, such as lower-cost funds, patented designs or raw materials. Establishment regulations by definition favour existing firms on the market, because they impose costs on potential entrants which the incumbents have already expended.[12] Establishment regulations can be in the form of educational requirements, certificates of craftsmanship, spatial zoning regulations, and permits in the areas of safety, health or the environment.

The third method relates entry and exit rates to profit rates to determine the strength of competitive forces (Kleijweg and Lever 1994). The more entry by new businesses occurs at a given (industry-wide or firm-level) profit rate, the more competitive the market. While entry should respond to profits, profits should also respond to entry in competitive markets. The link between entry and profits is therefore a two-way causal relationship.[13]

Entry may be of various kinds: by a newly created firm; by diversifying, either by buying or building a new plant or by altering the product mix of an existing plant; and entry may take place by a foreign-owned firm in one of the above ways. Entry by newly created firms tends to happen on a smaller scale than other forms of entry and has a significantly lower probability of survival (Mueller 1991, p. 11). By contrast, entry by an international competitor can have a substantial effect on existing firms. International differences in relative factor prices and production processes may be quite large, and foreign entrants are often well-established firms in their home or other foreign markets. This may enable them to enter the market by significantly underpricing their domestic competitors or by offering superior quality. Thus, the degree of import competition is another important indicator for the contestability of a market.[14]

Other market structure indicators
Other commonly used indicators of market structure are the export and import shares, capital intensity (i.e. investment as a percentage of value added or turnover), and the share of consumer goods in sales (Dijksterhuis et al. 1995). The export and import shares indicate the extent to which firms are exposed to foreign competition. Economic dynamism is influenced positively especially when firms are exposed to foreign competition both abroad (through exports) and on the domestic market (through import penetration). This is so because in the absence of import competition, for example due to trade barriers, large internationally operating firms may be able to charge higher prices on the domestic market (reciprocal dumping).

Capital intensity is an indicator which may be heavily correlated with buyer concentration. Sectors with a high capital intensity are often characterized by high fixed costs, and consequently decreasing average costs, which favours large firms *vis-à-vis* smaller ones (Lyons 1988, pp. 37—41). As a result, the minimum efficient scale is relatively high. In addition, new firms may have problems in raising sources of finance for entering these markets (because of imperfect capital markets), and the required capital goods are often too specific to be re-sold without loss of value. A high capital intensity may hence pose both entry and exit barriers.

Whether the product concerned is sold largely to other producers or to consumers determines several buying market characteristics, such as the number of buyers, the average size of buyers, the degree of professionality and expertise of the buyer and the degree in which middlemen are used to enable the sale (Kotler 1980, pp. 267—9). Each of these characteristics influences the division of market power between buyers and sellers. Sellers will have relatively more market power in consumer goods industries, where the number of buyers is usually large, and the size and expertise of buyers is low. As such, the share of consumer goods in sales is often strongly correlated with the concentration of buyers: the higher the proportion of consumer goods sold, the more buyers, and therefore the lower the concentration of buyers (Dijksterhuis et al. 1995, p. 653).

3.4   Indicators of Conduct

Conduct by firms which restricts competition is not easy to detect. This is especially true when one uses a macroeconomic or mesoeconomic approach. Above all, this is caused by the wide diversity of conduct that may or may not be the result of oligopolistic collusion. For example, just by looking at price changes in a cross-section of industries it is not possible to ascertain which industries engage in price-fixing agreements, because there simply may have been no economic reason to change prices. Collusion is also less traceable in the case of price leadership in a transparent market, when follower firms are willing to co-operate with the leader's decisions, or when all firms adhere to similar pricing rules. In general, the difference between tacit collusion and forms of co-ordination which are more or less inherent to the market concerned is very subtle. It is because of this complexity that the links between indicators of firm conduct and competition should be interpreted with caution. None of the proposed links is strictly deterministic, and other interpretations of empirical observations may also be valid.[15]

Price
For our purposes, the most important indicator of firm conduct is price. An efficient price mechanism co-ordinates economic activities by signalling (changes in) relative scarcity, thereby indicating the (in)compatibility of claims on given resources. Prices form the point of departure for all kinds of investment decisions. In addition, the price mechanism allocates production between relatively efficient producers and relatively inefficient producers. Prices, however, can only fulfil their co-ordinating role when they are sufficiently flexible to be 'up to date' and when they reflect actual differences in relative scarcity. This can only be achieved when markets are competitive, so that prices approach the level of marginal production costs. Cartels, for example, can fix prices at a relatively high level, given sufficient market power and barriers to entry. The consequence is that prices

cannot allocate production between the members of the cartel. The most efficient producer loses his or her competitive advantage *vis-à-vis* the other cartel members as his or her production is artificially limited. Differences in relative prices then no longer reflect differences in relative scarcity. Inflexible prices can therefore be the result of a lack of competition.

Theoretical explanations of price inflexibility are large in number. Prices in oligopoly may be less flexible because oligopolists fear the breakdown of implicit or explicit collusion. Especially when products are relatively homogeneous, small price changes can cause large fluctuations in market shares. A price war may be the result (Ross and Wachter 1975). In addition, cartels try to make market behaviour as uniform as possible, with price fixing as just one of the instruments in this respect. Cartel members, however, often differ in their price preferences, for example because of differences in costs or different estimates of the price elasticity of demand. This makes it difficult to reach an agreement. Once an understanding is reached, parties to the arrangement may be reluctant to suggest a price increase for fear of appearing weak to their 'partners'. As a result, there is a tendency to avoid price changes once agreements are reached (Scherer and Ross 1990, p. 244). More tacit forms of collusion resort to several facilitating devices as a way of communicating intentions to co-operate. Price changes may be announced in advance, prices may be recommended by a central agency, or some common pricing rule such as full-cost pricing may be adhered to.

The degree of price inflexibility can be measured in a number of different ways. Flexibility in this respect means the flexibility of prices to changes in demand, supply and costs. Changes in demand may, for example, be approximated by comparing differences in price changes during recessions and during upswings (Encaoua et al. 1983). During recessions, when demand is weak, price changes should be lower than during the expansion phase of the business cycle. The degree to which the average price change during the recession (or in the last year of the recession) is lower than during the upswing can be seen as a measure of the price response to changes in economic activity.[16] This analysis can be done at different levels of aggregation and sophistication, for example by examining the business cycle of a particular product and by correcting for differences in costs.[17] However, the method is inaccurate because it does not explicitly relate changes in prices to changes in demand or costs. In addition, the results may be sensitive to the determination of the business cycle. In Chapter 4, therefore, we will consider empirical investigations of the degree of price flexibility where changes in demand and costs are treated explicitly.

Quantity reactions
Another indicator of firm conduct can be found in the way firms expect rivals to respond to changes in their own output (Cowling and Waterson 1976). This so-called conjectural variation is the change in the output of all other firms in the industry with respect to the output of a single firm i:

$$\lambda_i = d(Q - q_i)/dq_i \tag{3.2}$$

where λ_i is the conjectural variation of firm i, Q is total market demand and q_i is the production of firm i. If the conjectural variation is zero, firm i thinks that other firms will not react to changes in its output (the so-called Cournot hypothesis). When the conjectural variation is equal to one, on the other hand, firm i believes that when it restricts its output by one per cent, rivals will do the same. If firm i maximizes its profits on the assumption that $\lambda = 1$ and when the other firms react in the manner perceived, the monopoly output will result. In this case, all firms in the market co-operate to restrict output. When the conjectural variation is minus one, rivals will compensate any attempt of firm i to pull output off the market, so that total industry output will not change. This is what happens in the perfectly competitive case. The estimation of conjectural variations thus provides information about the degree of market power that individual firms have. The higher the conjectural variation, the more market power firms have, with, for example, plus one as the monopoly result and minus one as the perfect competition result.

These elasticities can be estimated given information about the industry price elasticity of demand, and about prices, costs and the market share of a particular firm (see Bresnahan 1989 and Martin 1993a, pp. 534—43, for overviews of this literature). Given a firm which behaves as a quantity setter, the equilibrium price—cost margin of firm i satisfies the following equation:

$$(P - C)/P = s_i(1 + \lambda_i)/\epsilon \qquad (3.3)$$

where P is the price of the product concerned, C is marginal cost, s is market share, ϵ is the industry price elasticity of demand, and λ is the conjectural variation as defined in equation (3.2). The suffix i again refers to firm i. Rearrangement of expression (3.3) allows estimation of λ_i.[18]

An advantage of applying this procedure is that it makes it possible to measure market power at the level of aggregation where it is actually exercised. However, firm-level data are often difficult to obtain. This is one of the reasons why some researchers resort to the estimation of conjectural variations at the industry level.[19]

Non-price attributes
Other conduct indicators are the advertising intensity, and the research and development and investment efforts of firms.[20] Advertising may have both positive and negative effects on competition (Scherer and Ross 1990, pp. 405—6 and 435—7). On the positive side, advertising can provide valuable information to critical consumers about the existence of products, about prices, and so on. By expanding the available information about alternatives, demand curves may become more elastic so that market power may be reduced. On the other hand, advertising can influence economic dynamism negatively if it has characteristics of a fixed cost. If all firms in the market have to expend a certain amount on advertising, minimum efficient scale rises.[21] In addition, advertising is a sunk cost, as it is generally not recoverable upon exit.[22] Advertising may also act as an entry barrier when entrants have to advertise more per unit sold compared to established firms, in order to convince prospective buyers of the quality of their product. Finally, advertising is a means of differentiating products and establishing brand loyalty, which makes demand less sensitive to price changes. Market power rises as a result. Empirical evidence in this area is still inconclusive.[23]

The R&D and investment expenditures of firms share many of the characteristics of advertising expenditures. Both types of expenditures create barriers to entry when they become necessary to enter the market successfully (Lyons 1988, pp. 50—58). On the other hand, the R&D intensity is an indicator for the efforts that firms undertake to develop new products and processes. By analogy, the investment intensity serves to upgrade existing products and production facilities. With these new or better products and processes, firms hope to gain a competitive advantage. In other words, R&D and investment expenditures can be spurred by intense competition on dynamic markets, because firms which do not undertake these efforts will put themselves in an unfavourable competitive position. Many of today's most dynamic markets are characterized by large R&D expenditures, such as the semiconductor and aircraft industry, where rivalry is extremely strong. Whether or not R&D and investment expenditures promote competition is therefore unclear from a theoretical point of view.[24]

3.5   Indicators of Performance

Firm or market performance refers to the outcome of the competitive process, and is usually analysed jointly with indicators of firm conduct and market structure. Performance indicators of economic dynamism are the profitability of the firm or industry concerned, the productive and allocative efficiency which is achieved, the dynamic efficiency in terms of new products and processes and the growth in domestic or foreign sales.

Price—cost margin
A well-known indicator of profitability is the so-called Lerner index or price—cost margin $(P - C)/P$, which is a measure of the extent to which firms are able to raise their prices P above their marginal costs C. A Lerner index close to zero indicates intensive competition, while a relatively high value may indicate a lack of actual competition.[25]

The Lerner index can give a useful first impression of the degree to which possible abuses of market power have led to an increase in profitability.[26] This is even more so because figures on prices and costs are relatively easily obtained. In order to gain more insights into the causes of the high profits, profitability can be analysed jointly with a market structure variable such as concentration. The theoretical justification for these analyses is provided by Cowling and Waterson (1976). Given any number of identical firms producing a homogeneous product, with each firm behaving as a profit-maximizing quantity setter who anticipates no change in the output of rivals, the equilibrium price—cost margin satisfies the following equation:[27]

$$(P - C)/P = s_i/\epsilon \qquad (3.4)$$

where P is the price of the product, C is marginal cost, ϵ is the price elasticity of demand and $s_i = 1/n$ if firms are identical (n is the number of firms in the market). The larger the number of sellers and the higher the price elasticity of demand, the lower the market power (as measured by the Lerner index) of any firm in the market is expected to be. A positive correlation between the number of sellers and the price—cost margin is considered as evidence of collusive behaviour.[28] The consensus among industrial organization researchers, however, is that

> the correlation between industry concentration and either firm or industry profitability, if positive, is surely weak, and might very well be non-existent or even negative (Mueller 1991, p. 3).[29]

X-inefficiencies

One of the reasons for the weak relationship between concentration and profitability is that monopoly power may not only result in excessive profits, but could also lead to excessive costs. When competitive pressure is weak, managers may tolerate higher than necessary cost levels or may engage in 'rent-seeking' — which incurs substantial wasteful expenditures to obtain or strengthen monopoly positions. These activities have been labelled Directly Unproductive Profitseeking (DUP) activities (Bhagwati 1991, pp. 129—206). Essentially DUP activities generate shifts in income and profits at the expense of productive inputs: DUP activities dupe. Productive efficiency is therefore not optimal, which results in so-called X-inefficiencies (Scherer and Ross 1990, pp. 668—78). X-inefficiencies are one of the main reasons for the privatization of state-owned enterprises which are sheltered from competition (Ferguson 1988, pp. 157—9). Examples are outlays for emoluments, overmanning, maintenance of excess capacity, bribery and lobbying.

Figure 3.1 Illustration of the measurement of X-inefficiencies by estimation of the 'best-practice' isoquant Q*

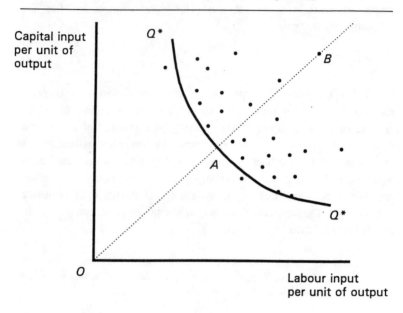

The degree of X-inefficiencies or productive efficiency is another possible indicator for the strength of competition. In a competitive environment, X-inefficiencies should be low and productive efficiency high. X-inefficiencies could, for example, be measured by comparing the capital and labour inputs per unit of output among different plants within an industry and across nations. By fitting a 'best-practice' isoquant Q^* through the observations using the least inputs at varying capital—labour ratios, a ranking of relative productive efficiency can be obtained. Figure 3.1 depicts the hypothetical case of a cross-country comparison of the efficiency in a given industry. The farther away an observation is from the estimated isoquant Q^*, the less efficient is the observed production point. A rough measure of X-inefficiency is therefore the extent to which actual practice departs from best practice, i.e. the distance *OB* relative to *OA* in Figure 3.1.[30] Empirical evidence suggests a positive correlation between productive efficiency and indicators of market structure such as the number of firms and the degree of import competition, thereby confirming the X-inefficiency hypothesis.[31]

Persistence of profits

A problem with the Lerner index is that it assumes that markets are in equilibrium. If high profits in concentrated industries are only a temporary phenomenon, because competition becomes fiercer in response to profit opportunities, economic dynamism is high. This means that not only the size of (excess) profits at a particular moment in time should be considered, but also the duration of excess profits.

A way around this problem is provided by the persistence of profits literature, which tries to measure how fast excess profits erode (Brozen 1971). The idea is that in a dynamic and competitive environment, high profits cannot persist long because other firms will want 'a piece of the cake'. High profits will trigger entry by new firms and increased competition between existing firms. As a result, profits approach their long-run equilibrium value relatively quickly. On the other hand, competition may be hampered by barriers to entry or collusive behaviour of incumbent firms so that profit levels are permanently high. The operationalization of the approach and the empirical results achieved in a cross-country comparison will be summarized in Chapter 4.

A criticism of the use of 'profits' as a measure of 'competition' which also applies to the Lerner index is that it suffers from problems of aggregation over different products and over different firms. Firms with many different products may have relatively high persistent profits, so the intensity of competition seems to be low. However, competition may in fact be very fierce if the profit per product can only be sustained for a short time span. By analogy, if profits in an industry are persistently high, this may be due to the fact that there are always a certain number of firms with high profits. But because of the intense competition in the industry, these may be different ones in each period.

Output indicators

The dynamic performance of firms and markets is usually measured by output indicators such as the number of new products, the number of new patents for innovations, or the number of quotations in scientific journals.[32] In dynamic high-growth sectors, firms need to invest continuously in new products and processes to maintain market share and profitability. The global consumer electronics industry is an example. Competition is fierce because of short product life-cycles, critical and demanding consumers and large differentials in costs and quality between different producers. Firms must continuously develop new products and processes in order to survive. Thus, a high innovative output of a sector can be an indication that competition is strong.

Dijksterhuis et al. (1995) also consider growth in domestic or foreign sales as an indicator of economic dynamism. Given that no large overcapacity exists initially, growth in sales creates room for new competitors to enter the market. In these markets, existing firms must continuously upgrade capacity through investment, because otherwise new competitors will try to enter the market. For the same reason, existing firms must keep prices in line with costs. However, it is important to keep in mind that growth in sales can be caused by many things. At the mesoeconomic level, a sector which grows strongly may be profiting from trade liberalization or an expansion in the demand for the product concerned. This does not have to go hand in hand with intensive competition *within* the sector. At the level of the individual firm, a dominant firm with superior products may have substantial market power, but at the same time experience a strong rise in sales.

3.6   Conclusions

Table 3.1 summarizes the different kinds of indicators of economic dynamism we have discussed in this chapter. In addition, we show the expected influence on competition of each of these indicators. For example, markets in which productive efficiency is relatively high are expected to be more competitive, and the same holds for markets in which prices are relatively flexible. In the case of advertising, R&D

and investment expenditures, the theoretical effect on competition is ambiguous.

Table 3.1   *Summary of structure, conduct and performance indicators of economic dynamism*

Structure	Expected relation to competition
Market concentration	—
Market mobility	+
Entry and exit	+
Import competition	+
Exports	+
Capital intensity	—
Consumer goods	—
Conduct	
Price flexibility	+
Collusion (Conjectural variation)	—
Advertising expenditures	+/—
R&D expenditures	+/—
Investment expenditures	+/—
Performance	
Price—cost margins	—
Persistence of profits	—
Productive efficiency	+
Output of innovations	+
Growth in sales	+

In order to measure the degree of competition on macroeconomic and mesoeconomic markets for goods and services, a large number of indicators can be used. In this chapter, three broad groups of indicators are evaluated: indicators of market structure, firm conduct and performance. One lesson from our discussion is that one should never look at any one indicator in isolation. Market structure, conduct and performance are so diverse in reality, that by focusing on just one indicator, one is bound to make errors of observation and/or interpretation. For example, a high concentration may be an indication that producers have market power, but one can only know this for sure by analysing other aspects of structure, conduct and performance such as buyer concentration, barriers to entry, profitability and productive efficiency. Consequently, no indicator taken by itself can be seen as evidence for abuses of market power or artificial limitations of the contestability of markets. Given the impossibility of performing an all-encompassing analysis, the usual approach is to combine, for example, a performance indicator with one or more indicators of market structure. Even then, however, the evidence is at best circumstantial so that further analysis of those sectors where competition seems to be suboptimal is required.

A second lesson is that with such a wide array of indicators, theoretical and empirical inconsistencies can easily occur. According to one indicator, for example, market A might be more dynamic than market B, but according to another indicator the reverse may be the case. In the next chapter, we look at how well empirical researchers so far have succeeded in avoiding these problems.

Notes

1.   See, for example, Kremers (1993, pp. 184—6).
2.   This theoretical result depends on two crucial assumptions (Marris and Mueller 1980, p. 32). The first is that competition is atomistic, which means that no competitor is relatively large compared to the other. The second is that all competition is price competition. Non-price competition, such as competition by research and development or by offering products with certain unique attributes, changes the implications of the invisible hand theorem, in the sense that less non-price competition, rather than more non-price competition, may be Pareto optimal. Later on, we will discuss the implications of a relaxation of the second assumption.
3.   See Schmalensee (1989) on the long run endogeneity of basic conditions, structure, conduct and performance.
4.   See Curry and George (1983) for a survey of concentration indicators and some explanations for the rise in concentration in the manufacturing sectors of the United States and the United Kingdom.
5.   Because observations on market shares are often not available, market concentration is usually proxied by employment shares (for example, the share of the four largest firms in industry employment).
6.   See also Scherer and Ross (1990, pp. 533—5) for a review of the empirical evidence on this topic.
7.   See Das et al. (1993) for an application.
8.   Actually, as long as there are at least two incumbent firms in an industry with decreasing average costs, prices cannot exceed marginal costs. See Lyons (1988), p. 31.

9. Baumol himself, however, seems to have little doubt that real-world markets constitute 'reasonable approximations to the efficient structures'. See Baumol (1982), p. 8.

10. See Love (1995) on the measurement of entry rates and OECD (1994d) and ENSR (1993) for a recent international comparison of entry rates.

11. This is especially so when incumbent firms are willing to respond quickly and aggressively to entry by price competition.

12. In some cases these regulations are almost impossible to circumvent. The French *Loi Royer*, for example, gives a committee of local politicians and existing store owners the power to block the creation of large stores. Since 1984 almost all projects were rejected as a result of this law (McKinsey 1994).

13. See Geroski and Schwalbach (1991) and Geroski (1991) for an overview of the theoretical and empirical literature.

14. Contestability with respect to foreign entrants can be measured directly by estimating the elasticity of imports to domestic price changes. A high elasticity indicates a relatively open market. Note, however, that the absence of import competition may also indicate the competitiveness of domestic producers. This may be the case if the products concerned are in fact traded internationally and the domestic market is not protected by import barriers.

15. See, for example, Jacquemin (1996) who deals with this problem from the point of view of competion policy makers.

16. More precisely, for each economic cycle (recession and expansion) the percentage change in the aggregate price index should be related to the change in industrial production. This makes it possible to determine the output elasticity of prices, i.e. the percentage change in inflation due to a fall in output.

17. See Bagwell and Staiger (1995) for a recent investigation into collusive pricing over the business cycle.

18. Actually, expression (3.3) links a performance indicator (the price—cost margin) with indicators of firm conduct (conjectural variation) and market structure (market share), as will be explained in the following section.

19. This requires two additional simplifying assumptions: (1) the product concerned is homogeneous and (2) the conjectural variation is equal among all firms in the industry (see Appelbaum 1982).

20. Legal strategies are also considered as an indicator of firm conduct. An example is the patenting strategy of firms, which may help firms to appropriate a larger part of the benefits of their research (Cohen and Levin 1989, pp. 1090—95). Whether advertising is considered an aspect of market structure or firm conduct, is rather arbitrary. As far as product differentiation through advertising is an intrinsic characteristic of the product concerned, it may be considered an aspect of market structure. However, because advertising is nowadays an integral part of company strategy and it is often consciously used both to create market niches for the own product and barriers to entry for competitors, we rank advertising under 'conduct'. The same holds for research and development efforts of firms, which may be classified both as 'conduct' and as 'performance'. Here, we make the distinction between the R&D input (conduct) and the

results of these efforts, the output of new products and processes (performance).

21. See the discussion on capital intensity as a barrier to entry in this chapter.

22. This depends on how successful the product and the advertising campaign concerned have been. No one would attach value to the advertising campaign of a flunked product, but a brand name of a successful product may have potential to be (re-)sold.

23. See Das et al. (1993) for a recent overview of the empirical evidence. In this paper, a measure of market share instability is used to test for the effects of advertising on competition. The empirical results show a statistically significant positive correlation between advertising intensity and market share instability in 163 US manufacturing industries during the period 1978—88. According to this investigation, therefore, advertising generally stimulates competition.

24. See Cohen and Levin (1989) for an overview of the — still inconclusive — empirical evidence concerning R&D expenditures.

25. Price—cost margins usually vary over the business cycle, as a better utilization of productive capacity results in lower unit costs during business cycle upswings. Any empirical investigation into the relation between price—cost margins and competition should therefore control for the effects of the business cycle.

26. See Hall (1986), Roeger (1995) and Felder (1995) for three more sophisticated versions of the Lerner index.

27. When sellers do expect reactions of competitors to changes in their own output, which means that the conjectural variations are non-zero, equation (3.3) is the result.

28. Another explanation is the hypothesis that efficient firms achieve both high market shares and high profits. The observed positive correlation between concentration and profit levels can therefore also be due to the superior efficiency of large firms. See Eckard (1995) for a recent investigation of this topic.

29. See also Schmalensee (1989), p. 976 on this conclusion.

30. Another method relies on a direct comparison of productivity levels using industry specific conversion factors to make the different sectoral productivity levels internationally comparable. See van Ark (1995).

31. See Scherer and Ross (1990, pp. 668—78) and Mayes et al. (1994) for an overview of the empirical evidence, and Donni and Fecher (1994) for a recent application to the insurance industry in the OECD countries. See also MacDonald (1994), who shows that import competition led to large increases in labour productivity growth in highly concentrated industries in the US during the period 1972—87.

32. The measurement of innovation output in terms of new products often requires the use of questionnaires. See Brouwer and Kleinknecht (1994) for an example.

4. Measuring the Speed of the Invisible Hand

The functioning of markets is an inherently dynamic process, very unlike the static world that is often suggested by traditional undergraduate microeconomic courses. In contrast with the motionless state of equilibrium that we know from introductory textbooks, we need words like rivalry, adjustment, strategy and disequilibrium to describe markets in the real world. Indeed, there is no reason to assume that the invisible hand is chained to a particular state of affairs. This dynamism, however, often breaks down when markets do not function properly, especially when prices do not adjust to clear markets. Carlton (1989, p. 918) argues that price rigidity may be a much more relevant phenomenon than the wage rigidity that features in macroeconomic theory and considers the emphasis by macroeconomists on wage rigidity as a cause of macroeconomic difficulty as 'misplaced'. Indeed, for a long time mainstream macroeconomics has paid little attention to the rigidity of prices, perhaps because the influence of price rigidity on unemployment was not seen as important as the effect of wage rigidity.

In this chapter we resort to the rich industrial organization literature that deals empirically with questions related to (the determinants of) the rapidity of market adjustment processes, providing an overview of empirical assessments of the speed of the invisible hand at the macroeconomic and mesoeconomic levels. We take a keen look at the potential applicability of the findings by macroeconomic analysts and model builders, focusing on four variables that play a key role in economic adjustment processes: profits, mark-up ratios, responsiveness to supply and demand shocks, and rigidity of prices. In doing so, we lean heavily on the concepts developed in Chapter 3. Our aim is to assess in which countries a lack of economic dynamism might pose a policy problem by discussing available internationally comparable evidence. The next sections are structured as follows. We start with a discussion of the theoretical background of the indicator; next we deal with estimation issues; and finally we discuss the findings and compare the results across countries. Section 4.1 takes a closer look at investigations of the persistence of profits. Section 4.2 uses mark-ups (or Lerner indices) to identify to what extent prices exceed marginal costs, i.e. real world departures from perfect competition. The following sections are concerned with different measures of the degree of price flexibility as an indicator of economic dynamism. In Section 4.3 we summarize the evidence on the flexibility of prices to changes in costs and demand. Applying the concept of hysteresis to the markets for goods and services, Section 4.4 identifies the extent of product market inertia in the OECD by means of a comparative analysis of macroeconomic price dynamics. Since this is a rather new application we discuss theory as well as measurement at the mesoeconomic and macroeconomic levels. The final section evaluates the usefulness of the indicators, discusses the main findings of this chapter and draws conclusions about the possibility of ranking countries according to a comprehensive set of indicators.

### 4.1	The Persistence of Profits

Theories of economic progress often point out dynamic aspects of rivalry and stress the need for sufficiently large profits as these provide the investment funds for research, product development and experimentation. Schumpeter (1943) and Galbraith (1952) have even argued that technological change is higher in a less competitive economy. In their view, persistently large profits are an indication that an industry is extremely successful in maintaining its position through heavy investment. This contrasts with the view that profits in a competitive industry will tend to be not much more than a normal rate of return on capital and that high profits will be a temporary phenomenon.

In the persistence of profits literature, competition is not seen as a process for allocating a given stock of resources. Rather it is a process through which the innovation of new products and processes creates temporary monopolistic positions. Such monopolies disappear over time as new firms enter the market and imitate and improve the new product. Markets are thus constantly in a state of flux, with temporary monopoly positions as an integral part of this process (Mueller 1990b, p. 1).

Since we want to say something about economic dynamism, the crucial question is: how fast will excess profits disappear in dynamic and competitive industries? This adjustment speed of profits to their long-run equilibrium value can serve as an indicator of the strength of competitive forces.

Estimation
Empirically, persistence of profits can be modelled as follows (Geroski 1990). First, assume that the evolution of firm-level profits during time can be separated into profit changes due to competitive forces (E_{it}) and profit changes due to other, non-systematic factors (μ_t). The variable E_{it} in equation (4.1) therefore describes the net effect of new firms entering the market, the presence of potential entrants which may discipline incumbent firms and competition between existing firms. The net effect of increased competition on firm-level profits is reflected in the coefficient γ_{1i}: net increases in competition by entry lead to lower profits for existing firms.

$$\pi_{it} - \pi_{i(t-1)} = \gamma_{0i} - \gamma_{1i}E_{it} - \gamma_{2i}\pi_{i(t-1)} + \mu_t \qquad (4.1)$$

where
π_{it} = profit of firm i at time t
E_{it} = profit change of firm i at time t due to competitive forces
μ_t = error term, $\mu_t \sim N(0, \sigma_\mu^2)$.

Note that if γ_2 were equal to zero, equation (4.1) would reduce to a random walk with a positive drift in the zero entry equilibrium. The steady-state value of profits may then approach infinity as t approaches infinity. Equation (4.2) indicates that entry occurs as soon as profits exceed the long-run equilibrium value π_i^*. Thus, θ_i reflects the magnitude of the effect of excess profits on competition. The higher θ_i, the more entry is attracted by those profits that can be bid away. The parameter γ_{2i} ($0 < \gamma_{2i} < 1$) ensures the stability of the system.

$$E_{it} = \theta_i(\pi_{i(t-1)} - \pi_i^*) + \epsilon_t \tag{4.2}$$

where

π_i^* = equilibrium level of profits at which all entry is zero
ϵ_t = error term, $\epsilon_t \sim N(0, \sigma_\epsilon^2)$.

Because E_{it} is a latent variable, the parameters of this structural model cannot be estimated directly.[1] A reduced-form equation can, however, be derived from the model. This reduced-form equation can be estimated with data on the evolution of the profits of individual firms through time:

$$\pi_{it} = \alpha_i + \lambda_i \pi_{i(t-1)} + \xi_{it} \tag{4.3}$$

where

$\alpha_i = \gamma_{0i} + \gamma_{1i}\theta_i\pi_i^*$
$\lambda_i = 1 - \gamma_{1i}\theta_i - \gamma_{2i}$
$\xi_{it} = \mu_{it} - \gamma_{1i}\epsilon_t,\ \xi_{it} \sim N(0, \sigma_\xi^2)$.

In order to correct for business cycle factors, each firm's profit rate should be taken as a deviation from the sample mean for each period.

Equation (4.3) contains two parameters (α and λ) that offer an indication of the strength of competitive forces:

● the long-run equilibrium level of profits $\pi_i^p = \alpha_i/(1 - \lambda_i)$; and
● the adjustment speed of profits to their long-run level $(1-\lambda_i)$.

The long-run equilibrium level of profits is the profit level of the firm to which short-run profits converge. A relatively high 'permanent' profit rate may indicate that competition is hampered, for example, due to barriers to entry or because newcomers are too small to actually threaten incumbent firms. Not only should the level of the long-run profit be relatively low if competition is strong, but the inter-firm differences in long-run profit rates should also be small. In the long run, capital should flow to those activities where the highest profit can be realized. Arbitrage on the product market is therefore the mechanism which should equalize long-run profits.

The adjustment speed of current profits to this long-run equilibrium level indicates how fast the long-run profit rate is reached. From λ_i, the time period can be determined in which half the adjustment of profits to their long-run equilibrium level is completed. This half-life of excess returns (T_i) can be calculated as follows (Geroski 1990, p. 23):

$$T_i = \log(\tfrac{1}{2})/\log\lambda_i \qquad\qquad 0 < \lambda_i < 1 \qquad\qquad (4.4)$$

The higher the persistence parameter λ_i, the longer the half-life of excess returns is. For example, if λ_i is one half, the half-life of excess profits is precisely one year. If, on the other hand, the persistence parameter reaches a value of 0.75, then the half-life of excess profits is almost 2.5 years. Thus, the persistence of profits methodology assumes that in a competitive environment, competitors are bound to react quickly to excess profits. Both the long-run equilibrium level of profits and the degree to which short-run profits persist are indicators of the strength of this reaction.

Findings
A number of estimates of the persistence of above-normal profit levels exist. A problem, however, with many of these estimates is that they are difficult to compare — either because the empirical model is not the same, or because of differences in both the level of aggregation of the analysis and the period that is investigated. In addition, differences in the chosen definition of profits hamper a proper comparison. The estimates published under the editorship of Mueller (1990a) are the best available material in this respect as the country studies deployed both a uniform methodology and a common profit definition. Even then, however, comparability is not guaranteed. Differences between economic profits and accounting profits, differences in accounting practices, differences in statistical definitions, differences in time period and differences in sample selection altogether warrant a serious caveat to the robustness of the inferences based on this material. Hence these results should be interpreted with caution.

Table 4.1 shows the empirical estimates of the strength of competitive forces according to both the spread in long-run profits and the half-life of excess profits. This was done by estimation of equation (4.3) with firm-level data.[2] We use the spread in long-run profits and not the degree of persistence of initial profits because the latter may be influenced by random factors. The spread in long-run profits is calculated by dividing the sample of firms into six equally large groups, ranked by the level of initial profits. The spread in long-run profits can then be easily determined as the difference in profits between the most profitable and least profitable categories of firms. Competition is strong when the spread in long-run profits is small. In that case, arbitrage on the product market is able to (almost) equalize inter-firm differences in profits, so that all profit opportunities are utilized. The half-life of excess profits indicates how fast this process works.

In all countries of the sample, permanent differences in profitability exist. Competition according to this measure is the strongest in Japan, West Germany, the United Kingdom and the United States in the period 1964—80, as a relatively high convergence in long-run profits is achieved. On the other hand, competition is weaker in Canada, France, the Netherlands and the United States in the period 1950—72.[3] No large differences exist in the adjustment speed of profits to their long-run level except for the case of Sweden. In general, half the adjustment is realized at 5—12 months (it takes 20 months to 4 years to realize 95 per cent of the adjustment).

Figure 4.1 offers a graphical representation of Table 4.1. The horizontal axis depicts the adjustment speed of profits to their long-run equilibrium level, λ. Higher values of the persistence parameter indicate lower adjustment speeds and therefore less competition. The vertical axis shows the spread in the long-run profit rate of two categories of firms: the most profitable and least profitable. The dotted lines in the figure denote the average values of the spread in long-run profits and in the persistence parameter. As a result, four quadrants can be obtained, which can be used to indicate whether a country is over- or underperforming on a particular indicator.

Table 4.1 Empirical estimates of the speed of profit adjustment: short-term persistence of current profits (measured by the half-life of excess profits T) and spread in long-run profit levels of most profitable and least profitable categories of firms ($\pi_{high}^p - \pi_{low}^p$)

Country	Survey	Number of firms	Estimation period	Spread in long-run profits	Half-life of excess profits T (months)
Japan	Odagiri and Yamawaki 1990	376	1964—82	1.5	11
Germany	Schwalbach and Mahmood 1990	290	1961—82	1.6	8
United Kingdom	Cubbin and Geroski 1990	243	1951—77	2.6	12
United States	Mueller 1990c	413	1964—80	3.7	11
Sweden	Odagiri and Yamawaki 1990	43	1967—85	6.1	34
United States	Mueller 1990c	551	1950—72	7.5	5
Netherlands	Kleijweg and Nieuwenhuijsen 1995	2085	1978—91	8.6	8
France	Jenny and Weber 1990	450	1965—82	9.7	8
Canada	Khemani and Shapiro 1990	161	1968—82	18.7	7

75

Only Germany is in the south-west quadrant where competition is relatively 'strong', i.e where both the spread in long-run profits and the short-term persistence of profits point to strong competition. For the other countries the results are ambiguous. There are no countries in the north-east quadrant where 'weak' competition could unambiguously be diagnosed.

Figure 4.1   Short-term persistence of current profits (λ) and spread in long-run profit levels of most profitable and least profitable categories of firms ($\pi_{high}^{p} - \pi_{low}^{p}$)

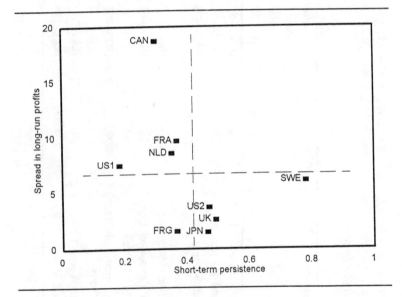

Notes: Estimation period: US1 United States 1950—72; US2 United States 1964—80; FRG West Germany 1961—82; JPN Japan 1964—82; CAN Canada 1968—82; SWE Sweden 1967—85; UK United Kingdom 1951—77; FRA France 1965—82; NLD the Netherlands 1978—91.

Country averages are unweighted averages of firm-level estimates.

Sources: See Table 4.1.

How can these results be explained? To begin with, no single variable stands out as the ultimate explanation for the observed patterns of adjustment speeds and permanent profit rates (Geroski and Mueller 1990, pp. 190—96). Differences in long-run profit levels were found to correlate with a firm's market share, product differentiation (operationalized by advertising or industry R&D), capital intensity and growth of demand.

The persistence of short-run deviations of profits from their permanent levels is found to be related to entry and exit barriers. A partial explanation for the relatively high permanent profits of the United States in the period 1950—72 may be the fact that many markets were relatively protected from competition, both from domestic firms and from abroad (Geroski and Mueller 1990, p. 190). The large firms which emerged after the Second World War often had dominant positions and also had access to favourable investment opportunities. Rising import competition, anti-trust actions and deregulation have caused a substantial increase in competition since the beginning of the 1960s (Gordon 1994, pp. 65—8).

Although Canada experienced relatively high levels of import penetration in the period 1968—82, this economy also had rather high tariffs and high levels of concentration (Geroski and Mueller 1990, p. 190). Industry concentration may also provide an explanation for the West German and French results, as concentration is substantially lower in West Germany than in France (Yamawaki et al. 1989, p. 116). In addition, both in France (Jenny and Weber 1976) and in West Germany (Neumann et al. 1985), a positive relation between concentration and profitability has been found.[4] However, concentration is even higher in Japan, and this economy is generally thought to be protected from foreign competition. For the case of Japan, specific national characteristics such as the relative abundance of capital, lifetime employment and overregulation of product markets may have caused allocative distortions especially in those sectors not exposed to foreign competition. These inefficiencies may explain the relatively low mean (initial and long-run) profits observed in Japan *vis-à-vis* the other countries in the sample. The most profitable category firms in Japan earn a long-run profit of only 0.7 percentage points above the sample average. In the other countries this figure is considerably higher, amounting to 1.5 in the United States (1964—80), 1.9 in the United Kingdom, 4.1 in

Sweden, 4.7 in the United States (1950—72), 5.0 in the Netherlands, 6.4 in France and 7.9 in Canada.[5] The results for the Netherlands correspond to the general perception that the degree of competition is low in the Dutch economy because of restrictive agreements, overregulation and barriers to entry (OECD 1993b).

4.2   Mark-up Ratios

The ratio between prices and marginal costs (the so-called mark-up ratio or Lerner index) is an important indicator for the existence of potential problems related to deviations from an optimal allocation. Profit maximization implies that the firm equates marginal revenue and marginal costs. Hence it sets its price level p at

$$p = MC/(1-1/\epsilon) \tag{4.5}$$

where ϵ is the absolute value of the price elasticity of the demand curve as perceived by the firm. We can write the mark-up ratio μ as $(1-1/\epsilon)^{-1}$. Although prices and marginal costs may also differ because of fixed costs (such as expenditures on research and development or on advertising), mark-up ratios are often used to identify wedges (between marginal costs and prices) that are due to market power and specific policies.

Estimation
Whereas prices can be observed directly, marginal costs can only be estimated indirectly. Hall (1986) developed a method that inspired many empirical investigations. This method allowed Hall to identify the mark-up ratio in some fifty US industries. Assuming that labour is the only variable input, Hall proposed to measure the marginal costs MC of firm i at time t as

$$MC_{it} = w_{it}\Delta L_{it}/(\Delta Q_{it}-\pi_{it}Q_{it}) \tag{4.6}$$

where w_{it} is the (industry) wage rate, L_{it} is employment, Q_{it} is the volume of production and π_{it} is the rate of technical progress. Combining equations (4.5) and (4.6), solving for the change in output and writing in rates of change we have

$$\Delta Q_{it}/Q_{it} = \mu_{it} (\Delta L_{it}/L_{it}) (w_{it}L_{it}/p_{it}Q_{it}) + \pi_{it} \qquad (4.7)$$

where the first term of the right-hand side is the mark-up ratio μ_{it} times the change of labour input weighed by its share in revenue $p_{it}Q_{it}$ and the final term represents technological change. If competition is perfect we have $\epsilon_i = -\infty$ (so $\mu_{it} = 1$) and the so-called Solow residual (the part of real growth not explained by the growth of the variable input L_{it}) measures technological change.[6] Assuming that technology shocks and short-term fluctuations are uncorrelated, equation (4.7) can be used to estimate the mark-up ratio μ_{it}. If the mark-up ratio is 1, competition is perfect. Hall (1986) finds that the mark-up ratios typically exceed the value of 1.5 in many industries.

Roeger (1995) improved on Hall's method, which often produced unreliable and inaccurate estimates. Roeger (1995) confronted Solow residuals that were calculated from the production function and the cost function, respectively, eliminating technological progress (a variable that could only be approximated very roughly). The difference between the two Solow residuals gives an equation from which ϵ can be estimated directly (equation (4.8)) and thus we can calculate the mark-up ratio μ.

$$\Delta y_{it} = \epsilon_i^{-1} \Delta x_{it} + v_{it} \qquad (4.8)$$

where

Δy_{it} = $\Delta Q_{it}\Delta p_{it} - \alpha(\Delta w_{it}+\Delta L_{it}) - (1 - \alpha)(\Delta r_{it}+\Delta K_{it})$

Δx_{it} = $\Delta Q_{it}\Delta p_{it} - (\Delta r_{it}+\Delta K_{it})$

α = labour share

v_{it} = error term, $v_{it} \sim N(0, \sigma_v^2)$

r_t = interest rate

K_{it} = capital stock.

Findings

Table 4.2 reports estimated mark-up ratios for total manufacturing in 14 OECD countries. It is important to note that all estimates are significantly larger than 1 at the usual confidence levels. Hence manufacturing in the 14 OECD countries departs (to different degrees) from the hypothetical perfect competition case. The estimated mark-up ratios again illustrate that competition is stronger in the United States than in the European countries, the United Kingdom being the exception.

Table 4.2   Estimated mark-up ratios for total manufacturing in 14 OECD countries (1971—90)

France	1.26
Finland	1.25
Australia	1.25
Japan	1.22
Sweden	1.20
Italy	1.20
Germany	1.18
Canada	1.18
Netherlands	1.18
Belgium	1.17
Norway	1.16
Denmark	1.16
United States	1.15
United Kingdom	1.14

Source: OECD Secretariat, based on STAN Database, using Roeger's (1995) method.

4.3 The Speed of Price Adjustment

The adjustment speed of prices to changes in costs and demand is the measure of price flexibility which we will discuss in this section. Excessively slow price responses to cost and demand shocks may give rise to a serious misallocation of resources and are likely to be an integral part of the mechanism that generates cyclical fluctuations in employment and output (Geroski 1992). In addition, price inertia may also signal an unwillingness to respond to new market developments, in terms of both technological opportunities and changes in demand (OECD 1987b).

Economic theory provides a wide range of explanations for the phenomenon that firms choose to postpone their price responses in the face of cost or demand shocks. Some explanations of inflexible prices focus on the costs related to price changes (Mankiw 1985), kinks in the demand curve (Stigler 1978), full- or normal-cost pricing (Geroski 1992) and incomplete information about costs and demand (Bhaduri and Falkinger 1990 and Garman and Richards 1991). However, many economists believe that prices are likely to be more inflexible in less competitive markets. One of the arguments is that firms in narrow oligopolies may be reluctant to upset fragile (implicit or explicit) pricing understandings or implement price-smoothing policies due to lower discount rates and a firmer commitment to the market (Phlips 1980 and Blinder 1982). Intertemporal profit maximization causes these firms to trade off current profitability for higher profitability in the future by delaying price changes due to supply or demand shocks.

The extent, however, to which firms are able to normalize cost and demand changes depends on the stability of their market positions in terms of market share and profitability. In dynamic industries characterized by intensive rivalry and continuous changes in products and processes, firms are uncertain about their future market position which gives them strong incentives to secure short-term profits. Therefore, a high responsiveness of prices to current shocks is required. On the other hand, in industries where the market positions of its members are relatively persistent, firms can afford to take a 'long view'. The intensity of competition may thus be an important determinant of the extent to which current market conditions affect prices. Martin (1993b), for example, shows in a theoretical model of price adjustment that the speed of price adjustment depends positively on the price elasticity of demand and on the number of firms in a market, and negatively on the degree of collusion between firms. The degree of collusion is measured by conjectural variation.[7] The extent of price inertia thus depends both on market structure and on firm conduct.

Estimation

The empirical analysis is usually conducted on the basis of a two-step estimation procedure. The first step is the estimation of the speed of price adjustment on the assumption that price changes are a weighted average of past price changes and current changes in costs and demand. If current changes in costs and demand are weighted relatively high, prices react quickly to external shocks.

The second step is to explain the inter-industry variation in adjustment speed, by relating these to other indicators of economic dynamism. Here, market concentration is the most commonly used explanatory variable. In addition, the length of the production period may also be relevant as firms with long production periods may have larger inventories. If these firms use the FIFO (First In, First Out) system of inventory management, then output prices will adjust more slowly to changes in input prices.

Assuming that the responsiveness of prices to changes in costs and demand is identical, the general price adjustment model can be written as follows (all variables in rates of growth):

$$p_{it} = \lambda_{it} p_{i(t-1)} + (1 - \lambda_{it})(\alpha_{it} + \beta_{it} D_{it} + \gamma_{it} C_{it}) + \varsigma_{it} \qquad (4.9)$$

where p_{it} is the actual price change, D_{it} is the change in demand, C_{it} is a matrix of cost variables, α_{it} is the change in current market conditions independent of changes in costs and demand, and ς_{it} is the error term. The size of β_{it} and γ_{it} reflect the relative importance of the cost and demand components for price-setting.[8] The parameter λ_{it} indicates the sensitivity of current prices to changes in current costs and demand. The higher the extent of price inertia (λ_{it}), the lower the speed of price adjustment $(1 - \lambda_{it})$.

Findings

Table 4.3 shows the results of some of the empirical evaluations of the speed of price adjustment. Not all investigators have used the general price adjustment model of equation (4.9), which assumes that the adjustment speed of prices to cost and demand changes is identical. While Domberger (1979) focuses exclusively on the relationship between price inertia and cost changes $(D_{it} = 0)$, Weiss (1993) sets up a price adjustment model where prices can react differently to changes in costs and demand. He does this by estimating separate inertia parameters for changes in costs and demand. In Austrian manufacturing, prices adjust more slowly to demand variations than to cost changes (see note a of Table 4.3). Prices seem to adjust relatively quickly in Japan, Sweden, Canada and Australia as half the adjustment to the new long-run level of prices occurs in two to five months.[9] In the UK, the US, Austria and Greece, adjustment takes between 6 and 21 months.

Table 4.3 Empirical estimates of the speed of price adjustment: average levels of price rigidity λ and influence of market structure variables

Country	Survey	Number of sectors	Estimation period	Average λ	Domestic concentration	Import penetration	Foreign direct investment
High adjustment speed							
Japan	Encaoua and Geroski 1986	67	1971–79	0.01	—	0	0
Sweden	Encaoua and Geroski 1986	36	1970–80	0.11		0	0
Canada	Encaoua and Geroski 1986	50	1970–80	0.11	0	0	—
Australia	Dixon 1983	43	1949–74	0.17	—	+	
United Kingdom	Encaoua and Geroski 1986	50	1970–79	0.26	—	+	
United States	Encaoua and Geroski 1986	430	1958–80	0.27	—/0[b]	0	
Austria	Weiss 1994a	17	1974Q4–88Q3	0.15/0.42[a]	0	+	
The Netherlands	Wijnstok 1995	19	1970–92	0.31	0	0	
United Kingdom	Domberger 1979	21	1963Q1–74Q4	0.49	+		
Greece	Bedrossian and Moschos 1988	20	1963Q1–77Q4	0.67	—		
Low adjustment speed							

Notes:
+ = Variable has a positive influence on the speed of price adjustment $(1 - \lambda_i)$;
− = Variable has negative influence on the speed of price adjustment $(1 - \lambda_i)$;
0 = Variable has no significant influence on the speed of price adjustment $(1 - \lambda_i)$;
a = Average of inertia parameters for cost $(\lambda_{cost} = 0.15)$ and demand $(\lambda_{demand} = 0.42)$ changes;
b = Effect of concentration on speed of price adjustment to cost and demand changes, respectively.

Table 4.3 also shows the relationship between the inter-industry variation in the speed of price adjustment and domestic concentration, import penetration and foreign direct investment. A high degree of market concentration may point to market power, which enables the leading firms to implement a long-term pricing strategy. The presence of competing imports *ceteris paribus* limits the possibilities of domestic firms to set prices independently. The physical presence of foreign competitors on the domestic market may also lead to an increase in competition if collusive behaviour is more difficult among international firms than among purely domestic firms.

These market structure variables, however, are not necessarily directly associated with the strength of competitive forces. For example, economies of scale in concentrated industries which relate to substantial fixed costs also lead to long planning periods so that price adjustment may be slower because of this effect. In addition, large enterprises are often highly diversified, both geographically and in terms of different kinds of products. The pricing of one product category may therefore be affected by pricing decisions in other markets on which the firm is operating. On the other hand, when firms have an international pricing strategy this may weaken the influence of purely domestic market developments on prices. Import penetration will not measure the actual presence of competing foreign products in a particular sector but may simply reflect deliveries by foreign suppliers of raw materials and pre-fabricated products. In summary, market concentration, import penetration and foreign direct investment at least in theory are only imperfect proxies of the state of competition, so that the empirical results must be interpreted with caution.

The balance of the evidence on market concentration suggests that the speed of price adjustment is lower in more concentrated industries, the only exception being the results of Domberger (1979) for the UK. Competition from imports has a positive or insignificant effect on the speed of price adjustment. The insignificance of this effect for Japan, Canada and the United States may be due to the relatively low degree of openness of these countries. The influence of foreign direct investment on price adjustment could be tested in two cases only. The insignificant effect for Japan can again be explained by the relatively low foreign presence on the Japanese market during the estimation period. On balance, however, the hypothesis of more price smoothing in less competitive industries is confirmed. For the case of the Netherlands, the insignificance of both domestic concentration and the rate of import penetration may be due to the relatively low number of observations (15) available for explaining differences in price flexibility between sectors. As a result, the estimated regression equations for the speed of price adjustment are insufficiently robust to slight changes in the estimation sample (Wijnstok 1995).

4.4 Product Market Inertia

The measure of product market inertia that we deploy here is based on the concept of hysteresis. Economists use this term to denote situations where the long-run equilibrium of a system is not only a function of the exogenous variables but also depends on the initial values of the state variables and on the values of the endogenous variables outside the long-run solution space. In practice this means that current values of endogenous variables also depend on lagged endogenous variables. The hysteresis concept is not new — reference to hysteresis of market prices can already be found in the first edition of Marshall's *Principles* (Cross 1993) — but the widespread application of hysteresis models is of more recent date and can be traced to theoretical and empirical analyses of labour market rigidities. Flexibility of labour markets became a topic in empirical research when Blanchard and Summers (1986, p. 71) in their seminal study concluded that:

> Periods of persistently high unemployment are not uncommon events in (a) broad historical context, yet standard macroeconomic theories have a difficult time accounting for them. ... [T]hey can only be understood in terms of theories of hysteresis that make long-run equilibrium depend on history.

So it became customary to include in wage equations prices and the present and lagged levels of unemployment in order to assess the impact of hysteresis on wage rigidity. The extent of hysteresis therefore determines the speed with which the labour market moves towards equilibrium. One mechanism which might cause hysteresis in unemployment rates is that workers who become unemployed lose the opportunity to maintain and update their skills by working (Blanchard and Summers 1986, pp. 27—9). This causes a decline in the productivity of the labour services they can provide, which reduces their chances of finding a job. According to the so-called insider—outsider theory, employed workers (the insiders) set wages so as to remain employed. After an adverse shock, however, some workers lose their insider status and become unemployed ('outsiders'). The new, smaller group of insiders again sets wages so as to maintain employment. As a result, small adverse shocks can have permanent effects as employment and unemployment show no tendency to return to their pre-shock value.

Recently, the concept of hysteresis has been introduced in the analysis of the behaviour of firms as well (see, for example, Dixit and Pindyck 1994). Suppose a firm considers both entry and exit into a new market, and that the firm's optimal decision under uncertainty is characterized by two thresholds. A certain, high, level of current profits justifies entry, while a sufficiently large level of current losses induces exit. Suppose furthermore that when the firm first arrives at the scene, profits are in the intermediate range, so that waiting is the optimal decision. When profits rise past the upper threshold, the firm invests. However, if after having entered the market, profits fall back again to the old intermediate level, this does not justify abandonment of the investment.

> Thus the underlying cause (current profitability) has been restored to its old level, but its effect (investment) has not. ... This phenomenon is called ... economic hysteresis (Dixit and Pindyck 1994, p. 17).

Analogous to the analysis of the long-run unemployment phenomenon, hysteresis on product markets can be determined by means of estimated price equations (Kuipers 1991). In our investigation of price rigidity, we also estimate price equations with both present and lagged levels of capacity utilization as explanatory variables. Strictly speaking, hysteresis on the product market occurs when changes in prices do not depend on the level of capacity utilization. A decline in capacity utilization has a negative effect on prices only once, so the underutilization is sustained. Hysteresis in a more general sense, which is the definition that we will use here, occurs when the level of capacity utilization does influence prices, but only to a limited extent. As a result, deviations of capacity from optimal levels are maintained for a relatively long time, because quantities rather than prices adjust.

Prices and capacity
An important question is why price rigidity, competition and capacity utilization are related phenomena. From a macroeconomic point of view the problem is essentially why demand or supply fluctuations do not lead to changes in the price level if the market structure does not meet the requirements of perfect competition. If effective demand decreases, capacity utilization goes down and — at least in theory — this will lead to lower prices in a competitive environment. In oligopoly, however, the oligopolists may be reluctant to disturb any co-operative equilibrium by changing price because they are uncertain about the reactions of their competitors. This reluctance is magnified in the face of transaction costs associated with price changes, causing prices to be relatively unresponsive to changes in market conditions. If price rigidity is the consequence of the fragility of oligopolistic collusion, it may be that this phenomenon is most pronounced at intermediate levels of concentration. At low levels of concentration, collusion will not be relevant and at high levels of concentration, knowledge of competitors may be large enough to reduce uncertainty about mutual behaviour. Although the empirical evidence is by no means unambiguous, cyclical pricing responses do seem to be more sluggish under oligopoly than in more atomistic markets (see, for example, Scherer 1980, p. 356, and Carlton 1986).

Excess capacity is often a necessary condition for collusive activity, as can best be explained by the example of a cartel. In a fully rationalized cartel, all the members of the cartel act as one entity in terms of prices and quantities in order to maximize collective profits (Scherer and Ross 1990, pp. 240—41). In order to achieve maximum profits, less efficient cartel members must reduce production capacity in favour of their more efficient colleagues. The incentive for the less efficient sellers to reduce production, however, is low because after rationalization the efficient producers may demand a larger share of cartel profits:

Maintaining production capabilities intact is a good bargaining counter against such demands. As a result, few cartels have gone very far towards the rationalization of production (Scherer and Ross 1990, p. 242).

Stiglitz (1984) argues that in an economy that is dominated by monopolies and monopolistically competitive firms, four channels will prohibit price reductions if effective demand decreases. First, in this economy prices will be set in order to equate marginal revenue and marginal costs, which results in the well-known inverse relationship between mark-up and demand elasticity. If the demand elasticity decreases in a recession (for example, when the share of necessities in total consumption outlays increases), the mark-up will rise. Second, limit pricing in order to prevent entry from new firms will become of less strategic importance during a recession. Third, as far as excess capacity acts as a deterrent to potential entrants, the recession induces additional excess capacity and hence deterrence increases, allowing for rising mark-ups.[10] Finally, those regulated industries which clearly do not possess natural monopoly characteristics are characterized by significant efficiency costs in terms of distorted (relative) prices, allocation and innovativeness. According to the OECD (1987a, pp. 300—301) prices in these regulated industries exceed both those that would have pertained in a competitive market and those corresponding to second-best optimizing:

> This has only partly been due to supra-normal profits — though these have been significant in a few cases. Rather, the additional profits created by regulatory protection have typically been dissipated in excess costs, as producers resort to non-price forms of competition — such as enhanced or more frequent service — to increase their market share.

All in all it is quite probable that excess capacity, price rigidity and competition are connected variables, so that the hysteresis concept which links price rigidity to capacity utilization may be a useful concept to assess the flexibility of a market economy.

Analogous to the analysis of the long-run unemployment phenomenon, we determine hysteresis in the product markets by means of estimated price equations (Kuipers 1991). In our equations, changes in prices do not only depend on costs and the price of competing imports, but also on the evolution of capacity utilization. Equation (4.10) is an example of the estimated price equations:[11]

$$p = \alpha_1 ULC + \alpha_2 p_M + \alpha_3 Q + \alpha_4 \Delta Q + c + v \qquad (4.10)$$

where p is the price level domestic demand, ULC is unit labour costs and p_M is the import price level. These three variables are measured as rates of change. Q is the level of capacity utilization, ΔQ is the change of capacity utilization ($Q_t - Q_{t-1}$), c is the constant term and v is the error term.

The expected signs of the α's are positive as higher unit labour costs, a higher import price level and a higher level of capacity utilization exert upward pressure on the domestic price level. As a measure of hysteresis, equation (4.11) suggests a product market inertia coefficient ($PMIC$), which by definition lies between zero and one hundred per cent.[12]

$$PMIC = \alpha_4 / (\alpha_3 + \alpha_4) \times 100\% \qquad (4.11)$$

In the case of complete or strict hysteresis ($\alpha_3 = 0$; $PMIC = 100$ per cent) neither excess capacity nor excess demand influences the rate of inflation. Consequently, an economy in the trough of a depression can experience accelerating inflation if its capacity utilization improves, no matter how low the level of capacity utilization. As a result, demand and supply on the goods markets will not equilibrate by means of price movements, as a central feature of the price mechanism is absent. In contrast, if changes in capacity utilization do not influence price movements at all ($\alpha_4 = 0$) hysteresis is virtually absent. The $PMIC$ now reaches its zero per cent floor. The speed of the invisible hand is high as prices react very quickly to the level of capacity utilization. Excess capacity induces price decreases and vice versa. Consequently market flexibility is high and the price mechanism allocates resources in an efficient way. In general the $PMIC$ lies somewhere in between: the larger its value, the slower the speed of the invisible hand.

Findings

Table 4.4 presents the results of estimated price equations for eleven industrialized economies in the period 1974—92 (compare equation (4.10) above). First- and second-order autocorrelation — denoted by $AR(1)$ and $AR(2)$ in Table 4.4 — was corrected using the Cochrane—Orcutt procedure for serial correlation. The bottom line of the table presents the point estimates of the $PMICs$, calculated using equation (4.11).

Table 4.4 Estimated price equations for the determination of the product market inertia coefficients (1974—92)

	Taiwan[a]	US	Canada	Australia	Denmark	UK	Germany[b]	France	Netherlands	Italy	Japan
Unit labour costs (ULC)	0.31 (1.27)	0.85[c] (13.3)	0.55 (6.10)	0.46 (4.52)	0.69 (7.06)	0.70 (11.70)	0.48 (5.14)	0.69 (9.48)	0.62 (5.49)	0.73 (7.16)	0.72 (9.27)
Import price (p_M)	0.60 (4.08)	0.11 (6.08)	— —	0.22 (3.11)	0.09[c] (1.36)	0.20 (5.44)	0.18[a] (3.60)	0.09 (7.55)	0.11[a] (2.24)	0.13 (3.63)	0.06 (3.24)
Capacity level (Q)	0.43 (1.96)	0.18 (2.36)	0.02 (1.96)	0.03 (3.71)	0.02 (2.27)	0.02 (2.00)	0.01 (3.27)	0.02 (2.91)	0.02 (3.06)	0.02 (2.10)	0.005 (1.26)
Change in Q (ΔQ)	0.13 (0.31)	0.13 (1.63)	0.11 (1.50)	0.29 (1.34)	0.32 (1.56)	0.29 (2.30)	0.25 (1.88)	0.37 (3.18)	0.45 (1.84)	0.68 (3.60)	0.42 (1.86)
Constant term	−0.35 (−2.15)	−0.18 (−2.29)	— —	— —	— —	— —	—	—	—	—	—
AR(1)	−0.69 (−2.16)	−0.57 (−2.25)	1.13 (4.87)	— —	0.40 (1.07)	0.85 (4.12)	—	0.70 (4.23)	—	0.39 (1.67)	—
AR(2)	−0.38 (−1.28)	−0.55 (−2.34)	−0.34 (−1.41)	— —	— —	−0.52 (−2.67)	—	—	—	—	—
adj-R^2	0.91	0.91	0.94	0.77	0.90	0.95	0.81	0.98	0.79	0.95	0.96
DW	1.94	2.23	1.82	1.69	1.95	2.01	1.77	1.88	1.92	2.03	1.69
product market inertia coefficient	23	42	83	90	94	95	95	95	97	97	99

Notes: [a] Estimation period 1976—94; [b] West Germany, estimation period 1973—91; [c] Variable has been lagged one period. adj-R^2 = adjusted R^2, DW= Durbin—Watson coefficient, AR(x) = autocorrelation process of degree x and (t-values between brackets).

Sources: OECD Economic Outlook data base on diskette and direct submission by Taiwanese authorities.

The calculations should only be seen as indications for the problems at hand. International conceptual and methodological differences in the construction of index numbers for prices, costs and especially of capacity utilization levels are a complicating factor in any comparative analysis and justify a serious caveat to interpret our results with caution. Moreover, being a ratio the *PMIC* itself is a source of indeterminacy as this measure has been defined as the quotient of two estimated coefficients, the standard errors of which in general will reinforce each other. Neglect of this aspect of the use of ratios of estimated coefficients is a general characteristic of the literature on price and wage dynamics. In order to prevent seemingly accurate measurement resulting in an overrated distinguishing power we proceed as follows.

Assuming that the OLS estimates of equation (4.10) yield unbiased estimates of the coefficients α_3 and α_4 and that the distribution is sufficiently normal, the variance of the ratio α_3 / α_4 can be approximated (Kendall and Stuart 1977, pp. 246—7) by:

$$\text{Var}(\alpha_3 / \alpha_4) = \text{Var}(\alpha_3)/\alpha_4^2 + \alpha_3^2 \text{Var}(\alpha_4)/\alpha_4^4$$
$$- 2\alpha_3 \text{Cov}(\alpha_3, \alpha_4)/\alpha_4^3 \qquad (4.12)$$

Equation (4.11) can be rewritten as

$$PMIC = 1/\{(\alpha_3 / \alpha_4) + 1\} \times 100\% \qquad (4.13)$$

so that the estimated variance of α_3 / α_4 can be used to determine a confidence interval.[13]

Figure 4.2 summarizes the results that Table 4.4 reports in detail. European and especially Japanese macro-markets for goods and services suffer from substantial hysteresis as the *PMIC*s are all at the 94 per cent level and higher. The low *t*-value of only 1.26 that we find for the estimated coefficient of the level of capacity utilization in the case of Japan, suggests that the 'level effect' is actually absent so that hysteresis on the goods market in this case is complete. On the other hand, hysteresis does not seem a problem for Taiwan, as the point estimate of the *PMIC* is only 23 per cent. In addition, the *t*-value and estimated coefficient of the change in capacity utilization imply that the 'rate of change' effect is virtually absent in Taiwan. The relatively low *PMIC*s (42 and 83 respectively) indicate that the price mechanism also seems to function relatively well in the US and Canada. Especially for Taiwan and the US the level effects are substantial as the elasticity of the change in prices with respect to the level of capacity utilization is on average about ten times larger than the elasticities that we find for the other countries.[14]

*Figure 4.2   Product market inertia coefficients: point estimates and
90 per cent confidence intervals*

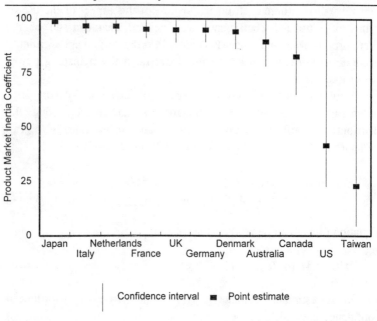

The estimates of equation (4.10) appear quite satisfactory on the basis of the t-values, the adjusted-R^2 and Durbin—Watson statistic, but it is difficult to present a clear ranking on other grounds than the point estimates. The evidence, however, clearly suggests that the macroeconomic markets for goods and services in, for example, Japan, Italy, the Netherlands and France suffer from substantial hysteresis because it can be asserted with 90 per cent confidence that their product market inertia coefficient exceeds a level of 90 per cent. The policy implication of this comparative analysis is that many countries may be able to improve on the flexibility of their markets for goods and services, possibly by pursuing an economic strategy that complements privatization, deregulation and a more vigorous competition policy with a more liberal attitude towards international trade and investment.

Table 4.5   Product market inertia in 19 Dutch SIC sectors (1971—92)

Industry class	Product market inertia coefficient
Rigid	
Crude petroleum and natural gas production; mining	99.2
Medical services	98.7
Electrical engineering	97.9
Paper and paper products	97.2
Banking and insurance	97.2
Wholesale and retail trade	97.1
Slaughtering and meat processing; dairy	95.9
Other services	95.7
Automobile industry and transport equipment	95.3
Other transport and communication	95.2
Agricultural processing	94.4
Metal products, machinery, instruments	94.1
Construction and installation on construction projects	92.3
Chemical and rubber products	87.4
Wood and building materials	86.8
Basic metal industry	84.1
Sea and air transport	80.5
Beverages and tobacco processing	42.0
Textiles and clothing	32.2
Flexible	

A significant advantage of the *PMIC* is that it can be estimated both at the macroeconomic level and at lower levels of aggregation. Table 4.5 reports *PMIC*s that were found in a comparative analysis of 19 Dutch sectors.[15] Macroeconomic product market flexibility is considerably lower in the Netherlands and other European countries than in Taiwan, the US and Canada. Table 4.5 confirms this result, as 85 per cent of Dutch sectors have mesoeconomic *PMICs* that exceed the macroeconomic *PMICs* of Taiwan, the US and Canada. In the Netherlands, the inertia problem seems to be economy-wide. Our results for the Netherlands are also confirmed by Kuipers (1991), who finds a *PMIC* of 95 per cent at the macroeconomic level for the period 1971—88.

As to the determinants of the *PMICs* at the mesoeconomic level, observations on market concentration and openness to international trade were only available for 15 sectors. As explained in the introduction to this section, concentration is expected to have a positive influence on product market inertia and openness a negative one. Equation (4.14) shows the regression estimates for a cross-section of 15 industries. The openness variable *OPEN* in equation (4.14) is defined as exports plus imports as a percentage of value added, and it has the expected positive impact on the speed of the invisible hand as measured by the *PMIC*. The elasticity of the openness variable with respect to the *PMIC* is 0.2. Market concentration *CONC* has a negative influence on the degree to which markets clear through price adjustment (a positive influence on the *PMIC*). The influence of concentration on the *PMIC* is larger than for the openness variable, as for average values of concentration the *PMIC* rises by 0.4 per cent when the degree of market concentration increases by one per cent[16] However, it should be kept in mind that these inferences are based on a limited number of observations only. Whether these inferences can be maintained when more data on concentration becomes available is yet unclear.

$$PMIC = 5.5 \; CONC - 0.4 \; OPEN \qquad\qquad (4.14)$$
$$\quad\quad (2.5) \qquad (-2.2)$$

adj. $R^2 = 0.41$; F-test $= 4.2$, t-values in brackets.

In summary, product market inertia seems to be a pressing policy problem in European countries and in Japan. Preliminary investigations at the mesoeconomic level suggest that in the case of the Netherlands, the lack of economic dynamism may even be an economy-wide problem. Product market inertia was shown to correlate with two indicators of market structure, namely the degrees of domestic market concentration and openness to foreign competition. Our empirical results therefore confirm the broad conclusion of Porter (1985, pp. 10—11), who asserts that:

> industry structure is fundamental to both the speed of adjustment of supply to demand and the relationship between capacity utilization and profitability.

4.5 Discussion

Internationally comparable research on the degree of competition on markets for goods and services is scarce. One of the explanations for this is the fact that competition obviously is one of those concepts that are hard to measure. Competition is often highly dependent on factors that are intrinsically difficult to observe (Kühn et al. 1992, p. 2). Statistical difficulties magnify these problems. Among the plagues of the empirical researcher are matters of comparability (differences in definitions, statistical sources, reliability) and availability (van Bergeijk 1995).

In this chapter, four different indicators have been used to assess international differences in product market competition. The major advantage of the persistence of profits indicator is that competition is measured at the level where it actually takes place, namely at the level of the individual firm. The underlying Schumpetarian view of competition — firms are rewarded for innovations by a temporary rise in profitability — has a strong intuitive appeal. One obvious disadvantage is the fact that a reduced-form equation is estimated, which makes it impossible to test the structural model on which the inferences are based. In addition, other factors which may influence the evolution of profits over time are neglected. Moreover, in order to obtain a measure of the macroeconomic speed of profit adjustment, firm-level adjustment speeds are averaged, giving observations on small and large enterprises an equal weight. A way out may be to weight each firm by its value added.

The mark-up ratio and our indicator of product market inertia do not suffer from this 'adding-up problem', but the high level of aggregation of the current analysis may obscure relatively dynamic sectors and emerging markets. On the other hand, the relatively limited data requirements is a clear advantage of these methodologies. Care must be taken to correct for possible asymmetries in pricing behaviour, as oligopoly theories suggest that the pricing behaviour of dominant firms may be pro-cyclical.

Table 4.6   Intensity of competition according to the four different indicators

Spread in long-run profits	Mark-up ratio (1971—90)	Product market inertia coefficient (1974—92)	Speed of price adjustment
	Strong Competition		
Japan 1964—82	UK	Taiwan[a]	Japan 1971—79
Germany 1961—82	US	US	Sweden 1970—80
UK 1951—77	Denmark		Canada 1970—80
US 1964—80	Norway		Australia 1949—74
	Moderate Competition		
Sweden 1967—85	Belgium	Canada	UK 1970—79
US 1950—72	Netherlands	Australia	US 1958—80
Netherlands 1978—91	Canada		Austria 1974—88
France 1965—82	Germany		Netherlands 1970—92
	Weak Competition		
Canada 1968—82	Italy	Denmark	UK 1963—74
	Sweden	Germany[b]	Greece 1963—77
	Japan	UK	
	Australia	France	
	Finland	Netherlands	
	France	Italy	
		Japan	

Notes: [a] 1976—94, [b] 1973—91.
Sources: Tables 4.1—4.4 above.

The problems of 'adding up' and cyclical price responses also occur in the case of the speed of price adjustment. Here the analysis may be hampered by the fact that not all relevant cost and demand developments are observed by the researcher, so that the 'current' price level to which prices supposedly adjust, may not be correct. Because of this joint hypothesis problem, it is impossible to determine whether price rigidity is the result of a wrong model for prices or of an actual lack of flexibility. All of the surveyed indicators more or less take the viewpoint of static efficiency, as they do not take the innovativeness of firms into account (at least not directly).

On the basis of the empirical studies, it is difficult to establish accurately the relative position of the countries in the sample in terms of market dynamism (Table 4.6). In part, this may be due to differences in the estimation period of the various studies, which makes the various estimates difficult to compare. Japan, for example, has both the lowest spread in long-run profits (1964—82) and the highest speed of price adjustment (1971—79), which points to strong competition. On the other hand, Japan has the highest degree of product market inertia (1974—92) and a high mark-up ratio (1971—90), which points to a rather weak relationship between prices and capacity utilization and to high market power.

Another part of the problem is that the inferences are based on a comparison of the relative position of each country in the study, and not of the absolute 'level' of competition. Competition on Canadian markets, for example, may not have changed substantially in the period 1968—92, so that changes in the relative rank of Canada may be due to institutional changes in the other countries that were studied.

In our view, however, the most important explanation for the observed differences is that in fact different dimensions of competition are examined here. Each indicator measures a different aspect of competition. For example, persistent excess capacity raises costs at the level of the individual firm, which may result in a long-run profit level no different from the competitive norm. Prices may react quickly to changes in costs and demand, but if firms maintain excess capacity for strategic reasons, the assessments based on the market inertia coefficient and the speed of price adjustment will not be the same. If this is true, any rank correspondence between countries would be largely coincidental. Subsequent analysis will have to provide an explanation in terms of an analysis of the determinants of economic dynamism as can be measured by indicators like the ones we have discussed in this part.

Still, our task is by no means hopeless and our findings are not futile. For example, competition in the US is never identified as weak and in three out of four cases the indicators point to strong competition. This contrasts with France, where competition is never found to be strong and where we identify weak competition in two out of three cases. Moreover, in discussing a number of ways in which the speed of the invisible hand can be determined empirically, we have illustrated some new and interesting approaches which may be useful for sharpening the perspective of macroeconomic analysis. Indeed one important finding is that rigidities and imperfections are relevant characteristics of many national product markets today. Consequently, it is important to consider the implication of imperfect markets for macroeconomic theory and applied modelling.

Notes

1.	For an example of the estimation of a structural model of entry, see Geroski and Masson (1987).

2.	For an estimation of equation (4.3) with industry data, see Kessides (1990) for the United States, and Kambhampati (1995) for India.

3.	These results do not change when the levels of the long-run profit rates are compared.

4.	See also Jenny and Weber (1990, p. 128), who explain that French industries with high permanent rents are typically relatively concentrated (such as pharmaceuticals and oil refining), while industries with negative rents (such as the textile and clothing sector) had low concentration, exhibited low economies of scale and faced severe import competition from South-East Asian products.

5.	Germany is an exception in this case, with long-run profits of only 0.5 above the sample average. However, in Germany the initial profit level is higher than in Japan.

6.	More in general: assuming perfect competition we can start from a set of nested CES production functions to arrive at an equation in which we decompose the growth of output into the growth of technological progress and the growth of the factors of production (labour, capital, land use, intermediate inputs, etc.) weighed by their respective factor shares.

7.	See Chapter 3 on the use of conjectural variation as an indicator of economic dynamism.

8.	The expected sign of β is *a priori* not clear as the direction of the price change due to a change in demand depends on the shape of the marginal cost curve. On the other hand, a profit-maximizing firm will respond to a rise in marginal costs by a rise in prices, so that for γ a positive sign is expected. See Wijnstok (1995) on these issues.

9.	Equation (4.4) was used to arrive at this estimate.

10.	See Lieberman (1987) for a survey of the empirical evidence on excess capacity as a barrier to entry.

11.	We drop the subscripts for industry i and time t for notational convenience.

12. Actually, the *PMIC* is equal to the Z-criterion in Blanchard and Summers (1986) which is defined as the ratio of the coefficient of the lagged variable to the coefficient of the present variable. This can easily be verified if one replaces ΔQ by $(Q - Q_{-1})$ and rearranges terms in equation (4.10). We prefer the *PMIC* to the Z-criterion because of its intuitive appeal.

13. As suggested in Leamer and Stern (1970), we present the respective confidence intervals in addition to the point estimates of the *PMIC*s in Figure 4.2.

14. The point estimate of the elasticity of the change in prices with respect to the level of capacity utilization is 15.3 for Taiwan and 3.0 for the United States. For the other countries, this elasticity is considerably lower, ranging from 0.1 (Japan) to 0.5 (the Netherlands).

15. The macroeconomic and mesoeconomic *PMIC*s have been tested for stability across time using dummy variables. Significant dummies were obtained only incidentally, in these cases causing relatively small variations in the *PMIC*. In addition, oligopoly theories suggest that the pricing behaviour of dominant firms may be cyclical, raising prices in times of undercapacity, but not lowering them in times of excess capacity. Again we used dummy variables to test for this asymmetry, but none of them were statistically significant. For the macroeconomic *PMIC*s, inclusion of a short-term interest rate to correct for international differences in the stance of monetary policy did not yield significant results. See also Haffner (1993) on these points.

16. A multiplicative model was also estimated but this did not change the qualitative results.

PART III
MACROECONOMICS

5. Structural Rigidity, Macro-economic Inefficiency and the Efficacy of Economic Policy

Before we can say something meaningful about the macroeconomic costs and benefits of deregulation, privatization and more competition, we need to consider the following question: How do microeconomic rigidities on the product market influence the performance of a macroeconomic system? This is not a question that has been on top of the list of empirical questions which has been produced by the neoclassical research agenda. The Walrasian or Arrow—Debreu approach in which product markets (goods and services) and factor markets (for land, labour, capital, etc.) are assumed to be competitive and clear instantaneously appears to have dominated the microeconomic foundation of neoclassical macroeconomic analyses.[1] Traditional Keynesianism focused on wage rigidity rather than product market inertia. Consequently, for a long time, product market disequilibria were ruled out by theory. Not all economists were satisfied with this situation. Okun (1981, p. 19), for example, wondered:

> But why should one cling to the maintained hypothesis that product markets are always in equilibrium in the short run? Perpetuating the hypothesis preserves the principle of conservatism about, and respect for, this classical model that has served for so long in so many dimensions. But it is difficult to find any other virtue. In particular, empirical evidence pulls the analyst in the opposite direction.

Whereas the question of the impact of market structure on the economy was neglected a bit by neoclassically inspired macro-economic practitioners, by now a rich body of literature exists on imperfect competition in related fields such as industrial economics, strategic trade theories and labour market theories which incorporate trade union behaviour.[2] In addition, Neo- (or 'post') Keynesians and Marxists have dealt intensively with the question of how monopoly power and co-ordination failures could influence the nature of the macroeconomic equilibrium. Fortunately, in the 1990s with the birth of modern 'endogenous' growth theory, the importance of the issue of distortionary policies as a determinant of economic slowdown was recognized more fully.

5.1 Three Questions and the Literature

There is now a large and rich literature that deals with these and related questions from different angles. This chapter takes stock of the literature dealing with a number of the theoretical topics that directly relate to economic policy. Our aim is modest. We want to illustrate mechanisms that have been or could be used to analyse the macroeconomic costs of malfunctioning product markets and that are potentially valuable in providing transparency about the costs and benefits of the removal of product market distortions, in particular privatization, deregulation and competition policy. Consequently, we analyse some simple models, use simplified approaches for a closed one-sector economy and discuss in a qualitative sense only the extensions to, for example, open multisector economies or an explicit treatment of government. In other words, this is not a detailed and balanced representation of the technicalities in the literature (these are provided by, among others, Malinvaud 1978, Bénassy 1982, Mankiw and Romer 1991, Silvestre 1993 and Dixon and Rankin 1994). Nor is it our purpose to discuss in detail the methodologies that have been used (the interested reader is referred to Peeters 1987 and van Ees and Garretsen 1993).

Figure 5.1 extends Silvestre's (1993) classification of the literature. We use three criteria to categorize the theoretical approaches followed in the literature:

- Do agents have market power?
- Do prices and wages adjust immediately to exogenous shocks?
- Does investment have a capacity effect (i.e. does the analysis have a short time horizon or does it deal with the long run)?

Figure 5.1 Classification of the literature

	(Immediate) price adjustment	
	Yes	No
Market power		
No	(Neo)classical	IS—LM
	(New) growth theory	Fix-price growth
Yes	Co-operation and co-ordination failures	Neo-Keynesian theories
	Overlapping generations extensions	Disequilibrium growth theory

Note: ▒ dynamic approach.
Source: Adapted from Silvestre (1993), p. 106.

In the upper left of Figure 5.1 we find theories that are characterized by a short-term Walrasian equilibrium in which all markets clear instantaneously. The bottom right entry represents disequilibrium growth models in which prices and wages adjust sluggishly. Commenting on the static nature of disequilibrium economics (such as Neo-Keynesianism) and on the equilibrium nature of growth theory, van Marrewijk and Verbeek (1993, pp. 6—7) note that analyses that are based on both 'old' and 'new' theories do not sufficiently integrate two basic facts of modern economic life. First, market disequilibrium is a preponderant characteristic of the economy. Second, growth effects are ultimately more important than level effects. Neo-Keynesian theories of market disequilibrium, however, neglect endogenous capital accumulation (the capacity effect of investment), while growth theory more often assumes a competitive market structure than a non-competitive one. Hence van Marrewijk and Verbeek (1993) pursue the tracks of disequilibrium growth theory as introduced by Ito (1980), alas, focusing on wage rigidity only, rather than considering product market inertia.

Some entries in Figure 5.1 at first sight might appear to be merely 'empty boxes', 'odd theories' or empirically irrelevant. An example of a seemingly 'empty box' is the fix-price growth model. In this box, however, we find the theoretical fix-price non-Walrasian models (see Silvestre 1987) as well as applied models which have been extremely influential in increasing awareness of major social problems and shaping policies. An example of the latter is the WORLD-3 model in the Club of Rome's *Limits to Growth* (Meadows et al. 1972), which has a core relating to capital—investment and natural resource use, but neglects the price mechanism and, consequently, treats the use of scarce resources inadequately (Parker 1986). An example of an approach that at first sight would seem to be too simple and hence unable to describe the data is the IS—LM model (well-known from introductory textbooks), which has played a central role in the making of Keynesian macroeconomic theory and policy. Recently, however, Gali (1992) estimated a highly stylized four-equations dynamic macroeconomic model for the United States for the years 1955—87 with quantitative responses that match the qualitative predictions of the IS—LM framework quite well, thus supporting the empirical relevance today of the IS—LM model.

5.2   Macroeconomic Efficiency and Policy Effectiveness

We will make only a shaded sketch of a colourful theoretical landscape. In doing so, we will follow Blanchard and Kiyotaki (1987, pp. 652—4), who distinguish two different channels through which product market inertia influences the economy. We will label these effects the macroeconomic efficiency effect and the efficacy of policy effect.

Macroeconomic efficiency
The first channel focuses attention on how a malfunctioning market mechanism influences key economic variables such as prices, production, trade, investment and employment. This is the macroeconomic inefficiency effect of product market inertia which can be either static or dynamic (Scherer and Ross 1990, pp. 19—29

and 438—9, and Davies 1988b, pp. 196—205). For example, monopoly power may influence the allocation of factors of production and the level of productive efficiency (static efficiency); it may also have consequences for the growth rate of the economy and the speed of technical progress (dynamic efficiency).

The standard neoclassical model of economic growth assumes that distortions which, for example, result in product market inertia will influence only the level of income but not its rate of growth. Graphically, the removal of a distortion in this model shifts the growth path up while leaving its slope unchanged (see the shift from *AA'* to *BB'* in Figure 5.2).

Figure 5.2 Growth paths: static versus dynamic efficiency

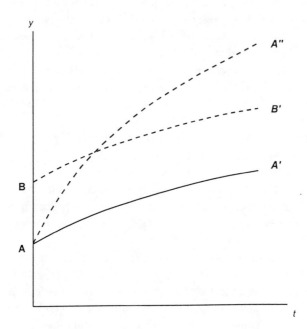

This 'exogenous growth' approach simply asserts that economic growth exists, leaving very little room (if any) for an analysis of the question of how government intervention may impact long-run growth. In this approach economic growth is by and large 'manna from heaven'.

Whereas the neoclassical growth model mainly considers long-run tendencies, another branch of the neoclassical growth deals with growth accounting (see, for example, Maddison 1987). This method tries to attribute economic growth not only to increases in the amounts of capital and labour employed, but also to a myriad of other factors (for example industrialization, number of hours worked, etc.) in a rather *ad hoc* manner. However, just like the neoclassical growth theories, growth accounting also generates a non-negligible residual which is hard to explain. This was a rather unsatisfactory situation from a theoretical point of view. New growth theories that came in vogue in the early 1990s and were developed in the mid-1980s by, among others, Romer, Rebelo, Barro, Grossman and Helpman, stressed that policies which improve the efficiency of resource allocation will have a positive impact on the rate of growth.[3] In Figure 5.2 such a policy will rotate the growth path counter-clockwise with the starting point serving as a hinge (from *AA'* to *AA"*).

Technically, the growth rate is endogenized by assuming a production function which features increasing returns or constant returns with respect to produced inputs such as capital and knowledge. The most important insight is that economic growth is the result of an intentional allocation of resources by private optimizing agents that react to incentives and operate within the borders set by institutions.

Obviously, these theoretical developments (which in addition to static efficiency gains highlight the potentially beneficial dynamic implications of structural reform policies) are relevant from a policy perspective. If policies can affect not only the level of income but also its rate of growth, then the gains from 'better' policies may be very substantial indeed. In the following sections, we will deal with the effects of product market inertia on static efficiency (Section 5.3) and dynamic efficiency (Section 5.4).

Efficacy of policy

The second channel through which product market inertia influences the economy relates to how a lack of price flexibility influences the efficacy of policy instruments, both in the short run and in the long run. Changes in demand elasticities may have real effects depending on the prevailing market structure. When imperfect competition prevails, government policies have the potential to alter relative prices through changes in demand elasticities. Some even see imperfect competition as the *raison d'être* for government policy. Rigidity, however, may also reduce the set of policy options, as well as the impact of specific instruments. Greater market flexibility may also impose economic costs on the economy. For example, price flexibility may give rise to larger and more frequent fluctuations around a trend at a higher level of economic activity, privatization may increase inflation and deregulation may impose adjustment costs that are prohibitively high.

The opportunity to exert some influence on economic activity through policy measures is influenced in several ways by functioning of the market mechanism. We will look at four specific issues:

●   Stabilization policy (Section 5.5): does imperfect competition increase the frequency and/or the amplitude of the business cycle?

●   Incomes policy (Section 5.6): do deregulation, privatization and competition policies benefit the wealthy?

●   Balance of payments policy (Section 5.7): does greater flexibility lead to higher imports and/or lower exports?

●   The effectiveness of the instruments of economic policy (taxation, spending, etc.) (Section 5.8): is imperfect competition the 'foundation' of macroeconomic policy?

Many attempts have been made to cover the theoretical grounds, but detailed descriptive models have so far been developed only in very rare cases (Hall 1986, p. 313; Silvestre 1993, pp. 109 and 136). Indeed, Sheffrin (1989, p. 125) observes:

> When theories collide, empirical work generally flourishes. But there is surprisingly little empirical work in support of the aggregate implications of the microfoundations of price stickiness.

Consequently, while there is ample empirical evidence for the presence of market power in many markets and sectors, the theoretical work on the implication of this fact of economic life can as yet hardly be empirically verified. Sections 5.5—5.8 will describe the available macroeconomic evidence, which as yet, however, by no means can be considered as conclusive. However, first we discuss the impact of product market inertia on static and dynamic efficiency.

5.3   Static Efficiency

Basically, economists agree that monopoly power in the product market leads to a situation in which the output price exceeds marginal cost. Hence a macroeconomy with imperfectly competitive product markets *ceteris paribus* has higher prices, a lower level of output and less employment than the hypothetical perfectly competitive (Walrasian) economy. Indeed, as Silvestre (1993, p. 108) states, 'inefficiency should not be surprising once one leaves the Walrasian ideal'.

Bénassy (1993, pp. 734—5) gives an example in a simple two agents—one good closed economy with a flexible wage rate in which unemployment and a lower level of production are caused entirely by the fact that the price level in the product market exceeds the market-clearing level. The price level is given for the firm in this model, because the market price is determined by the Walrasian 'auctioneer'; this is a specialized agent whose task is to find the equilibrium price that needs to be known before any trading can take place. The firm maximizes its profit:

$$\pi = pq - wl^d \tag{5.1}$$

in which p is the price level, q is production, w is the wage rate and l^d is labour demanded. The production process that is described by a function q only uses labour as an input $q = q(l)$. Maximization of equation (5.1) (the firm's profits) with respect to l requires $\partial q/\partial l = w/p$ and we may write labour demand as $l^d = q^{-1}(w/p)$. The household always supplies l_0 units of labour and maximizes utility

$$U = \alpha \ln c + (1-\alpha) \ln (m/p) \tag{5.2}$$

where c is current consumption and m is the quantity of money saved. The household's initial money holding is m_0, it earns a wage and receives all profits from the firm. Consequently, its budget constraint is $pc + m = wl + \pi + m_0$ which with (5.1) implies:

$$c = q + (m_0 - m)/p \qquad (5.3)$$

The maximization problem yields the macroeconomic demand function; in this case a consumption demand curve with unitary price elasticity $c^d = \alpha(q + m_0/p)$.[4] With labour supply given at $l^* = l_0$ and supply equal to $q^* = q(l^*)$, the auctioneer determines the Walrasian price p^* by equating supply q^* and demand c^d. This yields $p^* = \alpha m_0/[(1-\alpha)q(l_0)]$.

What happens if we leave the Walrasian world, not by making the usual assumption that the wage is rigid but by assuring that the price p is fixed at a level above p^*, for example because of government regulation? Since we assume that the labour market is flexible and competitive, too high a real wage will not cause a problem. In that case the wage level will go down until equilibrium in the labour market is restored (i.e. full employment). However, if the real wage is already less than or equal to its marginal product (so that we have $w/p \le \partial q/\partial l$; with market power the real wage understates the marginal product of labour), then too high a price will cause a problem, because if labour reduces its wage, no labour demand is forthcoming. Since unemployment exists there is no natural tendency for the wage to increase. This is a clear example of a co-ordination failure: a wage increase would result in the extra effective demand that is needed to restore the full-employment equilibrium.

Indeed, the firm faces a situation in which the demand for its products c^d is less than its Walrasian equilibrium level q^* which in its turn is less than or equal to the quantity that could be produced when the firm deploys labour up to the point where the marginal product of labour is equal to the real wage rate. If the firm decides to produce the quantity demanded ($c^d = q = \alpha m_0/[(1-\alpha)p]$), employment will decline to $l^d = q^{-1}(c^d) < l_0$, as long as $p > p^*$. This establishes a case where unemployment is caused by price inertia on the product market.

Admittedly, this is a simple model, but as Bénassy (1993, p. 735) argues, an important contribution is that it shows 'the importance of "spillover effects" through which disequilibrium in one market can actually be provoked by causes originating in another market', thus showing the need to analyse questions related to the macroeconomic impact of imperfect competition in a general equilibrium framework.

Bénassy extends his analysis for a closed economy with a public sector by endogenizing the processes of price and wage formation in the context of an imperfect competition framework and develops several macroeconomic applications. Introducing imperfect competition on the product and labour markets results both in unemployment and in an actual level of production that is less than the potential level (overcapacity), even though these outcomes are the result of voluntary and individually rational optimization problems.

5.4   Dynamic Efficiency

Giersch (1994) argues that the abolition of bureaucratic regulations, cartel arrangements and restrictive business practices may enhance economic dynamism. He defines economic dynamism as the ability of an economy to respond to changes in the environment and to make optimal use of its capabilities and opportunities. Easterly et al. (1991) have developed a simple model for a closed economy that can be used to illustrate how policies directed at improving economic dynamism may effect the efficiency of resource allocation. They show that even if the total volume of investment is not influenced by these policies, improved allocation will result in a larger level of production. Easterly et al. (1991) consider two types of capital K_1 and K_2 (for example, machines and human capital) in the production function which links output Y to capital K:

$$Y = AQ(K_1, K_2) \tag{5.4}$$

Here A is a technology fixed parameter and Q is a function which describes how the two types of capital can be combined in the production process.[5] If this production function is linearly homogeneous then equation (5.4) can be written as:[6]

$$Y = A\theta(\gamma)K \quad \text{with } \theta_\gamma < 0 \tag{5.5}$$

where K is the total capital stock ($K = K_1 + K_2$) and θ is a function of the (non-)tax wedge γ between the marginal products of the two types of capital ($\partial Y/\partial K_1$ and $\partial Y/\partial K_2$). In other words, the marginal wedge parameter $\theta(\gamma)$ indicates the degree to which the marginal products of the two types of capital K_1 and K_2 are not equalized. In a fully competitive economy, the marginal products of the two types of capital will be equal because of investments by the profit-maximizing private sector(s). The less competitive the economy, the larger the wedge between the two types of capital.[7] Browning (1994), who coined the phrase 'non-tax wedge', points out that non-tax market imperfections (comprising, among others, monopoly, monopsony and business regulation) may act as a hidden marginal tax which significantly influences resource allocation.[8] Indeed, the point of equation (5.5) is that the efficiency of the allocation matters even if the total level of capital does not change.

Moreover, if the economy-wide rate of capital accumulation is a fixed proportion i of production then the growth rate of output g becomes

$$g = iA\theta(\gamma) - \delta \tag{5.6}$$

where δ is the rate of depreciation, which is assumed to be equal for both types of capital. The growth rate is lower, the lower θ, i.e. the larger the distortion γ, and this result appears even when investment is unchanged. Consequently, distortionary policies will not just influence an economy's level of income, but also its rate of growth, which is too low from a social point of view. Solow (1992), however, warns that policy makers should not uncritically follow the modernist advice of new growth theorists as the empirical evidence in support of the new growth theory is scant at best: 'Excessive demands and rash promises are not a good basis for a commitment to a high growth policy' (Solow 1992, p. 14). Indeed, according to Solow (1992), it may still pay to design policies which, in terms of Figure 5.2, shift the potential trend of economic activity rather than exclusively focus on tilting it.

Innovation

The link between, on the one hand, privatization, deregulation and competition policy and, on the other hand, economic growth is a complex one. An important channel that needs to be considered is the possible link between market structure and economic performance (innovation, product quality, etc.) suggested by the industrial organization literature (see Scherer and Ross 1990). In particular, this literature relates endogenous technology to competition policy. Smulders (1994) illustrates various interrelations between the degree of competition and innovative activity in a theoretical framework. Modelling R&D as a fixed cost for firms, he finds that competition may harm technological progress as firms have insufficient means to innovate. This is in accordance with the Schumpeterian view that some sort of monopoly power may be necessary to provide the funds and incentives for R&D activities or to appropriate more fully the yields of technology. If so, then a more vigorous competition policy will reduce innovation and may lead to lower growth (see, for example, Davies 1988b). By contrast, tougher competition may also boost economic growth as innovation may yield a higher social rate of return because competition promotes the diffusion of innovations (Van Bergeijk et al. 1995). Another reason why the incentive to innovate may be higher in more competitive industries is that innovativeness may be a necessary condition to survive for individual firms.

This ambiguity is reflected in the Smulders and van de Klundert (1995) model in which growth is based on innovation. They show that growth is, on the one hand, higher in more concentrated markets because of scale effects and monopolization benefits. On the other hand this result that concentration may improve on growth performance in innovative industries is valid only when the initial market power of the firms in the market is not too high.

This discussion suggests that in some cases competition may actually be too vigorous and that dynamic inefficiencies may emerge because of an increase in competition. Although the empirical evidence on this question is still inconclusive, it is clear that sensitive balances exist between (OECD 1990, p. 10):

i) controlling the concentration of market shares with its potential for the exercise of market power; and *ii)* suppressing institutional or organizational innovation

and between

i) fostering innovation and diffusion by permitting firms to pool resources and share risks in undertaking R&D; and *ii)* tolerating cartel conduct that goes beyond the legitimate goal of an R&D joint venture or, worse, that merely serves as a cover for aggressive industrial policies.

Empirical evidence

Differences in market structures and demand conditions across countries (as reflected in mark-up variations, relative price distortions, etc.) may have a substantial impact on the growth dynamics of imperfectly competitive economies. In a cross-section of 46 countries and the year 1985, Gali (1994) uncovers a significantly negative relationship between the level of per capita income and the size of the average (macroeconomic) mark-up of prices over marginal costs: the higher the mark-up, the lower the level of per capita income. Easterly et al. (1991) develop a model in which investment is endogenous and adapt their model so as to be able to investigate specific distortions such as differential taxes, public spending financed by distortionary taxation, policy-induced uncertainty, monetary policy, trade intervention, exchange rate controls, policies on direct investment and sectoral policies. Next they set out a research strategy to assess empirically the impact of national policies on long-term growth and to find out along which channels structural adjustment has an influence in the long run. In this particular investigation only the black market premium of the exchange rate is used as a variable that represents relative price distortions. In contrast, Easterly (1993) includes several measures of relative price distortions in a cross-section investigation for a group of 51 countries and the years 1970—85. The empirical results show that the variance of a country's input price *vis-à-vis* the world market price structure has a strong negative impact on economic growth.[9] This implies that distortions of relative prices may lower growth substantially. According to Easterly's findings, increasing the variance of relative prices from the sample mean by one standard deviation will lower real annual growth by 1.2 percentage points. Barro (1991) introduced artificially high and artificially low investment prices as a proxy for relative price distortions and found a significantly negative relationship between, on the one hand, real per capita income growth and, on the other hand, the deviation of a country's PPP (purchasing power parity) adjusted investment deflator from the sample mean (i.e. the price on the world market). An increase of this deviation by one standard deviation reduces real annual per capita income growth by about half a percentage point. Unfortunately, several authors report that Barro's regression results — which *grosso modo* can be replicated quite well — differ from their findings with respect to the sign and significance of the coefficient of the deviation of the PPP investment deflator from its sample mean (see, for example, Englander and Gurney 1994, footnote 5).[10] Interestingly, in later articles (for example, Barro 1994), the investment price distortion was not included and Barro returned to the black market premium as an indicator for relative price distortions.

5.5 Economic Fluctuations

Many fears have been expressed that deregulation, privatization and more vigorous competition policy could run counter to the goal of stabilization policy. An early proponent is Zimmerman (1952) who argues that monopolization is 'badly needed for the stabilization of production and employment'. More recently, DeLong and Summers (1986) developed a rational expectations model in which the impact of a demand shock on output is larger when prices are more flexible (although the effect of the shock dampens quickly in such an economy). Basic economic logic, however, suggests that when prices and wages become more flexible, real variables such as output and employment do not have to bear the burden of adjustment or at least to a lesser extent. Also one would expect that an economy returns much more quickly to the long-run equilibrium path if its markets are flexible. Sheffrin (1989) reviews theoretical models in which a too rapid adjustment of prices and wages destabilizes output. The overview of available empirical evidence he presents, suggests that increased price flexibility in normal times stabilizes the economy.

The intuition that macroeconomic flexibility leads to smaller output fluctuations can be illustrated using a simplified closed economy version of the macroeconomic model that Barbone and Poret (1989) developed to analyse the effects of wage and price flexibility. In this economy, firms set prices P so as to reflect both the level of costs C and a mark-up on average costs which depends on the supply—demand gap. The supply—demand gap is represented by Y, i.e. the deviation of real output from its long-run trend value. The price equation therefore is: $P = CY^\beta$. Costs are described by a particularly simple average-cost function $C = W^\varphi$ which uses only the wage rate W as an input. Third, aggregate demand is described by $Y = D/P$ in which D is a nominal demand-push variable. If we write these equations in growth rates (indicated by lower-case symbols), we have the following simple model:

$$p = c + \beta y \tag{5.7}$$
$$c = \varphi w \tag{5.8}$$
$$y = d - p \tag{5.9}$$

To these equations we add a Phillips curve mechanism in order to determine the wage rate.

$$w = \alpha y + p \tag{5.10}$$

The solution of the model which describes the reaction of the economy to a demand shock is for p, w and y, respectively:

$$p = d(\varphi\alpha+\beta)/\{1+\beta+\varphi(\alpha-1)\} \tag{5.11}$$
$$y = d(1-\varphi)/\{1+\beta+\varphi(\alpha-1)\} \tag{5.12}$$
$$w = d(\alpha+\beta)/\{1+\beta+\varphi(\alpha-1)\} \tag{5.13}$$

We can now determine the multipliers of the endogenous variables with respect to the demand shock for three different 'levels' of product market inertia (Table 5.1). The larger the multiplier, the larger the volatility of the variable will be if the system of equations is subjected to a series of random demand shocks.

Table 5.1 *Multipliers of an increase in nominal demand for the price level, output gap and wage rate and different assumptions about the flexibility of the product and labour markets*

	Product market flexibility $(0 < \alpha < \infty)$		
	No flexibility $(\beta=0)$	*Intermediate flexibility* $(\beta>0)$	*Perfect flexibility* $(\beta=\infty)$
Price level p	$d\varphi\alpha/\mu$	$d(\varphi\alpha+\beta)/(\mu+\beta)$	d
Output gap y	$d(1-\varphi)/\mu$	$d(1-\varphi)/(\mu+\beta)$	0
Wage rate w	$d\alpha/\mu$	$d(\alpha+\beta)/(\mu+\beta)$	d

	Labour market flexibility $(0 < \beta < \infty)$		
	No flexibility $(\alpha=0)$	*Intermediate flexibility* $(\alpha>0)$	*Perfect flexibility* $(\alpha=\infty)$
Price level p	$d\beta/\lambda$	$d(\varphi\alpha+\beta)/(\mu+\beta)$	d
Output gap y	$d(1-\varphi)/\lambda$	$d(1-\varphi)/(\mu+\beta)$	0
Wage rate w	$d\beta/\lambda$	$d(\alpha+\beta)/(\mu+\beta)$	d/φ

Note: $\mu = 1 + \varphi(\alpha - 1); \lambda = 1 + \beta - \varphi.$

Two polar cases illustrate a very rigid and a very flexible macroeconomic product market. First, if $\beta = 0$, the price level only indirectly reacts to changes in capacity utilization (namely via the wage rate) and the economy adjusts through large quantity changes. Second, if $\beta \to \infty$, the impact of excess demand and excess supply is very strong and likely to be directly eliminated by price movements so that adjustments in y are very small. From Table 5.1 it follows directly that in this model real macroeconomic fluctuations and product market inertia are related phenomena. The demand shock clearly does not translate into an output gap in the case of perfect flexibility as the multiplier equals zero.

We can now also demonstrate that the flexibility of the labour market may provide an alternative cushion for demand shocks in an economy which suffers from product market inertia. The lower side of Table 5.1 shows the same multipliers with different degrees of labour market flexibility. When the reaction of wages to changes in capacity utilization is very strong, the output gap reduces to zero just as in the case of perfect product market flexibility. On the other hand, when both prices and wages are inflexible ($\alpha = \beta = 0$, not shown in Table 5.1), a demand shock feeds entirely into aggregate demand.

Barbone and Poret (1989) extend this model and investigate the implications of rigidities for supply shocks and in the context of a small open economy as well. They show that the responsiveness to external price competition increases output instability (as prices are more or less dictated for a small open economy) and that the sign pattern of the multipliers is identical for internal and external demand and supply shocks. In general, increases in α and β (representing greater flexibility of labour markets and product markets, respectively) stabilize output at the expense of greater price variance.

Empirical evidence

Barbone and Poret (1989) go on to analyse the results of increased flexibility in the empirical relevant context of the OECD's INTERLINK model, substituting the relevant parameter values of the United States (price and wage elasticities) in the INTERLINK equations for the United Kingdom, France, Germany and Italy. The calculations indicate different degrees of rigidity across countries illustrating that the challenges posed by privatization, deregulation and more vigorous competition policies will differ by country. Extensive simulations of changes in exogenous variables reveal that a greater flexibility of wages and prices results in a smaller variance of gross domestic product, while the volatility of prices increases. Noting that the costs and benefits from greater flexibility in the labour market and the product market in terms of output and prices are almost additive in the case of a demand shock, Barbone and Poret (1989, p. 155) point out that this is not the case for relative factor costs and, consequently, not for (un)employment. Both a restrictive demand shock and an adverse supply shock

> might be more costly in terms of employment losses when product markets alone are deregulated, compared with cases where competition in the labour market increases (Barbone and Poret 1989, p. 155).

Other investigations have found similar results. Using parameters for a representative economy, Schmidt-Hebbel and Serven (1994) find in a rational expectations general equilibrium framework with intertemporally optimizing economic agents that their neoclassical benchmark economy adjusts smoothly and often monotonically to external shocks such as foreign transfers, international prices of intermediate imports and foreign real interest rates. In contrast, economies with liquidity constraints and rigidities show an adjustment pattern with large cyclical responses to external shocks.

Hall (1986) actually made good use of macroeconomic fluctuations as these fluctuations allow him to identify the mark-up ratio on marginal costs in some fifty US industries, as we discussed in Section 4.2. Moreover, Hall shows that market power can play a major role in the propagation of shocks and may explain the cyclical behaviour of productivity. For example, if competition is imperfect then the mark-up is larger than one. Now if the mark-up is sufficiently large, technology shocks and the cyclical implications of monopoly power cannot be distinguished. Indeed, in the absence of technological progress, we would have a cyclical Solow residual reflecting cyclical movements in labour demand. However, although market power and output instability are positively correlated, 'plainly market power is not the prime determinant of instability' (Hall 1986, p. 301).

The responsiveness of an economy to demand and supply shocks is also a major theme of Neo-Keynesian economics. The Neo-Keynesian microeconomic foundations of price stickiness acknowledge the fact that production decisions are made by monopolistically competitive firms. Keynesian research, however, has not led to readily accessible empirical output, other than the survey article by Gordon (1990).[11]

Gordon (1990) distinguishes three dimensions of price rigidity: (*i*) inertia effects, (*ii*) rate of change effects and (*iii*) level effects. The inertia effect basically relates to serial correlation in prices. The rate of change and level effects relate price movements to changes in the utilization of capacity, respectively the level of capacity utilization. In a situation of excess capacity the level effect exerts a downward pressure on prices. If firms see excess capacity increase, then the rate of change effect assures that they adjust prices downwards. Note that the level effect and the rate of change effect may sometimes work in opposite directions, for example when an economy recovers from a recession: in this case capacity utilization is low, but improving.

The three effects can be identified and summarized by the following equation:

$$p_t = \lambda p_{t-1} + \alpha x'_t + \gamma Q'_t + z_t \qquad (5.14)$$

where p is the rate of inflation, $x' = x - q^*$ is the excess of real GNP growth (x) over trend real GNP growth (q^*), $Q' = Q - Q^*$ is the excess of real GNP (Q) over trend real GNP (Q^*) and z_t is an external shock.

According to Gordon (1990), price rigidity occurs when λ is relatively high and α and γ are relatively low. No statement is made on the relative importance of these effects. A high λ reduces the adjustment speed of price reactions to external shocks because past inflation determines current inflation to a greater extent. When $\alpha=0$, inflation will not react to changes in x'. Therefore, for given values of γ and λ the acceleration of inflation because of an overcapacity of, say, five per cent will always have the same magnitude, irrespective of whether the excess of real over trend GNP growth is rising $(x'>0)$ or falling $(x'<0)$. When $\gamma=0$, production does not converge towards its long-run trend value because of price adjustments.

Gordon's findings, which relate to the United States, United Kingdom, France, Germany and Japan in the years 1873—1986, suggest a large variability along the three dimensions of price rigidity, not only between countries and between (sub)periods but also within countries depending on the specific dimension that is the focus of the analysis.

Table 5.2 Ranking of price rigidity 1974—88 based on six adjustment parameters for 23 OECD countries

Rank	Inertia effect		Rate of change		Level effect	
	Nominal	Real	Nominal	Real	Nominal	Real
1	DEN	**NOR**	AUT[a]	**NOR**[a]	SPA[a]	ICE[a]
2	US	BLEU	BLEU[a]	GRE[a]	UK	JAP[a]
3	BLEU	FRA	DEN[a]	BLEU[a]	JAP	DEN[a]
4	GER	US	CAN[a]	SWI[a]	FIN	TUR[a]
5	AUS	NL	GER[a]	AUT[a]	SWI	FIN
6	CAN	SPA	AUS[a]	CAN[a]	TUR	SWE
7	ITA	DEN	US[a]	AUS[a]	NL	UK
8	GRE	AUS	SWI	IRE[a]	GER	POR
9	AUT	CAN	FRA	NZ[a]	ITA	NL
10	FRA	GER	NL	FRA[a]	DEN	SPA
11	NZ	GRE	ITA	DEN[a]	SWE	GER
12	NL	ITA	FIN	NL[a]	ICE	NZ
13	SWE	IRE	POR	GER[a]	POR	ITA
14	SWI	AUT	GRE	SPA[a]	IRE	SWI
15	POR	SWE	**NOR**	US[a]	GRE	US
16	FIN	POR	IRE	POR[a]	US	BLEU
17	UK	FIN	JAP	SWE[a]	FRA	FRA
18	**NOR**	UK	NZ	FIN[a]	NZ	AUS
19	SPA	NZ	SWE	ITA	AUS	AUT
20	JAP	JAP	UK	JAP	AUT	IRE
21	ICE	ICE[a]	SPA	UK	**NOR**	GRE
22	TUR	SWI[a]	ICE	TUR	CAN	CAN
23	IRE	TUR[a]	TUR	ICE	BLEU	**NOR**

Note: [a] Coefficient contradicts theoretical expectations.
Source: Van Schaik (1991).

This variability or indeterminateness is well illustrated in Table 5.2 which reports on an investigation by van Schaik (1991) who estimates equation (5.14) for the OECD countries, using alternatively nominal and real variables. As a result, six different parameters are available to indicate the extent of price stickiness.

Table 5.2 presents the rankings of 23 OECD countries based on van Schaik's (1991) findings for each of the individual parameter estimates. It is difficult to establish a clear ranking of the degree of market flexibility.[12] These results vividly illustrate the measurement problems at hand. Countries shift along the spectrum depending on the criterion for price rigidity one wishes to adopt and the extent of indeterminacy is very large. Indeed, the estimates offer little guidance for actual policy analysis (compare, for example, the spread of Japan, Norway, and the United States). All in all, it is rather difficult to assess whether price and quantity movements are comparatively low for a specific country.

Even the ranking of country pairs is prohibited because of non-transitivity of the outcomes (compare the rankings of the United States, Japan and France). So an important caveat that is to be derived from van Schaik's findings is that it is rather difficult to assess whether and how price rigidity is related to the business cycle (i.e. the level and rate of capacity utilization).

All in all, indications exist which support the intuition that deregulation, privatization and more competition will not increase an economy's instability with respect to income. The evidence, however, is not very strong and may allow for other interpretations.

5.6 Incomes Policy

An equitable income distribution is an important goal of economic policy in the modern welfare state. Structural change influences relative prices and, consequently, the primary distribution of income. In addition, this distribution changes due to the fact that some sectors will lose although the economy as a whole will gain from structural change. An example is the implementation of a specific anti-trust policy measure which prohibits (the workers of the firms that form) a cartel from reaping monopoly rents and at the same time improves on the well-being of consumers in general because of a lower market price and a better product quality. According to Bovenberg (1985, pp. 37—8),

> [w]ith ... segmented markets and other factors that impede adjustment, larger changes in relative prices are required to achieve quantity adjustment. Relative price movements, however, not only reallocate resources, they also redistribute income.

Clearly, the impact that policies aiming at structural change exert on the income distribution needs to be taken into account. This is true not only from the philosophical perspective of equity, but also from both the economic perspective of efficiency and the policy perspective of feasibility. Implementation of structural policies needs to take into account that the pattern of losers and gainers may give rise to pressure groups which oppose deregulation, privatization and more vigorous competition policies. We will return to the policy maker's point of view in Chapter 7, and consider the philosophical issues related to equity beyond the scope of this book.[13] Hence we presently concentrate on the economic issue of the relationship between income distribution and dynamic macroeconomic efficiency.

The distribution of income (and saving) may actually be more important than the level of savings for the level of economic activity in a country. Schumpeter (1934 (1983), p. 72) pointed out that entrepreneurial profits provide for an economy's investment funds, while savings are not a sufficient condition for economic growth. Economic growth prospects to a large extent depend on the distribution of income between capital owners and labour, because the saving and investment rates may be different for different types of income earners. Van Marrewijk and Verbeek (1993, pp. 99—103) develop an interesting disequilibrium model for an open two-sector economy and although the source of disequilibrium in their model is sluggish wage adjustment rather than price inertia, their findings are instructive for our discussion as well. In the van Marrewijk— Verbeek model one sector (consisting, for example, of firms producing consumption goods) is not rationed in its labour and product markets and the zero profit condition applies. The other sector (for example, the capital goods industry) is 'rationed' and making an (excess) profit. The results of the model in terms of the growth path achieved critically depend on the questions of who receives these profits and who saves relatively more (capital owners versus workers).

Indeed, an indirect mechanism that links economic growth to imperfect markets is the distribution of income, especially of rents, which may be influenced through anti-trust legislation. Bertola (1991) develops the argument that non-contestable monopolists and other so-called rentiers do not save when the economy moves along a balanced long-term growth path. In order to increase economic growth through larger volumes of investment, aggregate saving needs to increase. This suggests that a growth-orientated economic policy should seek to increase the share of producible factors of production (physical and human capital). Rent-protective legislation and institutions, according to Bertola, may cripple potential growth. Such an indirect mechanism between economic activity and market structure may actually be quite important.

Empirical evidence
Some indirect empirical evidence exists that regulation, lax law enforcement and protection may redistribute income in such a way as to be detrimental to economic growth, although it is often difficult to observe the relevant distributive policies (see Persson and Tabellini 1994). The more skewed the primary income distribution, the higher taxes *ceteris paribus* must be to arrive at the same measure of equality in the secondary income distribution. In many cases the skewedness of the income distribution results from insider—outsider phenomena in the labour market (employed—unemployed), product market (restrictive business practices), and in the markets for produced inputs (for example, schooling). In these cases deregulation, privatization and competition policies may help to reduce distributional conflict. This suggests that structural reform, through privatization, deregulation and competition policy, can also be turned into an important instrument to arrive at a more egalitarian income distribution, and as a by-product may help to lower taxes and via this mechanism enhances economic activity.

5.7 The Balance of Payments

Disequilibrium of the balance of payments has been identified by a number of authors with the prevalent market structure on domestic markets. Bovenberg (1991) and Kremers (1991) argue that an increase of the dynamism of the non-traded and sheltered sectors of an economy will enhance investment and increase labour demand. Production in the non-traded and sheltered sector, will only react quickly to new opportunities when markets function efficiently. Hence a country that combines a surplus on the current account of its balance of payments with product market inertia and high unemployment should follow a strategy that tackles the three problems in one stroke through a policy that improves on the functioning of domestic markets.[14] Examples of countries where this policy proposal could be effective according to Bovenberg and Kremers are the Netherlands and Germany (see, for example, Lipschitz et al. 1989). Essentially, Bovenberg and Kremers consider a surplus on the current account as an indicator for a lack of flexibility of an economy. This is, however, not a strictly logical conclusion. Thirlwall (1992), for example, following similar reasoning uses the deficit on the current account as an indicator for lagging supply-side performance in the United Kingdom.

Let us consider the determinants of a balance of payments surplus in somewhat more detail.[15] The link between the balance of payments and an economy's flexibility runs via competitiveness and (net) exports. In a Keynesian analysis balance-of-payments-constrained economic growth is linked to export demand which is either classified as being exogenous or depends on some measure of competitiveness, such as the exchange rate, unit labour costs, etc. (a recent application is Atesoglu 1994). In contrast, a supply-side approach to exports explains the volume of trade on the basis of the available production capacity (the so-called home-pressure-of-demand effect; see, for example, Draper 1985). The implication is that competition most probably improves competitiveness, resulting in a surplus on the current account of the balance of payments. However, when structural reform includes the removal of barriers to trade such as import quotas and tariffs as well, a movement towards equilibrium of the balance of payments is ambiguous (see, for example, several simulation results in Srinivasan and Whalley 1986).

Empirical evidence
Brakman et al. (1988) show that flexibility of the economy is an important determinant of international competitiveness as supply-side flexibility (both at mesoeconomic and the macroeconomic level) contributes significantly to the explanation of the development of international market shares in Germany, France, the Netherlands and Belgium/Luxembourg. Investigating over 100 industries in Denmark, Germany, Italy, South Korea, Singapore, Sweden, Switzerland, the

United Kingdom and the United States, Porter (1990a) shows that excellence on world markets depends on related groups of successful firms and industries ('clusters') that operate in the context of healthy competition. According to Porter (1990a):

> Among the strongest empirical findings from our research is the association between vigorous domestic rivalry and the creation and persistence of domestic competitive advantage in an industry (Porter 1990a, p. 117).

5.8   The Instruments of Macroeconomic Policy

Do changes in the market structure influence the impact of macroeconomic policy instruments? At first sight it would seem that in an economy with a responsive and self-equilibrating supply side, government intervention in reaction to exogenous demand and supply shocks would be suboptimal. Indeed, such an economy mimics the neoclassical paradigm so that government would seem to be less potent than in the Keynesian case of sticky prices, essentially because it is the slowness of price adjustments which makes policies aimed at influencing aggregate demand effective (in a flexible economy demand shocks feed into prices). This mechanism is illustrated by Gelauff's (1992, pp. 185—8) sensitivity analyses in which he compares two versions of MIMIC, an applied general equilibrium model for the Netherlands in which the labour market is modelled by either assuming wage bargaining or market clearing. Although this is primarily a theoretical exercise as it compares two extreme cases, Gelauff's calculations illustrate that assumptions about the labour market structure are relevant for policy makers in two respects. First, the size of the impact of taxation depends on the labour market regime. For example, a decrease in the first bracket tax rate equal to 0.4 percentage points of GDP increases employment by 0.27 percentage points in the wage-bargaining model, whereas the same measure yields an increase of 0.07 percentage points only in the market-clearing wage model (Gelauff 1992, pp. 168 and 186). Second, the assumptions about the functioning of the labour market influence the ranking of tax instruments, especially since supply-side effects are relatively more relevant in the market-clearing model than in the wage bargaining model.

This mechanism has been amended by recent research. To be sure, most economists agree that a slow speed of the invisible hand is the *raison d'être* of the Keynesian analysis. Markets do not clear instantaneously and this means that output is often constrained by effective demand, as Tobin (1993, p. 46) notes:

> Any failure of price adjustments to keep markets cleared opens the door for quantities to determine quantities, for example real national income to determine consumption demand, as described in Keynes' multiplier calculus.

There is also wide agreement about the fact that market structure matters for macroeconomic policy. Discussing intertemporal disequilibrium extensions that focus on the implications of future quantity constraints on the effectiveness of economic instruments, Rankin (1994) points out that the nature of the equilibrium in markets is the crucial factor that determines the efficacy of economic policy.[16] Most economists would seem to agree with that position, but substantial differences of opinion exist about the actual size and sign of the multipliers of the economic policy instruments in different market regimes.

In the Bénassy (1993) disequilibrium model which describes an economy that exhibits the property of Keynesian allocative inefficiency, government policy in many cases turns out to work quite differently from a traditional Keynesian model. For example, in Bénassy's model a reduction of lump-sum taxation neither influences production nor employment; the only impact being an increase in inflation and higher nominal wages. In contrast, an increase in government expenditure results in more employment and higher prices (as expected), but fully crowds out consumption. Obviously, these results are related to the particular structure of Bénassy's model (for example, supply-side effects are neglected and the model does not study investment). Still, its lesson for the real world is clear. Market structure influences both the static efficiency of the allocation and the multipliers with respect to government policies.[17]

Dixon and Rankin (1994) point out that the elasticity of demand matters when competition is imperfect. Government policies that change demand elasticities thus have an additional channel to influence relative prices *vis-à-vis* the perfect market economy. If government expenditures have a lower price elasticity than private

demand (for example, because spending is fixed in real terms with
zero elasticity or in nominal terms with unit elasticity), then an
increase in government expenditure decreases the elasticity of
macroeconomic demand. This increases market power and the firm's
mark-up will increase, reducing output and employment and
increasing the price level as we saw before. This phenomenon that
government spending typically makes the demand curves faced by
sellers more inelastic, according to Silvestre (1993, pp. 136—7)
points to an interesting paradox:

> One can say that, paradoxically, government spending enhances market power
> while trying to alleviate its consequences.

Moreover, the Keynesian multiplier process depends on the notion
that an increase in effective demand in demand-constrained regimes
has positive externalities. The multiplier is a process that essentially
takes place in real time, so that the speed of the process matters (cf.
Keynes 1936, pp. 122—5). If such demands do not spill over to other
markets (or take a very long time to spill over), for example because
of a specific agent's inertia, then the multiplier process will come to
a halt and the externality no longer exists.[18] So supply-side policies
may enhance the impact of demand management, and structural
adjustment policies aimed at more flexible markets may also enhance
the effectiveness of the government's box of economic policy tools
via this mechanism.

This is the Keynesian paradox: we do not have a Keynesian
problem if markets are too flexible, but at the same time the
Keynesian answer will not suffice if markets are too rigid. The new
Keynesian paradox is well illustrated by the general equilibrium
simulations for a small open economy which are reported in Table
5.3. The outcomes of the simulations are represented as departures
from a baseline which is assumed to reflect the long-run growth path
of the economy. The calculations have been made with the MESEM
model, an applied general equilibrium model for a small open
economy which is parameterized for the Netherlands in 1985 (van
Sinderen 1993). A main characteristic of MESEM is that it takes into
account the 'incentive effect' of taxation through explicit modelling of
the tax wedges on labour and capital.[19]

*Table 5.3   Product market inertia and the efficacy of macroeconomic
policy (cumulative, per cent departure from long-run
growth path)*

		Production		Employment	
	Years	Product market hysteresis	Market clearing	Product market hysteresis	Market clear-ing
Labour tax reduction	4	0.4	0.8	0.5	0.6
(1 per cent of GDP)	10	0.5	1.2	0.6	0.8
Capital tax reduction	4	0.4	0.8	0.2	0.3
(1 per cent of GDP)	10	0.5	1.1	0.1	0.3
More public consumption	4	0.1	0.2	0.1	0.2
(1 per cent of GDP)	10	0.1	0.1	0.0	0.2
More public investment	4	0.2	0.4	0.1	0.2
(1 per cent of GDP)	10	0.2	0.5	0.1	0.2

Source: Van Bergeijk et al. (1993).

Table 5.3 shows the cumulative impact of a permanent net impulse of 1 per cent of GDP in the short (4 years) to medium term (10 years). Tax reductions have a relatively high yield in terms of both employment and production, as is to be expected given the Dutch high marginal and average labour taxes and the very large share of the Dutch public sector in GDP. Although the impact of the respective economic policy instruments differs considerably it should be noted that both the short-run and long-run multipliers in many instances double once markets clear. We find multipliers that exceed the value of 1 only when the product market clears instantaneously and the demand stimulus results from tax cuts (which also improve the supply-side behaviour of the economy). Indeed, in a world with flexible markets one would expect that a reduction of the labour wedge will result both in an improvement of macroeconomic performance because of a more efficient allocation and in higher welfare. The employment effects of fiscal policies work through the supply side which is modelled explicitly in the MESEM model and this may explain why the results differ from those obtained by new Keynesian simulation models such as Gelauff's (1992) MIMIC model.

This suggests that economic policy should not attack unemployment by means of increased government spending, but rather via the supply side of the economy: taxes should be lowered and markets should be made more competitive.

5.9   Conclusions

Central to the understanding of the macroeconomic consequences of imperfect markets (and hence of the costs and benefits of privatization, deregulation and more vigorous competition policy) is the time horizon that is being adopted in the analysis. In the short term when we neglect the capacity effects of investment and other supply-side considerations, the perspective is Keynesian and the efficiency losses of malfunctioning markets are static in nature. In the short run the instruments of economic policy appear to be more effective in an economy with rigidities than in a flexible economy.

In contrast, when we take the cumulation processes of producible factors of production (such as investments in physical and human capital) into account, the analysis of the macroeconomic effects of imperfect markets in the long run allows us to investigate dynamic (in)efficiencies and to take supply-side effects into account which influence the effectiveness of economic policy instruments. Although the empirical evidence as yet is inconclusive, recent developments in theory and applied research suggest at least that policy does not become less effective when the speed of the invisible hand increases. In general, the endogenous growth approach suggests that policy instruments do have a long-term influence on the growth rate, whereas the short-term approach focuses on the impact of policies on the level of economic activity only. Anyhow, it would not seem to be farfetched to assume that the long-run effects will ultimately dominate the short-term effects so that contradictions between short-term and long-term analyses could ultimately be reconciled. Even if the short-term approach is right, in the end a positive impact on the rate of growth will cancel a negative economic impact on the initial level of economic activity.[20]

Although our overview has shown some contradictions with respect to the multipliers (i.e. the efficacy and even the direction of the impact) of demand management and taxation when we adopt a different time horizon, three conclusions can unambiguously be derived if re-allocation costs are absent or negligible and if the potentially negative impact on innovation is not too strong. These conclusions are valid independently of the time horizon that is being adopted:

●   per capita income is *ceteris paribus* higher in the deregulated, flexible economy with competitive markets;
●   the price level is *ceteris paribus* lower in the deregulated, flexible economy with competitive markets;
●   employment is *ceteris paribus* higher in the deregulated, flexible economy with competitive markets.

Hence an important policy conclusion is that flexibility improves on macroeconomic performance. An equally important caveat is that we need to qualify this policy conclusion in the sense that reallocation costs may be prohibitive and that the pace of innovation can be hampered by too much rivalry. Hence a careful and detailed analysis of transition costs and an empirical assessment of the relevance of the competition—technology relationship should accompany any policy proposal related to privatization, deregulation and competition policy.

The finding that flexibility is an important determinant of macroeconomic performance suggests that privatization, deregulation and competition policy can be developed into important instruments of economic policy in most European countries where both labour and product markets are much more rigid than in, for example, northern America. The *White Paper* of the Commission of the European Communities (1994) on the unemployment problem stresses that the challenges that policy makers in the whole of Europe have to meet are in general caused by a lack of economic dynamism. According to the Commission, European economies lack flexibility. This inertia is related to the lack of internal and external competition both in labour markets and on the markets for goods and services.

In addition, as to the proper methodology that is to be deployed in analysing these issues, many authors stress spill-over effects between markets and sectors and, consequently, argue that the 'costs of non-competition' should be properly analysed in a general equilibrium framework. Focusing on the long-run equilibrium solutions of macroeconomic models in analyses of issues related to deregulation, privatization and a more vigorous competition policy would seem to be appropriate, as the theoretical and empirical evidence that was reviewed suggests that such policies may help to dampen economic fluctuations. Hence it may be appropriate to focus on the long term in our analysis.

In the next chapter we will review the available evidence from general equilibrium analyses, discussing the modelling strategies that were actually followed by policy analysts with respect to four major programmes aimed at deregulation, privatization and a more vigorous competition policy.

Notes

1.   See the December 1987 Special Issue of *De Economist* devoted to the microfoundations of macroeconomics and van Ees and Garretsen (1993).
2.   See, for some examples, Bresnahan (1989), Krugman (1986) and Hersough (1984).
3.   See, for example, Sala-i-Martin (1990) for a review and Crafts (1992) for a more speculative and critical assessment.
4.   Proceed as follows. The Lagrangian version of the objective function is $Z = \alpha \ln c + (1-\alpha)\ln(m/p) + \lambda[c-q-(m_0-m)/p]$. The first order conditions require $Z_c = \lambda + \alpha/c = 0$; $Z_m = (1-\alpha)/m + \lambda/p = 0$ and $Z_\lambda = c - q - (m_0 - m) = 0$. Next, using $Z_c = Z_m = 0$, we find $m = pc(1-\alpha)/\alpha$; substitution in the budget constraint (equation (5.3)) yields the expression for c^d.
5.   Note that static gains can be represented in this model by a shift in the efficiency parameter A.
6.   For example, if Y is a CES (constant elasticity of substitution) production function of the type $Y = A[\alpha K_1^{-\rho} + (1-\alpha)K_2^{-\rho}]^{-1/\rho}$, then $Y_{K1} = \alpha/A^\rho][(Y/K_1)^{1+\rho}]$ and $Y_{K2} = [(1-\alpha)/A^\rho][(Y/K_2)^{1+\rho}]$. The wedge between the two types of capital γ assures that $Y_{K1} = (1+\gamma)Y_{K2}$. Now we can solve for $K_2/K_1 = [(1+\gamma)(1-\alpha)/\alpha]^{(1/1+\rho)}$, substitute this in the production function using $K = K_1 + K_2$ and arrive at $Y = A\theta(\gamma)K$, where $\theta(\gamma) = [\alpha+(1-\alpha)\omega]^{-1/\rho}/(1+\omega)$ and $\omega = K_1/K_2$. It is left to the reader to check that $\theta(\gamma) > 0$ and $\theta_\gamma < 0$ as long as α is not too small.
7.   In addition, tax systems in many countries tend to treat different types of capital differently, which is another reason why (gross) factor rewards are not equalized.

8.   Posner (1971) has already identified regulation as an indirect form of taxation.

9.   The world market price therefore is assumed to be the 'undistorted' competitive price level. Note that it is advisable to correct the variance of relative prices across commodities for international differences in natural endowments, as done by Easterly et al. (1991).

10. Replication and duplication efforts at the Ministry of Economic Affairs for a sub-group of 24 OECD countries also failed (see van Bergeijk, Hiddink and Waasdorp, 1995).

11. A non-technical introduction to the main issues is provided by the *Journal of Economic Perspectives'* 1993 symposium on Keynesianism today. Mankiw (1990, p. 1657) argues that 'this line of research is still too new to judge how substantial its impact will be or to guess what problems will be judged most important'.

12. Note, moreover, that a procedure that excludes the most probable outliers (i.e. the highest and the lowest ranking that each country achieved on the basis of each of the six parameter estimates) still does not produce a clear-cut impression on the basis of an average ranking although from such an exercise North-West Europe (the Netherlands and Scandinavia) appears to be among the most rigid European countries.

13. For a transparent egalitarian analysis one may wish to consult Roemer (1994), who also deals with privatization and deregulation (especially in the context of the changes in Eastern Europe).

14. See for analyses of the current account when markets are modelled as being imperfectly competitive, for example, Persson and Svensson (1983) and van Wijnbergen (1987). They use a two-period framework in which the first period is typically characterized by Keynesian unemployment while the state of the world in the second period is either uncertain or characterized by a Walrasian equilibrium. Unfortunately, these models do not shed light on the actual relationship between market structure and current account.

15. See Brakman (1991) for an overview of (applied) trade modelling.

16. See also Heijdra (1995) for a demonstration of the quantitative significance of the assumption of an imperfectly competitive market structure. Heijdra (1995, p. 29 and Tables 5 and 6) finds substantially lower multipliers when markets are competitive.

17. This is confirmed by Heijdra and Broer (1993) who show that rigidity may reduce the set of policy options as fiscal policy multipliers go to zero when market power increases.

18. We are convinced that Keynes would not have been interested in a situation where government spending via a slow multiplier improves on the economic performance in the long run only.

19. The MESEM model and the procedures are discussed in more detail in Section 6.4 below.

20. However, the short-run effects may be extremely relevant from a political point of view, even when the long-run effects are positive. Chapter 7 elaborates on this topic.

6. Modelling Strategies for Structural Reform

Competition policy, privatization and deregulation became international topics in policy making when the OECD launched its structural adjustment programme in 1987. This programme aimed at creating more flexibility in the economy as a whole by increasing competition in product markets, improving the responsiveness of factor markets and improving the efficiency and effectiveness of the public sector. The OECD's (1987a) structural adjustment programme was initially quite successful in generating awareness of the question of how market structure, competition policy, government procurement and so on may influence the adjustment process of the markets for goods and services. Unfortunately, empirical estimations of the economy-wide effects of rigidity on the markets for goods and services are difficult and scarce. The costs of non-competition have so far been mainly asserted on a case-by-case basis for narrowly defined industries (see, for example, Winston 1993).

This case-by-case approach has left many observers with the wrong impression that structural problems — which are often micro-economic in nature — do not have macroeconomic repercussions. A second problem is that microeconomic analyses are simply insufficient to say something meaningful about the macroeconomic consequences of microeconomic reform. In discussing the case of Eastern Europe, Welfens (1993, pp. 42—6) notes that economy-wide privatization and deregulation may yield ambiguous results for the economy at large even if a microeconomic analysis points in only one direction. For example, the average savings rate could be influenced by counteracting changes in either the unemployment rate or the budget deficit. Very little, however, is as yet known about the relationship between structural 'microeconomic' rigidities and the macroeconomic performance of an economy.[1]

Lucas critique

One reason is that macroeconometric models may be improper tools for questions that relate to qualitative economic policies such as structural reform. Any exercise in qualitative policy analysis is rather vulnerable to the Lucas (1976) critique, that actual policies change the behaviour of individuals, for example, because of changes in expectations formation. Invoking the *ceteris paribus* clause means that such changes are not considered, the implicit assumption being that product market inertia could have been improved upon without influencing other behavioural parameters. Taking the Lucas critique fully to heart implies that the consequences of institutional change can never be ascertained empirically. To some this may seem to be a logically valid position which invalidates the macroeconomic assessment of the benefits of deregulation and competition. An example is Kuipers (1990, p. 251) who argues that

> Qualitative policy and reforms imply changes in the social organization ... Hence, policy measures of these kinds are not of a routine character, and will therefore change the stochastic environment. If attempts are made to assess their consequences by means of models estimated with past data, the Lucas critique holds.

Indeed, structural reform often renders the lessons that can be derived from econometric models useless. For example, the Reserve Bank of New Zealand (1994, p. 2) in discussing the forecasting and modelling issues related to its new structural macroeconometric model 'Model XIII' points out that this exercise became a necessity because its predecessor ('Model XII') was found to perform very poorly out-of-sample, possibly because of the fundamental and wide-ranging reform of the New Zealand economy:[2]

> This re-estimation process has involved a substantial reformulation of the structure of the model to account for the widespread deregulation and liberalization of the New Zealand economy since 1984. It is in the nature of structural change that equations estimated on samples including pre-reform data are unlikely [to] perform well as forecasting tools.

To others the Lucas critique is an important caveat which implies that the results of such exercises should be interpreted with caution. Mayer (1993, pp. 93—101) discusses the views that the economic profession holds on the Lucas critique and reviews empirical studies of specific regime changes. These studies yield mixed results (Mayer 1993, p. 95): 'They suggest that the Lucas critique is fully applicable to financial markets, but that its applicability to labour markets is more problematic'.

General equilibrium approach
In this chapter we will describe and discuss five recent quantitative investigations which may shed some light on the macroeconomic costs and benefits of structural adjustment. These investigations were initiated against the background of major qualitative policy shifts towards privatization, deregulation and competition in the European Community, Germany, the Netherlands and Australia, respectively.

In contrast with the individual country studies which use applied general equilibrium approaches, the European Commission uses a partial equilibrium analysis. At the time of writing the Emerson report applied general equilibrium models under imperfect competition were not yet available, so that the choice for a partial equilibrium model would seem to have been dictated by the state of the art in the economic profession in the mid-1980s. Emerson et al. (1988, p. 202), however, argue that the difference between a 'partial' and a 'general' equilibrium estimate (i.e. the impact of a sector on the supply and demand conditions of other branches of the economy, the so-called second-order effects due to changes in relative prices between sectors) is an 'open empirical matter'. Moreover, the trade-off between the research effort needed for theoretical rigour and the political time constraint leads Emerson et al. (1988) to opt for an aggregate estimate based on partial analyses rather than an estimate based on a general equilibrium model.[3]

The preference, however, for general equilibrium approaches is not only guided by fundamental theoretical considerations. Nor is a general equilibrium approach impossible as shown by the following discussion of the four studies that deal with the potential benefits of structural change in Germany, the Netherlands and Australia. The choice of the economic tool of general equilibrium analysis is in the first place a logical one (see, for example, Bovenberg 1985, Borges 1986, Hamilton et al. 1988 and Gelauff and Graafland 1994, p. 6). General equilibrium models have a solid theoretical foundation as the

optimizing behaviour of microeconomic agents is explicitly modelled.
Consequently, a general equilibrium model might be less affected by
structural change as long as agents optimize behaviour given various
constraints. In addition to the robustness of the analysis with respect
to structural changes, the general equilibrium approach considers the
economy as a complete system of interrelated actors (government,
firms, households, etc.), recognizing that (Dixon et al. 1992, p. 1)

> economic shocks impacting on any one component can have repercussions
> throughout the system and that accounting for these repercussions may be
> essential in assessing the effects of the shocks — even on the components upon
> which they impact initially.

These effects are very relevant because deregulation, privatization
and more vigorous competition will have a different impact on
different sectors. A partial analysis, for example relating to a specific
industry that is to be deregulated, may show a loss for this specific
industry, while the overall effect on the economy is beneficial.

6.1   The Macro Paradox

Actually, our interest in the topic of the macroeconomic
consequences of microeconomic reform derives from the paradox that
the OECD (1993b) notes with respect to the macroeconomic impact
of the relaxed competition policy in the Netherlands. The OECD
asserts that the Dutch comparative macroeconomic performance over
the last decade or so in terms of either economic growth or the price
level does not provide clear-cut evidence of the harmful effects of a
lax competition policy.

It is, however, more likely that the OECD has been looking in the
wrong direction. In its country report on New Zealand, the OECD
(1993a, pp. 134—6) presents an empirical investigation *à la* Barro
(1991). The original study by Barro (1991) uses a sample of 98
countries to investigate in a cross-section the question of how average
annual real per capita GDP growth over the years 1960—85 is
influenced by variables like the 1960 level of income per head,
investment, public expenditure, fertility rates and school enrolment.[4]
The OECD Secretariat re-estimates slightly adjusted Barro equations
for the group of 24 OECD countries and investigates the residuals of

the estimated equations. Interestingly, the OECD notes that New Zealand consistently stands out as 'one of the economies' where actual growth performance falls short the most of what is predicted and that this

> points to a substantial adverse impact of structural rigidities associated with the protected and non-competitive nature of the economy up to the mid-1980's (OECD 1993a, p. 136).[5]

In the OECD investigation, however, the Netherlands stands out as *the* economy where actual growth performance in all regressions falls short the most (largest residual). Actually, the OECD regressions suggest that Dutch annual per capita income growth in the years 1960—85 fell short by half a percentage point, thus confirming the findings that will be presented in Table 6.6.

By way of illustration, Table 6.1 replicates the OECD Secretariat's exercise for 24 OECD countries in the period 1960—85 on the basis of Barro's data set.[6] We use this equation and the observed values of the explanatory values to make 'in sample' predictions and to calculate the residuals that are reported in Figure 6.1 below.

Table 6.1 Factors determining the average annual percentage growth of per capita GDP in 24 OECD countries over the years 1960—85 (ordinary least squares method)

	Sample mean	Estimated coefficient	t-value	Elasticity on average
GDP per capita in 1960	4.3	—0.5	—8.4	—0.8
Secondary school enrolment	0.50	1.4	2.4	0.2
Public consumption to GDP	0.15	—4.4	—2.0	—0.2
Fertility rate	2.4	—0.8	—4.0	—0.6

Note: All coefficients are significant at the 95 per cent confidence level and better, the constant term is 7.1, R^2 is 0.81 and the F-statistic is 20.

Table 6.1 shows that the growth rate of GDP per capita is larger the lower the initial level of GDP per capita (the so-called 'catch-up effect'), the lower public consumption in relation to GDP, the lower the fertility rate and the higher the level of education. The equation provides a useful description of economic development in the OECD over a quarter of a century. First, the estimated coefficients are highly significant. Second, the standard error of the equation is 0.4 per cent (the average annual growth rate is 3 per cent). Third, the equation is able to explain more than 80 per cent of the variance observed in the growth rates of the 24 per capita GDPs over the period 1960—85.

Figure 6.1 shows the residuals of this exercise in growth accounting. We have specifically marked the countries which will either be studied or serve as a point of reference in the present chapter. Just like the OECD Secretariat, we find rather substantial negative residuals for New Zealand, the Netherlands and Australia (0.6 per cent, 0.4 per cent and 0.3 per cent, respectively).[7] The residual for Germany is negative, but small (0.05 per cent only). Large and positive residuals are found for Japan, Norway, the United States and Canada.[8]

So where does this leave us? We have not established a causal link between, on the one hand, structural rigidities (a deficient competition policy, market inertia, the extent of public sector involvement, etc.) and, on the other hand, growth performance. Syrquin (1995, p. 35) rightly argues that 'differences in growth performance may indicate where to look for measures of flexibility, but by themselves cannot be taken as such measures'. Levine and Zervos (1993, pp. 426—7) point out that 'cross-country regressions do not solve causal issues ... [T]hey should be viewed as evaluating the strength of partial correlations, and not as behavioral relationships that suggest how much growth will change when polices change'. Another conceptual problem of this manner of comparison is that variations in one economic performance indicator (i.e. per capita GDP) may not only be due to structural features, but also to different policy goals (Bruno and Sachs 1984). This conceptual problem makes the proper identification of the impact of structural factors often ambiguous.

*Figure 6.1 Dispersion of the residuals from the growth equation
(actual growth minus growth estimated on the basis of
the equation in Table 6.1, figures on an average annual
basis in per cent)*

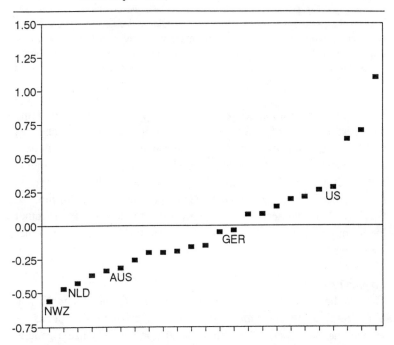

Note: AUS: Australia; GER: West Germany; NLD: the
Netherlands; NWZ: New Zealand; US: United States.

So establishing a causal relationship between structural reform
(privatization, deregulation and more vigorous competition policy)
will be one of the topics of the next sections. Using the OECD's own
methodology, however, we have now succeeded in illustrating that
the growth experience of the Netherlands was below the country's
potential.

The need for counterfactual analysis
Indeed, the starting point of this chapter is that straightforward
inspection of the historical data is an insufficient basis to assess the

effects of privatization, deregulation and more vigorous competition.[9] Winston (1993, p. 1270), for example, is very explicit in his prescription of how to measure the effects of deregulation:

> [S]imply comparing the economic welfare of affected groups before and after deregulation, as is frequently done in the popular press, fails to account for the effects of contemporaneous changes in other economic factors, such as the business cycle and technological trends, that also affect welfare ... Empirical assessments of the actual effects of deregulation therefore require a counterfactual approach.

Discussing privatization, Galal et al. (1994) point out that comparing the performance of the enterprise before divestiture and its performance after divestiture 'is applicable only in a stationary environment'. In reality economic conditions are constantly changing and therefore any observed changes could be the results of changes in the macroeconomic environment. These judgements by Winston and Galal et al. would seem to be equally valid for the benefits of other kinds of structural reform, be they national or *vis-à-vis* other countries.

Common methodology
The studies that we will discuss all deploy a counterfactual framework, using the same configuration of exogenous variables. A second characteristic of the country studies is that they use a general equilibrium model to link structural microeconomic rigidities to macroeconomic performance, thus providing an alternative approach to traditional growth-accounting techniques *à la* Maddison (1987, 1991). In a sense these studies follow up on the seminal article by Hamilton et al. (1988), which calibrate general equilibrium models for the United States, India and the Soviet Union in which distortions feature that change over time. Essentially, these exercises by Hamilton et al. (1988) provide an alternative explanation of below potential growth in the three economies, focusing on the way in which institutional arrangements and their changes over time influence performance. The country studies that we discuss differ from the *ex post* approach by Hamilton et al. (1988) as they provide an *ex ante* evaluation of proposed qualitative policies.

6.2   The European Community

Policy background
In 1985 the European Commission launched its *White Paper* on the completion of the internal market by 1992 in which the Commission identified barriers to the free flow of goods, services, capital and labour. These barriers can be subdivided into five economic categories (Emerson et al. 1988, p. 21): (*i*) tariffs, (*ii*) quantitative restrictions, (*iii*) cost-increasing barriers, (*iv*) market-entry restrictions and (*v*) market-distorting subsidies and practices. The *White Paper* identified 278 measures to be taken. This plan of action proved to be very successful in producing progress in terms of political decisions on major issues related to structural reform. Part of this success was due to the report by Emerson et al. (1988), which provided estimates of the economic benefits of 'Europe 1992'.

Methodology
The European Commission followed a two-trail approach. The macroeconomic costs of non-Europe were assessed on the basis of:

● an aggregation of microeconomic findings from sectoral and firm-specific studies (these studies were often performed by outside consultants); and

● the macroeconomic repercussions (distributive, accumulation and multiplier effects) of microeconomic shocks in key parameters (such as productivity, costs of intermediate inputs etc.) calculated with the aid of macroeconometric models.

We focus on deregulation and competition and will not consider the Commission's analysis of trade-related barriers (i.e. tariffs, quantitative restrictions and cost-increasing barriers such as customs handling). Economic integration involves not only a reduction in transport and transaction costs (just like trade liberalization), but in addition entails deregulation of markets.[10] This dramatically changes the rules of the competitive game and in itself is a positive economic force (see, for example, Smith and Venables 1988 and Haaland and Wooton 1991). Taking account of the market structure, Norman (1990) and Venables (1990) show in the context of European integration and under conditions of imperfect competition that the threat of foreign competition alone can already be enough to persuade companies to be more alert on their markets and that the reduction of non-tariff barriers may convince companies that they can no longer directly influence prices in their home markets. As argued by van Bergeijk and Kabel (1993), in such models an increase in competition will have a positive welfare effect, not so much because of an increase in the international division of labour but rather because of a reduction in production inefficiencies arising from protective (semi)-monopoly positions. An important reason not to investigate trade-related barriers is that by 1985 the European Community had already eliminated such barriers, at least in principle.[11]

Fortunately, the methodologies deployed by Emerson et al. (1988) allow for the separation of trade-related and competition effects.[12] As illustrated in Figure 6.2, microeconomic and macroeconomic effects are being studied. The microeconomic evidence relates to

● the costs of barriers affecting all production (typically limiting market entry and/or competition), such as government procurement restrictions, national technical regulations etc.; and
● competition effects and the effects on so-called X-inefficiencies (related to suboptimal allocation within firms), such as excess capacity, overemployment, etc.

In the case of the macroeconomic evidence, the analysis deals with

● the opening up of public procurement,
● the liberalization of financial services; and
● supply effects, such as the strategic reactions of firms faced with a new competitive environment.

Emerson et al. (1988) distinguish two phases in their investigation. Based on the assumption that the *White Paper* proposals will be implemented, relevant market-entry restrictions and market-distorting subsidies and practices are identified at the industry level. Abstracting from comparative advantage, the core assumption of the analysis is that a reduction in direct and indirect market barriers enhances competitive forces, thus reducing X-inefficiencies through economies of scope and scale. Many empirical data sources and methods are deployed so as to use all available information and to be able to cross-check the microeconomic evidence.

Figure 6.2 Methodology to assess the macroeconomic benefits of market integration and deregulation in the EC

---

1. Scenario Assumptions:
Effective implementation of the *White Paper*, a positive attitude by firms in their strategic response to the new post-1992 business environment and an unchanged macroeconomic policy.

2. Microeconomic Evaluation:
Collection of information on market-entry restrictions and market-distorting subsidies and practices through opinion surveys and questionnaires about the likely response of individual firms, through industry case studies and through partial equilibrium analyses.

3. (a) Aggregation of Microeconomic Evidence
(b) Multisector Macroeconometric Models
(a) Aggregation of the findings for sectors and branches. Checks for double counting and gaps in coverage.
(b) Counterfactual analysis (forward looking) of opening up public procurement, liberalization of financial services and supply effects.

Source: Based on Emerson et al. (1988), pp. 194—212 and 251—61.

Next these first-order effects were used as an input in the analyses with two macroeconometric models.[13] The Commission's macroeconomic multisectoral HERMES model was used in the analysis of public procurement practices and supply effects. The OECD's INTERLINK model was used to analyse the liberalization of financial services, as it contains a disaggregated description of monetary and financial mechanisms. According to Emerson et al. (1988, p. 204),

[thus] the inability of the econometric models to describe the primary effects was circumvented; on the other hand, full use was made of their ability to

simulate secondary effects, i.e. all normal macroeconomic mechanisms (multiplier and accelerator effects, income-sharing effects, price competitiveness
effects, inflation mechanisms, capital accumulation, growth potential, etc.).

According to the microeconomic evidence, the opening-up of public
procurement would reduce input prices of public service producers
and lead to restructuring aimed at higher productivity in supplier
branches. This was inserted into HERMES via the level of import
penetration in public markets (an average increase of 5.6 per cent)
and by exogenous changes in the prices of production and imports
(depending on the sector up to 8.5 per cent). The liberalization of
financial services was estimated to lead to reductions in the prices of
representative financial services that could be inserted in
INTERLINK through reductions in the cost of credit (0.3 to 2 per
cent), the costs of intermediate use of financial services by firms (12
per cent) and the price of final consumption of households (10 per
cent). The microeconomic evidence on supply effects was translated
into lower prices of intermediate inputs, larger market shares, an *ex
ante* increase in the productivity of capital (reflecting scale economies
and the removal of X-efficiencies) and in lower sales prices (0.7 per
cent) and profit margins (reduction of monopoly profits).

Results

Table 6.2 summarizes the macroeconomic consequences of the non-
trade-related measures in the *White Paper*. The calculations are based
on the primary microeconomic shocks wich amount to 3.6 to 4.0 per
cent of the EC's GDP. The range depends on the approach to evaluating effects on competition which is being used in the analysis (the
barriers affecting all production contribute a little bit more than the
competition effects on X-inefficiency and monopoly rents, see
Emerson et al. 1988, p. 208). Table 6.2 should be interpreted with
caution for two reasons (Emerson et al. 1988, p. 27). First, the
margin of error is substantial and, second, the table deals with the
medium-term effects (say, after six years) only: it 'describes the
destination; not the journey'.[14] The impact of liberalizing financial
services and the reduction of monopoly profits and X-inefficiencies
actually reduce employment by 0.4 per cent in the first year of
implementation because of the costs of adjustment and reallocation.

Table 6.2 Macroeconomic consequences of completion of the internal market (excluding the removal of trade barriers) (total effects for the EC in the medium term, per cent)

	Opening up public procurement	Liberalizing financial services	Supply effects (monopoly rents, X-inefficiency)	Total effect[a]
GDP	0.4/0.8	0.8/2.1	1.7/2.5	4.1
Consumer prices	—0.9/—1.9	—0.8/—2.0	—1.8/—2.7	—5.1
Employment	0.2/0.4	0.2/0.4	0.5/0.8	1.3
Budgetary balance[b]	0.2/0.5	0.6/1.5	0.5/0.8	2.0
External balance[b]	0.1/0.2	0.2/0.5	0.3/0.6	0.8

Notes: [a] 'Point estimate'. As illustrated by the ranges for the component parts, the margin of error is about 30 per cent.

          [b] per cent of GDP.

Source: Emerson et al. (1988), Tables B1 to B5, pp. 262—4.

The macroeconomic impact of microeconomic adjustments translates into a substantial increase in GDP (the medium-term average annual real growth rate increases by more than 0.5 per cent) and substantially lower consumer prices (inflation decreases by almost 1 per cent on average). Generally speaking the driving force behind these favourable results is cost reduction which improves on Europe's competitive position, increases the purchasing power of European consumers and stimulates investment. Interestingly, the supply side effects due to more competition turn out to be the most important component in the Commission's macroeconomic analysis. Higher growth and the (admittedly modest) improvement in European employment ease the fiscal constraint.

6.3 Germany

Policy background
In 1991 a special government commission on deregulation and competition published a detailed report on the institutional impediments to flexible adjustment and the functioning of markets in

Germany.[15] Some of its recommendations are being implemented because the guidelines for the EC's internal market already prescribe similar policy changes. Other measures were discussed by a parliamentary commission chaired by the Minister of Economic Affairs and in June 1992 the Federal Government decided to implement 58 out of the 97 measures proposed by the German Deregulation Commission. Pressure group activities by vested interests have, however, become an important force against structural change (Held 1993). In addition, the problems posed by the German unification for the moment seem to have gained priority over structural issues such as competition policy (OECD 1994a). Still, the analytical approach that was followed with respect to privatization, deregulation and competition in Germany may be instructive.

Methodology
Costs and benefits of specific institutions have been the subject of a number of investigations, especially with respect to trade liberalization. The most prominent analysis has been performed by a team of IMF experts. This to the best of our knowledge is the only study that deals with the macroeconomic benefits of deregulation and stronger competition in Germany.

The IMF approach to 'reach judgments on the costs and benefits of the various microeconomic characteristics' (Lipschitz et al. 1989, p. 1) combines a dynamic macroeconometric model with a comparative static multisector applied general equilibrium model. The main reason for this two-step approach is that the available dynamic macroeconomic models for Germany were not capable of dealing with relative price effects at a disaggregated (sectoral) level. Sectoral developments are used to approximate structural adjustment processes which are essentially microeconomic in nature. This suggests that the analysis should use a multisector general equilibrium modelling strategy:[16]

> microeconomic, structural effects work through a network of interrelated markets and can only be captured by a multisectoral general equilibrium model (Robinson and D'Andrea—Tyson 1984, p. 244).

Essentially, the IMF approach blends the microeconomic structural analysis which is prescribed by economic theory and the macroeconomic analysis which is often central to the economic policy debate. Three phases can be discerned in the IMF's approach to assess the costs and benefits of deregulation and enhanced flexibility in Germany (Figure 6.3).

Figure 6.3 Methodology to assess the macroeconomic costs and benefits of microeconomic reform in Germany

---

1. Scenario Assumptions:
More market-orientated pricing policy in agriculture and coal mining (lower administered prices), dismantling tariff and non-tariff protection (iron, steel, shipbuilding, textiles and clothing), deregulation in goods and services markets, reduction of labour market rigidities.

2. Applied General Equilibrium Model:
Impact on output, employment, exports, imports, prices for four sectors (basic goods, protected goods, traded goods and non-traded goods).

3. Dynamic Macroeconometric Model:
Baseline based on announced fiscal policy stance, constant real exchange rate and partner-country demand. Projections for key macroeconomic variables (GNP, domestic demand, exports, imports, current account, employment and inflation) for alternative scenarios.

Source: Based on Lipschitz et al. (1989), pp. 52—4 and 94—101.

The first phase consists of a detailed analysis of both literature and statistics which sheds light on the impact of mesoeconomic rigidities on the German economy (for example, the development of total factor productivity, pension schemes, medical insurance, unemployment insurance, industrial policy). The findings inform the empirical translation of the scenario assumption that pricing policy in agriculture and coal mining becomes more market orientated. This leads to an assumed reduction in relative prices by 4 per cent or a

nominal (actual) price cut of 2 per cent in the basic goods sector. A
second scenario assumes liberalization of international trade by a
rather substantial reduction of the tariff equivalent of all barriers to
trade from 32 to 8 per cent. In addition both scenarios assume
substantial deregulation in product markets and reductions of labour
market rigidities so as to make the adjustment of the German
economy to structural changes rather flexible.

*Table 6.3   Combined influence on selected sectoral variables
according to the AGE analysis*

	Basic goods	Protected goods	Traded goods	Non-traded goods
Output	—1.0	—0.9	1.5	1.7
Employment	—2.4	—1.1	2.3	2.7
Exports	—16.4	4.0	1.0	n.a.
Imports	0.5	12.5	0.4	n.a.

Source: Lipschitz et al. (1989), Table A65, p. 95.

The second phase consists of the analysis of the consequences of
these impulses in an applied general equilibrium model of the
Johansen type, which was calibrated on a 1982 data set for West
Germany.[17] This model has four sectors: basic goods (agriculture
and mining), protected goods (iron, steel, shipbuilding, textiles and
clothing), traded goods (other manufacturing and traded services) and
non-traded goods (mainly services).

It is noteworthy that the findings of this exercise, which assumes
fully flexible markets, indicate that reallocation takes place from the
sheltered sectors of the economy to non-sheltered manufacturing
industry and services (Table 6.3). The predicted overall developments
point in the direction of more employment, more output, less
inflation and equilibrium in international exchange (trade balance and
current account).

The third phase requires the translation of the findings of the
applied general equilibrium model into a coherent set of impulses that
can be handled in a dynamic macroeconometric model. The channel

through which the two model exercises are linked in the first scenario is the development of consumer prices. A reduction of consumer prices by half a percentage point increases real consumption through real income and real balance effects. The increase in real consumer demand and the reduction in the price level feed into an improvement of the return to capital which triggers both real investment demand and the demand for labour.

Results

Table 6.4 compares three simulations with the Lipschitz et al. (1989) dynamic macroeconomic model. The first column of Table 6.4 shows the projections for key macroeconomic variables (GNP, exports, imports, employment and inflation) in the baseline scenario. These projections are predictions that have been based on the assumptions that the announced German fiscal policy stance will remain unchanged, the real exchange rate will remain constant and that partner-country demand is not influenced by the exercise.

The second column reports projections for an alternative scenario. This scenario assumes deregulation in goods and services markets, a reduction of labour market rigidities, as well as a more market-orientated pricing policy in agriculture and coal mining (lower administered prices). The third column reports a scenario which in addition assumes the dismantling of tariff and non-tariff protection in sheltered sectors like iron, steel, shipbuilding, textiles and clothing. The fourth and fifth column assess the macroeconomic benefits of flexibility as the difference between the baseline and the two simulations for the alternative economic policy scenarios.

The benefits of deregulation and more flexibility (column 4 of Table 6.4) consist of 0.3 percentage points higher GNP growth, 0.6 percentage points more employment growth (resulting in a 1.1 percentage points lower unemployment rate in 1991) and 0.4 percentage points less inflation. There is, however, a small cost in terms of export growth (0.3 percentage points) mainly due to the increase in domestic absorption.[18] Average labour productivity decreases by 0.3 percentage points.

Table 6.4   *Macroeconomic benefits of deregulation and flexibility*
              (Germany, projections 1990—91, per cent)

	Baseline	Deregulation and liberalization scenarios		Macro-economic benefits	
	(1)	DF (2)	+TL (3)	DF (2—1)	+TL (3—1)
GNP	2.7	3.0	3.4	0.3	0.7
Exports	4.5	4.2	4.6	—0.3	0.1
Imports	5.4	5.5	6.3	0.1	0.9
Employment	0.4	1.0	1.4	0.6	1.0
Inflation	2.2	1.8	1.3	—0.4	—0.9
Unemployment	7.2	6.1	5.3	—1.1	—1.9

Notes: *DF:* Deregulation and larger flexibility.
            +TL: Including trade liberalization as well.
Source: Based on Lipschitz et al. (1989), p. 94, Table A64.

Extending the policy options by including trade liberalization in the deregulation package turns the export loss into a small gain and reinforces the other beneficial results of the alternative policy stance. Indeed, it is to be noted that the impact of trade liberalization according to these calculations for most variables seems to be stronger than the influence of deregulation and a more flexible economy (employment is the exception). From a policy perspective this suggests that the completion of the EC's internal market is of major importance for the German economy.

6.4   The Netherlands

Policy background
In 1993, Dutch authorities overhauled competition policy and intensified the enforcement of competition rules (van Rooy 1994 and Van Gent 1996).[19] Horizontal price agreements were prohibited in July 1993, with similar measures with respect to market sharing and

collusive tendering and the introduction of a new sharply liberalized Establishment Law as a follow-up. In 1994 a project was started in which a number of Ministries worked together aiming at, investigating and suggesting measures to improve on competition, deregulation and the quality of legislation. An important aim of the abrupt policy change was to align Dutch and EC competition laws. Another important goal was to increase economic dynamism by creating a more healthy and competitive domestic business environment. No empirical analyses, however, were available about the costs and benefits of these major operations.[20]

Methodology
In order to provide estimates of the economy-wide benefits of competition and deregulation, the Dutch Ministry of Economic Affairs followed a general equilibrium approach (van Bergeijk, Haffner and Waasdorp 1993). The modelling strategy was to introduce the product market inertia coefficient (*PMIC*) into the price equation of a single product market applied general equilibrium model.[21] Essentially four reasons can be discerned for this modelling strategy. First, a sound empirical basis existed for building scenarios for the *PMIC* under alternative scenarios so that a counterfactual analysis both was possible and could be justified. Second, the sensitivity of the model's results with respect to the assumed increase in flexibility could readily be checked since the simulation was to be made with respect to one parameter, *in casu* the *PMIC*. Third, this methodology permitted privatization, deregulation and competition policy to affect non-price attributes, such as overcapacity.[22] This is important because non-price competition is increasingly being recognized as an essential strategic business instrument (Koutsoyiannis 1982, Scherer and Ross 1990, pp. 571—92).[23] Fourth, the traditional policy models in the Netherlands are built in the Tinbergen tradition of large econometric disequilibrium models. These models show only small effects of changes in microeconomic behaviour and/or the institutional setting. The reason is that these models lack the microeconomic foundations which are necessary to analyse the effects of increased competition on individual incentives and market behaviour. In such models only limited attention is paid to the functioning of markets and the theoretical underpinnings are

weak (Haffner and van Bergeijk 1994). Hence the option to use the comparative static results of an exercise with a computational general equilibrium model as an input for a macro-model did not occur in the Netherlands.[24] This means that the IMF approach could not be followed in this case and that a new modelling strategy had to be looked for.

Figure 6.4   Methodology to assess the macroeconomic benefits of market flexibility in The Netherlands

---

1. Empirical Assessment of Rigidity:
Estimation of product market inertia coefficient for different countries and for 20 major Dutch sectors.

2. Scenario Assumption:
Economy-wide deregulation and introduction of new competition and establishment laws lead to an increase in flexibility so as to make the Dutch markets comparable with those in Northern America (a reduction of the product market inertia coefficient by 50 per cent).

↓

3. Applied General Equilibrium Model:
Counterfactual analysis (backward looking). Benchmark based on actual development of exogenous variables. Projections for key macroeconomic variables (GNP, domestic demand, exports, imports, current account, employment, inflation, government balances) for an alternative scenario.

Source: Based on van Bergeijk et al. (1993).

Figure 6.4 summarizes the Dutch modelling strategy. The first phase is the econometric identification of the problem at hand. The choice to use the product market inertia coefficient is favoured by the limited data requirements and the fact that this indicator can be estimated at microeconomic, mesoeconomic and macroeconomic levels. The first step of the first phase was to assess differences in the extent of product market inertia between countries. The results of this investigation have already been discussed in Chapter 4. The second step of the first phase is an assessment of the extent of rigidity of different (sectoral) parts *within* the Dutch economy. Econometric investigations for the years 1971—92 by Haffner (1993) showed that 85 per cent of Dutch sectors had mesoeconomic *PMIC*s which exceeded the macroeconomic *PMIC*s in flexible economies such as Canada and the United States (i.e. larger than 83, see Tables 4.4 and 4.5). In addition a number of non-industrial sectors (such as agriculture) show substantial inertia because of institutional arrangements (such as the EC's Common Agricultural Policy). This finding is important for the exercise, as it is the *general* inertia of the Dutch economy which justifies a single product market approach. Indeed, the fact that the mesoeconomic findings show substantial uniformity implies that the aggregate or macroeconomic relationship that is built into an applied general equilibrium model is rather convincing from an empirical point of view.[25]

The second phase is drawing up the scenario assumptions for the investigation. An economy-wide scenario suffices because (*i*) the inertia problem is in fact economy wide and (*ii*) the solution (i.e. the new pro-competition and deregulation policies) works economy wide as well.[26] A simple scenario is used: the contemplated policy change at best leads to an increase in flexibility so as to make the Dutch product markets comparable with those in Northern America. This assumption requires that the value of a structural parameter (the *PMIC*) for the United States is substituted for the relevant Dutch parameter in an empirically orientated model for the Netherlands. This procedure is also followed by Barbone and Poret (1989). It boils down to the assumption that the *PMIC* is reduced by 50 per cent.

The third phase is the incorporation of the *PMIC* into a general equilibrium model (MESEM) and the calculation of the impact of the change in economic structure on the growth path of the economy. MESEM is an applied general equilibrium model for a small open economy, which was built at the Dutch Ministry of Economic Affairs. A detailed description appears in van Sinderen (1993). The model was calibrated on a 1985 data set for the Netherlands. MESEM is generally used to investigate the economic impact of taxation and government expenditures on the Dutch economy. In the original version of MESEM the goods market clears as no idle production capacity exists ($PMIC = 0$). Although MESEM has many properties of a general equilibrium model, the labour market does not always clear. In particular short-run disequilibria occur because of sticky real wages and other market imperfections, so that unemployment may result. Accordingly, real wages will not react instantaneously to disequilibrium conditions in the labour market. Analogously to the possibility of labour market disequilibrium, product market disequilibrium was introduced in the model, essentially by dropping the assumed equality between production and production capacity.

An interesting question is how changes in the extent of labour market flexibility may influence the estimated benefits of structural change. Related questions are (*i*) whether synergy is to be expected if labour markets and product markets are liberalized simultaneously and (*ii*) whether the sequence of liberalization influences the outcomes (should labour markets be liberalized first or should primogeneity be granted to product market liberalization, i.e. deregulation, privatization and competition policy?). Finch (1994) points out that the question has not yet been analysed whether we need to place higher priority on the labour market in future radical reform in market economies that are characterized by systematic government intervention.

These questions were addressed by van Sinderen et al. (1994) for the case of the Netherlands. Using four different versions of the MESEM model, van Sinderen et al. (1994) follow up on the method used by van Bergeijk et al. (1993). They distinguish four different structural regimes in the model MESEM based on two possible states of the labour market and two states of the product market:

● labour market flexibility/rigidity; and
● product market flexibility/rigidity.

As before, macroeconomic rigidity and flexibility are investigated by assuming different values for structural core parameters which depict the speed of the invisible hand on the respective macro markets (see Table 6.5). A mark-up in the price equation was also used as a scenario variable to simulate the effects of increased competition on price—cost margins.

Table 6.5 Four different structural regimes of MESEM

	FLEX	Model version LFLEX	PFLEX	INERT
Product market	Flexible	Rigid	Flexible	Rigid
Labour market	Flexible	Flexible	Rigid	Rigid

		Scenario assumptions		
Phillips curve	Strong	Strong	Weak	Weak
Labour elasticity	0.45	0.45	0.15	0.15
PMIC	50%	100%	50%	100%
Mark-up	0.5	1	0.5	1

Source: Van Sinderen et al. (1994), p. 276.

Labour market flexibility is assumed to influence the economy through two different channels. The first channel is the labour supply elasticity which is allowed to assume different values (a comparable procedure has been followed, for example, in the studies by den Butter and Compaijen 1991 and by Barbone and Poret 1989). More flexibility implies that labour supply reacts more quickly to changes in (relative) rewards. This is an interesting research strategy since the elasticity of labour supply to a large extent depends on institutions. Relatively generous social benefits enable unemployed to search longer for an appropriate job: the reservation wage increases. The second channel is the Phillips curve which links (changes in) the level of unemployment to wage claims which influence labour demand and thereby unemployment in the long run. The investigation by van Sinderen et al. (1994) uses a wage equation with the so-called weak Phillips curve to represent a rigid labour market. Layard et al. (1991) argue that hysteresis on the labour market may occur because of efficiency wage structures, excessive union power, insider—outsider behaviour and excessive corporatism in an economy. In the presence of these labour market rigidities, high and persistent unemployment levels may continue for long periods of time (cf. Graafland 1992). The alternative assumption is that the Phillips curve effect is strong.

In that case, the unemployment level itself, rather than changes of that level, affects the wage-rate developments.

The costs of labour market rigidity can now be assessed for a given period (say 1984—90) as the difference between the sets of simulated variables in LFLEX and INERT, respectively. The costs of a combination of rigid labour markets and product markets can be ascertained as the difference between INERT and FLEX.

Results

Table 6.6 compares two simulations with MESEM. The first column reports the calculations with INERT. Essentially, it shows the MESEM predictions on the assumption of a Dutch *PMIC* of about 100 per cent, as suggested by the relatively high value of the *PMIC* of the Netherlands.

Table 6.6 Macroeconomic benefits of flexible product markets (the Netherlands, counterfactual analysis 1984—90)

	INERT PMIC=100 (1)	PFLEX PMIC=50 (2)	Macro benefits (3=2—1)	Flexible labour markets
Private production	3.0	3.5	0.5	1.1
Private employment	1.8	1.9	0.1	1.1
Private consumption	3.4	3.4	0.0	0.4
Private investment	6.6	5.6	—0.9	0.3
Consumption price level	1.4	0.8	—0.6	—0.7
Exports	4.0	4.9	0.9	1.7
Imports	4.8	4.8	0.0	0.0

Source: Van Sinderen et al. (1994).

The second column reports a counterfactual simulation with PFLEX on the assumption that the flexibility of the Dutch markets in the period 1984—90 would have been characterized by a *PMIC* of 50, for example, if the Dutch markets had been comparable to those of the United States. Admittedly, this is the most spectacular comparison that one can come up with, because economic inertia within Europe would seem to be more or less comparable across countries.

The third column assesses the macroeconomic benefits of more competition and deregulation in the case of rigid labour markets as the difference between these two simulations. The fourth column reports the macroeconomic benefits if the labour market is flexible as well. Detailed simulations illustrate the point that synergy can be obtained if labour market rigidities and product market rigidities are dealt with simultaneously. For example, van Sinderen et al. (1994, p. 278) show that making the labour market more flexible does not influence the level of private production (because of the rigidities imposed on the product market) and that making the product market more flexible increases the annual average growth rate of private production by 0.5 percentage points, but that a strategy that aims at more flexibility at both labour and product markets yields an increase of this growth rate of 1.1 percentage points.

The quantitative results of the simulations suggest that the Dutch medium-term annual real growth rate of private production could have been about half a per cent higher and export growth could almost have been one per cent larger, if the Dutch product markets had been characterized by the kind of flexibility pertaining in the United States. These results obviously follow from higher productivity due to a more efficient allocation of capital, which results in more production at a lower level of investment. This also reflects that risk premia are lower in a market that is protected and sheltered by competition-reducing institutions: the cost of capital increases as capital commands a higher average risk premium in a competitive environment. The potential improvement in inflation performance appears to have been substantial (0.6 per cent). The disinflation due to more flexible markets results from the associated reduction in concentration as well as from basic cost considerations (less capital is needed to produce a larger volume of production).

6.5 Australia

Policy background
In 1993 the Committee of Inquiry into National Competition Policy issued a report that investigated the barriers to internal trade and recommended many reforms to enhance competitive practices in sheltered sectors (see, for example, Fane 1995).

Traditional Australian protectionism already in the mid-1970s, had called forth policy proposals to engineer a gradual shift towards openness and integration into the world economy (Garnaut 1994). In 1974 the Industry Assistance Commission was created as an independent statutory authority (see Vincent 1990 and Powell and Snape 1993). In order to provide estimates of the economy-wide effects of industry assistance (comprising traditional border protection measures as well as taxes, subsidies and institutional arrangements which protect one sector of the economy at the expense of another). In 1992 an independent Committee of Inquiry was established which was asked to make recommendations on the implementation of a national competition policy. Its report — the so-called Hilmer report — was published in August 1993 (Independent Committee 1993) and was followed up by the Industry Commission in a very detailed report on its growth and revenue implications (Industry Commission 1995).

Methodology
The Australian approach offers by far the most comprehensive analysis of structural adjustment issues. Its orientation from the start on the economy-wide effects of 'assistance' fostered a policy climate that was receptive to policy advice based on applied general equilibrium models. In the 1980s and early 1990s general equilibrium models were applied to some 300 policy issues ranging from the effects of protectionism to policies combating greenhouse gas emissions (Powell and Lawson 1990 and Dee 1994 provide a bibliography). In addition the inquiry process encourages participation of all interested parties in the Industry Assistance Commission's policy advisory procedures. This offers policy analysts the opportunity to get better and more specific information.

Again three phases can be discerned (Figure 6.5). The first phase consists of econometric investigations, engineering studies and international comparisons aimed at identifying (inter)national best practices so as to assess the scope for improvement for a specific industry. This information-gathering process is complemented by the Industry Assistance Commission's inquiry process. The aim is to build an empirical basis for adjustments of the core applied general equilibrium model so as to reflect the specific characteristics of the investigated sector or activity. A second goal is to build convincing empirical cases for the scenario assumptions. The second phase of the analysis of the economy-wide impact of structural adjustment involves developing relevant scenario assumptions. Typically, the scenario variables are exogenous changes in productivity improvements so as to meet national or international best practices. Also changes in implicit taxes are considered for the sector or activity that is subjected to the inquiry process.

Figure 6.5 Methodology to assess the macroeconomic benefits of microeconomic reform in Australia

---

1. Assessment of a Particular Industry or Activity:
Identification of the scope and means for improvement based on (inter)national best practices, engineering studies and comparisons of total factor productivity and rates of return.

2. Scenario Assumptions:
Exogenous productivity improvements in public and private enterprises so as to match (inter)national best practice standards.

3. Applied Multisector General Equilibrium Model:
Counterfactual (forwardlooking) macroeconomic impact as deviation from unpublished control path with aggregation of the macroeconomic results of individual studies into a 'total' figure.

Source: Based on Dee (1994), pp. 18—20.

The third phase consists of running the applied general equilibrium model which typically is an adapted version of the detailed multi-sector ORANI model of the Australian Economy (Dixon et al. 1982) in which the labour market does not clear in the short term. The 'off-the-shelf version' of this model deals with more than 100 separate commodities, 30 service industries, 66 manufacturing industries, 6 mining industries and 13 agricultural industries. This tool box allows for the detection of the economy-wide effects of specific policy

changes that aim at an individual sector. The effects are published as
percentage deviations from a control path. The control path itself is
not published. The reason is one of presentation: policy advice is
meant to be 'relatively robust to where Australia is in the business
cycle' (Dee 1994, p. 21). Incidentally broad-ranging microeconomic
reform proposals are put to the fore while the assessment of their
total effect is calculated by aggregating the individual sector studies.

Results

Table 6.7 summarizes the total effects for the results of a number of
investigations that have been packaged together by the Industry
Assistance Commission in order to demonstrate the economy-wide
effect of the so-called Hilmer report (Industry Commission 1995).
The investigation covers a broad-ranging programme of microeconomic reforms for product markets, the government sector and
regulation with respect to occupations and professions. It does not
deal with labour market reform, but a sensitivity analysis is reported
in which the natural rate of unemployment is allowed to decrease
because of the reform measures. The simulations that are summarized
in Table 6.7 are made under the assumptions that aggregate
government expenditure on goods and services is held constant in real
terms and that monetary policy is accommodating in the sense that
consumer prices are held constant through an endogenous money
supply.

The calculations have been based on estimates of productivity
gains that can be reaped through better work and management
practices and more vigorous domestic competition and use the rate of
return on real assets as an additional parameter to simulate the
consequences of a more competitive environment. The calculations,
however, neglect the costs of reallocating the factors of production.

Interestingly, the long-run effects that pertain to a forward looking
counterfactual are much larger than the effects that are estimated in
the German case, which deals with the short term. The results,
however, are more or less in line with the Dutch case. Strong gains
in productivity exert a substantial downward pressure on the GDP
deflator (—1.0 per cent) and improve on the international
competitiveness of the Australian economy as exports increase by

almost 16 per cent. The economic growth consequences of the reform package are substantial (5.5 per cent).

Table 6.7 Projected long-run effects of the Hilmer report on National Competition Policy and related reforms (Australia, percentage deviations from control path)

	No impact on labour market	*Reduction in natural rate of unemployment*
Real GDP	5.5	8.3
Aggregate employment	0.4	3.0
GDP deflator	—1.0	—1.1
Real investment	6.0	8.6
Exports	15.8	24.3
Imports	1.3	2.5

Source: Industry Commission (1995), Table A4.7, p. 63.

Introducing labour market flexibility in addition to product market reform leads to more employment as was to be expected and to a substantially better growth performance. Interestingly labour productivity is also a bit higher when labour markets are flexible.

6.6 The Macroeconomic Impact of Privatization, Deregulation and Competition

Having set out the basic tools of the analyses, the macroeconomic benefits of structural reform can next be summarized. The benefits of product market flexibility are valued in terms of key economic variables such as prices, production and employment.[27] The costs of product market inertia and/or structural 'microeconomic' rigidities in general result from a suboptimal allocation of the factors of production due to an inadequate functioning of the market mechanism. The benefits result from removing these microeconomic distortions. In an empirical sense they are the mirror image of the costs of non-competition.

Table 6.8 summarizes the findings of the five studies which were discussed. Obviously, the order of magnitude of the quantitative results of the study is not comparable. For example, the policy proposals and the period that is being investigated differ substantially. It should also be noted that the results for the EC most probably already embrace part of the results that are reported in the studies on Germany and the Netherlands. Still, the qualitative agreement of the studies is remarkable and valuable.

Table 6.8 Macroeconomic effects of structural change (per cent deviations from base run)

		Production	Employment	Consumer prices
EC	cumulated and medium term	+4.1	+1.2	—5.1
Germany[a]	annual	+0.3	+0.6	—0.4
Netherlands	annual	+0.5	+0.1	—0.6
Netherlands[a]	annual	+1.1	+1.1	—0.7
Australia	cumulated and long run	+5.5	+0.4	—1.0[b]
Australia	cumulated and long run[a]	+8.3	+3.0	—1.1[b]

Notes: [a] Assuming a flexible labour market.
         [b] GDP deflator.
Sources: See Tables 6.4 to 6.7.

The studies agree that economy-wide structural change has a macroeconomic impact. All studies demonstrate increases in production, employment and exports and a decrease in inflation. In contrast to the findings for Germany, flexibility on the product markets in the Australian and Dutch analyses does not spill over to the labour market. Indeed Dutch and Australian labour productivity increases and this translates into higher real wages. It is not clear whether this difference is due to implicit or unreported assumptions in the Lipschitz et al. (1989) model with respect to the structural adjustment in the labour market or to differences in the models in the respective investigations. The calculations for the Netherlands show that deregulation of the labour market should be an important element of any economic policy that aims at more flexible product markets. In the Dutch case more dynamic good markets do not induce additional import demand. Actually, the export surplus increases mainly because the improvement in allocation reduces investment demand and consequently domestic absorption decreases. The national account identities logically imply that where investment goes down and domestic saving increases due to an increase in income, net export cannot but increase. Moreover, flexibility of the economy seems to be a major determinant of international competitiveness (Encaoua and Geroski 1986, Brakman et al. 1988 and Porter 1990a). This is reflected in the model simulations, that predict a substantial increase in exports, among others because price competitiveness improves. So whereas the IMF exercise with respect to Germany predicts that consumption increases immediately, the findings in the Dutch case, much like the simulations by the European Commission, suggest an increase in *future* consumption as the gains from deregulation, privatization and competition feed almost fully into savings and into an increase of net foreign assets. The Australian case also predicts an increase in savings and net exports due to increased competitiveness, but this is accompanied by a surge in private investment, although at the sectoral level indications exist that productivity improvements allow industries to economize on capital (Dee 1994, p. 31), as in the Dutch case.

6.7 Discussion

Although substantial progress in structural adjustment has been made, the impact that government activity exerts on the economy via its influence on competition and market structure is still a very relevant research topic. The approaches that were discussed in this chapter attempt to provide transparency about the macroeconomic costs of microeconomic rigidities and their mirror image, the benefits of structural reform (privatization, competition and deregulation). It should, however, be clear that these quantitative exercises are illustrations at best, given that numerous simplifying assumptions had to be made. The model exercises are, as Lipschitz et al. (1989, p. 52) rightly stress, 'more controlled laboratory experiments than forecasts of actual developments'.

Obviously, these modelling efforts are not perfect. From a policy perspective it is important that these studies shed light neither on the costs of transition nor on the welfare effects of an increase in the quality of products and employment. From a theoretical point of view a relevant question is whether relative prices and wealth effects drive the economic system (in which case general equilibrium models are the appropriate tools) or whether quantities and income are the moving forces (in which case a new Keynesian approach would seem to provide the appropriate — yet underdeveloped — analytical tool box).

Moreover, a number of methodological issues are at stake with respect to the individual studies. For example, the IMF approach which combines a dynamic macroeconometric model and a comparative static applied general equilibrium model into one tool, may give serious trouble as logical inconsistencies are to be expected. For example, the exercise with the applied general equilibrium model yields changes in output, employment and prices. However, the choice of the price impulse as the only relevant channel through which deregulation affects macroeconomic variables is rather arbitrary and neglects non-price elements. Moreover, the outcome of the dynamic macroeconomic simulation may contradict the other findings of the general equilibrium analysis. Logical inconsistency is less a problem for the Dutch investigation into the benefits of competition and deregulation, as this exercise is performed in the context of a single model. One crucial assumption of the Dutch exercise, however, is that both the policy problem and the policy solution are economy wide. The combination of empirically established overall product market inertia at the sectoral level and the change in competition policy that characterizes the Dutch case may be exceptional.[28]

Another problem is aggregation of sectoral results into one total figure for the macroeconomy (see, for example, Willenbockel 1994, pp. 2—3). The aggregation of the macroeconomic results of separate sector studies into total long-run projections for key variables is at the heart of the Australian and EC approaches. The aggregation implicitly assumes complete independence of the investigated policies. This assumption should be questioned because in a second-best world the removal of one distortion may actually aggravate other distortions. The assumed independence, however, also neglects the issue of synergy, for example, between labour market reform and product market reform. Indeed the effect of the total reform packet may exceed the sum of the individual policy measures. This suggests that the Australian and EC approaches substantially underestimate the actual impact of the *combination* of the policy proposals, but also that they may underestimate the counteracting impact of, for example, labour market distortions.

Despite these shortcomings the studies may help to provide transparency of the potential benefits of structural reform as they allow a first assessment of the efficiency gains that can be generated for the economy as a whole (cf. OECD 1994a, p. 12). Clarity about the benefits and the costs of microeconomic arrangements is an essential input for the public debate on privatization, deregulation and competition policy.

Notes

1. An early study by Barbone and Poret (1989) investigates the question of how product and labour market flexibility influence the impact of demand and supply shocks in Germany, France, Italy and the United Kingdom over the years 1980—89. This study, however, does not deal with the impact of flexibility on the baseline so it does not provide information about the macroeconomic benefits of deregulation.
2. Eric Hansen, personal correspondence. See, however, Siklos (1995) for a contrary opinion. A description of Model XII containing a discussion of the econometric problems encountered and some *ad hoc* solutions is Brooks and Gibbs (1994, esp. pp. 12, 15, 17 and 22). Swamy and Tavlas (1989) point out a similar breakdown of the money demand equation in Australia due to deregulation.
3. In addition, Emerson et al. (1988, p. 202) state that 'there are reasons to suppose that this possible source of measurement error is not so important, compared to many other primary issues'. Unfortunately, these reasons are not made explicit.
4. See Crafts (1992) for an alternative exercise in growth accounting that is critical of Barro's findings, and Levine and Renelt (1992) and Sala-i-Martin (1994) for two studies on the robustness of cross-country growth regressions *à la* Barro.

5.   Interestingly, New Zealand's rigorous deregulation and privatization programmes were carried out without any quantitative research and with benign neglect for the costs of structural change (Bollard 1994).

6.   The calculations have been derived from Van Bergeijk, Hiddink and Waasdorp (1995).

7.   See also Gruen (1986, p. 186) who, using a comparable methodology, argues that '[r]igidities in product markets probably used to be the major factor retarding faster growth in Australia.'

8.   Norway and Japan, obviously, are not prototypes of deregulated and flexible economies. In the case of Norway the developments in the oil and gas sectors play an important role; in Japan the high savings rate and the organization of national innovation activities may explain the residual (see, for example, Amsden and Singh 1994).

9.   See also Khan (1990) for some related issues in the context of evaluation of IMF adjustment programmes.

10.   Note that the move towards an internal market involved both negative integration (the elimination of obstacles) as well as positive integration (the creation of equal conditions for the functioning of the integrated parts of the European economy). Only the former requires deregulation and liberalization, while the latter requires harmonization and re-regulation.

11.   Exceptions were the so-called agricultural monetary compensatory amounts, production quotas in agriculture, fishery and steel, licensing in some services (road and air transport) and customs handling (often related to differences in VAT treatment).

12.   See Catinat and Italianer (1988) for a detailed account.

13.   See Brandsma et al. (1991) on HERMES and Richardson (1988) on INTERLINK.

14.   The problem that the short-run effects have an opposite sign appears to be relevant for employment only in the cases of the liberalization of financial services and of the supply effects. For the other variables and for opening up public procurement, Emerson et al. (1988) report smaller values in the short run, which move in the direction of the medium-term estimates.

15.   Unabhängige Expertenkommission zum Abbau marktwidriger Regulierungen, *Marktöffnung und Wettbewerb*, Poechel Verlag, 1991. See also *Report on Germany's Deregulation Policy* Bundesministerium für Wirtschaft (BMWi Dokumentation nr. 333), Bonn, 1993. See also Audretsch (1989, pp. 66—76) for a discussion of German competition policy in the 1970s and 1980s.

16.   See, however, Adelman and Taylor (1991) for a contrary opinion. They argue that a fixed price social accounting matrix may be used to assess economy-wide implications of alternative structural adjustment strategies.

17.   A full description of the computable general equilibrium model appears in Mayer (1989), where the model is used to investigate an appreciation of the Deutschmark under four alternative structural policy scenarios.

18.   More import growth is rightly considered as a benefit since this translates into a consumer welfare gain.

19.   See also Maks (1995) and Asbeek Brusse and Griffiths (1995) on the Dutch pre-1995 competition regime.

20. The Dutch Ministry of Economic Affairs (1990) prepared an in-depth sectoral analysis of the strengths, weaknesses, opportunities and threats to the Dutch economy much along the lines of Porter (1990a). The Dutch study pointed out the important channel between, on the one hand, vigorous competition policy and flexibility of markets, and on the other hand, international competitiveness. This study, however, did not offer a quantitative assessment of the possible benefits of deregulation and competition.

21. See Section 4.3 for a discussion of the *PMIC*.

22. Obviously, overcapacity is not an issue in an applied general equilibrium model. Overcapacity, however, can occur in the non-market-clearing version of the MESEM model.

23. A permanent exogenous increase in the consumption price level can also be simulated by the MESEM model and will result in underutilization of capacity. However, if the IMF modelling strategy were to be followed in this respect the non-price effects would not be incorporated.

24. Keller's (1980) applied general equilibrium model for the Dutch economy was recently expanded by Cornielje and Zeelenberg (1991) to allow for price rigidities and rationing. The Keller model, however, neglects the capacity effect of investment.

25. This provides in a very practical sense a microeconom(etr)ic foundation for a macroeconom(etr)ic relationship.

26. Note, however, that in general a macroeconomic approach to a problem that is essentially microeconomic in nature may not be appropriate.

27. Theoretically speaking this could and should be analysed within a traditional welfare analysis. However, as yet the analysis is too complicated and demands too much from scarce modelling capacities.

28. See, however, Weiss (1993 and 1994a). His findings suggest that this method may also be used in the case of Austria.

PART IV
POLICY

7. The Art of Reform

A reform programme will only have a chance to succeed when it is both economically and politically sound. How does a reform programme become economically and politically 'sound'? Of course, no universal receipt is yet available. Generalizations from the numerous experiences are not easy to make as the results of structural adjustment may depend on a myriad of factors, such as the initial conditions in the countries involved, the timing and speed of the reforms, and the political climate at the moment the reforms are announced and implemented. Even so, the literature on these political and economic aspects of policy reform is growing by the day and the sheer number of 'lessons' which are drawn is simply dazzling. To list just a few: the *World Development Report* of the World Bank (1991b) needs seven lessons to summarize its advice on policy reform, the OECD (1994a) study *Assessing Structural Reform* arrives at ten lessons and Douglas's *Unfinished Business* (1993) sums up a total of 16 political lessons.

In this chapter we will not try to increase the number of policy lessons; instead we try to distil the most important and most basic insights from the literature. Section 7.1 discusses the issue of credibility, which is a necessary condition for any reform policy to succeed. Section 7.2 looks into the question of the optimal sequencing of structural reform. Because of time and resource constraints, in practice it is hardly possible to reform all markets at the same time. Hence a certain order of reform must be chosen. Section 7.3 discusses the pros and cons of gradual reforms versus shock-like reforms. The following section looks at some of the political considerations which should be taken into account when attempting to implement structural reform policies (Section 7.4). Here we discuss some recent developments in the political economy literature on policy reform. Finally, Section 7.5 presents some empirical evidence on the factors which determine the success of structural reforms.

173

7.1 Credibility

The credibility of structural policy measures is a necessary condition for successful reform. Following Funke (1993), we define credibility as a situation in which private expectations about future policies are in accordance with the government's explicit or implicit announcements. Credibility is so crucial because uncertainty about the determination of the government to carry through reforms or about the exact actions which will be taken, may cause the private sector to just wait and see. Private agents may fear that policies will eventually be reversed and postpone investments as a consequence.[1] This brings the main objective of the reform programme into jeopardy — to reallocate resources towards more efficient activities. The reform programme may fail for this reason alone.

An example is the lifting of capital controls when the budget deficit is high. This requires domestic real interest rates to be high enough by international standards to keep foreign capital within the country. When the foreign exchange and capital markets are liberalized, expectations of inflation, exchange rate devaluations and higher government borrowing will exert an upward pressure on real interest rates. This would increase the government budget deficit and contribute to further macroeconomic instability. In other words, the reform is unsustainable in the long run, which raises expectations of a policy reversal.

Rodrik (1989) distinguishes three reasons why the public may fear a reversal of new policies:

● Policy inconsistency with other government activities and plans.
● Time inconsistency. The optimal strategy before starting to implement the reforms differs from the optimal strategy during implementation of the reforms. For example, once the private sector is convinced that inflation will be low, and sets wages and prices accordingly, it may be tempting for the government to disinflate less to realize some temporary output gains.
● Imperfect information. Private sector decision makers may simply not know whether the government is really serious about implementing structural reform.

Note that in the case of the time-inconsistency problem, the private sector is perfectly able to understand the government's motivations and objectives, whereas with imperfect information, the private sector is in the dark about the true motives of government.

How can policy makers enhance the credibility of reforms? In order to avoid inconsistent policies, the economics of the programme should make sense. For example, the sequencing of reforms can be inadequate because of inconsistencies within the reform package itself, thereby increasing the costs of adjustment and reducing credibility. Hence, reform proposals should be carefully evaluated in terms of internal consistency and should be part of an overall policy framework.

Solutions of the time-inconsistency problem are not easily found and are seldom costless (Rodrik 1989, p. 757). Publicly announcing the commitment to new policies, for example, reduces the ability of the government to respond to unforeseen circumstances. Building a reputation — another possible solution of the time-inconsistency problem — costs valuable time to gain sufficient credibility.

The problem of imperfect information may be alleviated by making the reform proposals as transparent as possible. This can be done by providing an insight into the costs and benefits of reform and by mapping out a clear timetable for implementation. In addition, reforms should be framed in a medium-term context. This reduces the uncertainty for forward-looking private sector decision makers. Another fact which may help improve the credibility of reforms is a speedy implementation. If reforms are carried through in a very gradual way, for example because each incremental reform is only decided upon after lengthy discussions in parliament, this may undermine the credibility of the entire reform programme. Finally, policy overshooting (the implementation of farther-reaching reforms than required from an economic point of view), may also signal the willingness of the government to actually carry through a reform programme.[2]

7.2 Sequencing

One of the first issues a policy maker is asked to deal with is the appropriate sequencing of reforms. The setting of priorities in reform is relevant not only when a piecemeal approach in reform is followed ('step-by-step') but also when more far-reaching reforms are discussed ('reform package'). The essential difference between the 'step-by-step' and 'package' approaches is that in the latter case, the issue of proper sequencing is dealt with more explicitly. The sequencing of reforms is especially important in developing economies and in the countries which are making the transition from centralized decision making to market economies. For the developing countries, the sequencing literature focuses on specific issues, such as the proper sequence of macroeconomic stabilization, reform of financial markets and external trade, or on the interaction between trade and reform and the liberalization of capital flows. For the economies in transition, the focus is much broader as the lack of market institutions and the sheer number of firms that have to be privatized have put forward a whole new range of questions to be addressed by the economic profession.

In industrialized countries also, issues of sequencing have relevance as many OECD countries are considering and implementing far-reaching reform proposals. In Japan, for example, increased emphasis has been put on microeconomic reform since the early 1990s. In part this reflected the recognition that macroeconomic measures alone would not be enough to get the Japanese economy out of the recession. Estimates indicate that about 42 per cent of the domestic value added was affected by the extensive government regulations especially in the sheltered sector of the economy, resulting in a cost of living about 20 per cent above the OECD average (OECD 1994b). As a consequence, the government embarked on a wide-ranging reform programme in areas such as financial services, competition policy, privatization, openness to international competition, and in the distribution, transportation, and energy sectors (see OECD 1994b, pp. 59—72 for an overview).

Improper sequencing of structural reforms can create problems. Privatization without a lifting of barriers to entry, for example, cannot be successful because this is equivalent to creating a private monopoly. Such a monopolist would have no incentive to produce efficiently because increases in costs can easily be passed on to consumers by charging higher prices. The same holds for the incentive to improve quality.[3] Another example is a reform of the financial sector without macroeconomic stability. If this reform requires a restructuring of financial institutions, government spending may rise in the short run. However, if the budget deficit is high to begin with, doubts will soon arise about the commitment and ability of the government to bail out insolvent credit institutions. In other words, the reform will not be credible because of the inadequate sequencing of the policy measures undertaken. Achieving fiscal stability in this case should therefore have a higher priority than reforming the financial sector.

Whereas structural reform in one market is unambiguously welfare improving when all other markets are undistorted, this changes when other markets are affected by government regulation, subsidization or taxation, for example. According to the theory of second best, reforming only one distorted market may aggravate the distortions on the other markets, thereby raising the costs of adjustment (Lipsey and Lancaster 1956). In theory, when determining whether the reform of one market is welfare improving, it is necessary to assess the welfare consequences of reform on all other markets as well. Three different categories of welfare effects arise (Edwards 1989):

- Direct welfare effects in the reformed market.
- Indirect *intra*temporal welfare effects. These arise from the interaction between the distortions at the time the reform takes place, because reform in one market spills over to other distorted markets.
- Indirect *inter*temporal welfare effects. These are due to the fact that most reforms will not only affect the economy at the moment the reform is implemented, but also before (when the reform is first proposed) and afterwards.

The total change in welfare of all these direct and indirect effects is not clear *a priori*. Note that according to the theory of second best, there is no guarantee that the total welfare effect of an isolated reform in one market is positive, as it depends on factor intensities, elasticities, and so on. These informational requirements needed to apply the second-best theorem make the formation of 'optimal' policies from a welfare theoretic point of view extremely difficult:

No central authority could conceivably obtain the masses of information on demand elasticities, cost functions, and prices needed to devise fully articulated second best pricing strategies for even a single major industry richly interconnected with other sectors (Scherer and Ross 1990, p. 37).

Partly as a result of these theoretical and empirical difficulties, the sequencing of reforms is one of the most highly debated issues among economists. Many opposing recommendations exist, which is probably due to the large differences between countries in initial conditions such as the institutional setting, the extent of the distortions and the macroeconomic environment (Funke 1993). So one result of the literature is that no generally applicable 'optimal' sequence exists. Another result is that when distortions prevail on more than one market, the optimal policy is to reform all distorted markets at once (Edwards 1989, p. 66). However, because this policy advice is difficult to follow in the real world, naturally a certain order of reform must be chosen.

By contrast, the interest of policy makers in sequencing issues appears to be rather modest. A recent evaluation (IMF 1995) of IMF-supported economic adjustment programmes in 36 countries, for example, finds that:

the actual sequencing of reforms has reflected political and administrative constraints, rather than considerations of 'optimal' sequencing (Morrison 1995, p. 236).

Sir Roger Douglas, the political leader of the structural reforms in New Zealand, also downplays the role of sequencing issues in practical policy making. He notes:

A great deal of technical debate has gone on worldwide about the best order for reform and the alleged sequencing errors of governments, both here and elsewhere. Those armchair theorists postulate the desirability of tackling the labour market or the tradeable goods market before embarking on the deregulation of sectors such as financing, for example. At a purely analytical level the debate is entertaining but no clear-cut answers emerge. Moreover, as a practitioner of reform, I find the question fundamentally irrelevant. Before you can plan your perfect move in the perfect way at the perfect time, the situation has already changed. Instead of a perfect result, you wind up with a missed opportunity (Douglas 1993, p. 224).

In contrast we find that the sequencing of reforms is an important policy issue both from an economic and from a political point of view. A politician might argue that reforms should be undertaken in such a sequence that the level of support from the electorate is maximized. This could imply that reforms with the highest expected outcome in the short run should be implemented first, because this would make people more willing to engage in further reforms (Roland 1994, p. 1163). An economist would perhaps adopt another perspective and focus on the need to let the adjustment process take place as efficiently as possible. Since widespread structural change implies major resource shifts from declining to growing sectors, the speed of the process depends on the ability to divest and reinvest resources quickly and efficiently. However, a problem is that the response to structural change often has an asymmetric nature (Savage 1990a, p. 28). For example, stopping production takes no time at all, while developing new products and processes can take considerable time; supporting infrastructure (utilities, transport systems) is easily abandoned in one industry, but cannot be developed just as quickly elsewhere. These asymmetries also have an impact on the labour market as workers can be laid off before new jobs are created.

To illustrate these issues and the possible consequences of an improper sequencing of reforms, we will look at the reforms in New Zealand in some detail. Until 1985, New Zealand was one of the most interventionistic and protected economies in the OECD. The economy was sheltered from international competition by a complex system of trade barriers and capital controls, resulting in an import penetration of only 32 per cent in 1985. These structural difficulties were reflected in the weak macroeconomic performance of the New Zealand economy: between 1950 and 1990, GDP per capita dropped from 26 per cent above the OECD average to 27 per cent below that average (Bollard 1994, p. 75).

The change of government in 1984, however, brought an administration to power which soon became convinced that there was no alternative to a programme of fundamental change (Kelly 1995). By 1985, New Zealand had embarked upon the most radical programme of structural adjustment of any OECD economy. It involved the liberalization of financial and foreign exchange markets, making the Central Bank independent, and the establishment of a free trade area with Australia. Trade was also liberalized by a drastic reduction in import tariffs and quantitative restrictions. Export subsidies were abolished. The product market deregulation programme involved the elimination of most market entry restrictions, price controls, regulatory monopolies and operating restrictions. Finally, government interference was reduced through corporization and privatization of numerous state enterprises. The corporization activities involved the setting up of a board of directors, and giving managers both real business objectives and full control over staffing and investment (see Bollard 1994, pp. 75—81 for an overview).

The results of the reforms are promising as the New Zealand economy is currently one of the fastest growing economies in the OECD area. The rate of inflation is also relatively low. However, this success was achieved at the cost of a long and protracted adjustment process in the years following the reforms. Table 7.1 summarizes some indicators on the macroeconomic development in New Zealand in the period 1985—91. The reforms have been successful in accomplishing a steep decline in the rate of inflation and an increase in the exposure to international competition. In agriculture, the effective rate of protection was dramatically reduced.[4] However, employment in industry dropped by more than 20 per cent, growth in real gross domestic product was erratic and the competitive position was eroded by an appreciation of the exchange rate.

At a sectoral level, a reallocation of labour took place from the tradeables sectors to the nontradeable sector. The shock-like exposure of industry and agriculture to (international) competition caused an enormous rationalization of employment. One of the reasons why the decline in employment was so large is that the increase in flexibility due to the reforms did not immediately result in improved international competitiveness (Grimmond 1989). Thus, increases in employment had to be realized in the sheltered sector. Employment increased most notably in community, social and personal services, the financial services sector and the trade, hotels and restaurants sector (OECD 1993a, p. 154). Between 1981 and 1989, the share of the nontradeable sector in employment rose by almost ten percentage points.

Table 7.1 Benefits and costs of reform in New Zealand, 1985—91

Benefits	1985	1991
Inflation	14	1
Import penetration[a]	32	40
Openness[b]	60	80
Effective rate of protection (%)[c]		
industry	37	19
agriculture	34	—6
Costs		
Real GDP[d]	100	101
Employment[e]	1544	1451
of which: industry[e]	444	341
of which: agriculture[e]	164	156
Nominal exchange rate[d]	100	116
Real effective exchange rate[d]	100	109

Notes: [a] As a percentage of domestic demand.
[b] Exports plus imports as a percentage of GNP.
[c] Percentage of value added protected, taking tariffs on imported inputs into account.
[d] Index 1985 = 100.
[e] Thousands.

Source: Bos and van Bergeijk (1994).

Note that Table 7.1 does not present an evaluation of the costs and benefits of structural reform in New Zealand. Ideally, such an evaluation should be a counterfactual analysis, because only then is it possible to assess the development of the New Zealand economy in the absence of reforms. In addition, Table 7.1 reports only on the medium-term economic development after the initiation of the first reforms. As the goal of structural reform is to improve upon the long-run growth perspectives of the economy, a much longer time horizon may be needed for a proper evaluation (Ostry 1993). Table 7.1 does indicate that structural reform is not a free lunch: especially in the short and medium term, adjustment costs can be high.

One of the reasons why the adjustment costs were so high in New Zealand is the combination of inadequately sequenced structural reforms with a strong currency policy (Bollard 1994, pp. 96—8,

Finch 1994 and OECD 1994c, p. 32). The early liberalization of the financial sector facilitated excessive and misdirected capital inflows. The lax fiscal policy, coupled with a tight monetary policy and high interest rates encouraged this inflow of foreign capital. At the same time, the demand for credit by both the government and the private sector surged — in less than two years from 1985, the volume of credit doubled (Kelly 1995, p. 336). The inflow of foreign capital also caused an appreciation of the exchange rate, to the detriment of export growth while the excessive borrowing allowed inflationary pressures to gain fresh momentum. The lack of labour market flexibility made it difficult to efficiently reallocate labour to the high-growth sectors, resulting in a rapid rise in unemployment. This in turn enlarged the budgetary burden because of increased spending on social security. Empirical investigations in the firm-level obstacles to better performance also tend to cite the lack of labour market flexibility as one of the barriers in this respect (Savage and Bollard 1990, p. 50, and Savage 1990b, pp. 139—45). All in all, the liberalization of both product markets and financial markets, the mounting fiscal deficit and the lack of structural measures in the labour market are important elements which may explain the costly adjustment process.

Political factors may have been more important than economic ones in determining the issues to be addressed first. This is reflected in the fact that the earliest reform package succeeded in creating losers with an incentive to support subsequent change (Kelly 1995, p. 336). For example, farmers who lost agricultural support found it in their best interest to support reforms which would reduce the costs of their inputs. Consistently with policy intentions, matters such as tariff reform and taxation became important issues. However, this logic in the sequence of reforms was broken by not addressing labour market inflexibilities. Radical action in this area was virtually absent until 1991, when a new structural policy framework was adopted (OECD 1993a, p. 55).[5]

7.3   Speed

The issue of the speed of structural reforms has played an important role in debates on privatization, deregulation and a more vigorous competition policy. Concern has arisen about how fast the sequential implementation of different reforms should proceed — the 'big-bang' versus the 'gradualist' approach. This is especially so in countries where a large number of areas qualify for reform. Examples are the Central and Eastern European economies which have all adopted massive privatization programmes, but where the speed of privatization varied considerably.[6]

Among the OECD countries also, large differences exist in the speed at which structural reforms are implemented. On the fast side of the spectrum, extensive reforms took place in New Zealand. The time span during which these reforms were formulated and implemented was extremely short, especially when the breadth of the reforms is also taken into account. On the other hand, Germany has adopted a more piecemeal approach, gradually reforming selected product and labour market rigidities over many years. Inherent in this approach is that agreement has to be reached on each separate reform proposal, rather than on a reform package, which makes the reform effort vulnerable to the opposition of special interest groups.

From an economic perspective, it is not clear whether a gradual or 'shock-therapy' approach should be preferred (World Bank 1991b, p. 117). As the initial conditions differ in each economy, the adage 'different speeds for different purposes' also applies here. Gradualism is more appropriate when the economy is characterized by a high degree of wage and price rigidity. In this case, shock-like reforms may lead to high adjustment costs because the reallocation of factors of production is hampered. Second, gradualism allows policies to be adjusted during the reforms. Structural adjustment often takes place under conditions of considerable uncertainty as to the outcome and the optimal institutional design of reforms. Through 'learning by doing', future policies can be made more effective. Even a return to the status quo ante becomes a policy option in the case of gradualism, which may improve the political support of the reforms (Roland 1994, pp. 1162—3). The reason is that when policies do not have the desired effects, the cost of a policy reversal after massive restructuring would be much higher. The existence of the extra policy option of a reversal of the reforms may increase the *ex ante* expected outcome and the willingness of the population to undergo experimentation with reform.[7] Dewatripont and Roland (1992) also find that gradualism is the appropriate strategy when governments need to maintain electoral support for their policies. In their theoretical model, some workers become redundant because of reform. These workers differ in ability due to differences in education level. The government finds itself in a situation where: *i*) it has to compensate workers who become redundant to maintain support; *ii*) support is only maintained if workers are compensated according to ability.

However, because the government cannot observe ability, high-ability workers must receive the same compensation as low-ability workers in a 'big-bang' reform at high budgetary cost. In a more gradual approach, however, reform can be implemented in such a way that in the first period, only the high-ability group is induced to be laid off. In the next period, the next highest ability group should leave, and so on, at much lower costs to the government budget. For this reason, gradualism is optimal. Finally, gradualism may be preferable when new institutions have to be developed (World Bank 1991b, p. 117). New institutions necessarily take time to devise, while a reform of pricing policy or taxation can be carried through fairly quickly. Excessive speed may prove counterproductive when new institutions need to be developed. For example, when the domestic capital market is underdeveloped, speed in the privatization of state enterprises may lead to an underpricing of assets and a suboptimal allocation.

Speeding up reforms also has some advantages. First, the faster reforms take place, the earlier the benefits of reform can materialize. If action is not taken fast enough, support for the reform programme may collapse because of the absence of tangible benefits. Second, in the case of a crisis, a sense of urgency often arises. The government does well in capitalizing on this sentiment by pushing the reforms through parliament as quickly as possible. When the business cycle is moving upwards again, it becomes much more difficult to communicate the necessity of structural reforms. Finally, a speedy implementation of reforms may help the new policies gain credibility and prevent the joint assault of special interest groups against the reforms (Douglas 1993, p. 224). Simply stating that reforms in a specific industry are being studied, without indicating what is supposed to happen or when the final decisions on reform will take place, will breed uncertainty. The longer this uncertainty is allowed to build up, the more resistance the government is bound to encounter. For example, Hirschman (1990) shows that gradualism inherits the danger of getting stuck at one stage of political and economic development because counteracting forces are given time to gain strength. Gradual reforms give pressure groups time to team up and strengthen their grip on the regulatory process. Van Wijnbergen (1992) shows that a lack of credibility in the case of gradual price reforms would create incentives for speculative hoarding. This is so because due to the price liberalization, prices are expected to rise in the future. The low supply response early on in the reform, however, causes the median voter to revise downwards his expectations of the benefits of reform, leading to a negative vote for the reform.

7.4 The Political Economy of Structural Reform

In the discussions of the sequencing and speed of reforms in the previous sections, political considerations have (implicitly) played a large role. The goal of this section is to make these considerations more explicit by discussing some of the findings in the literature on political—economic models with respect to the implementation of structural reforms. The standard neoclassical orthodoxy is based on the assumption that a well-informed, altruistic government tries to maximize social utility subject to certain administrative or technological constraints. Reform takes place whenever a policy is beneficial to the representative voter in the economy. Both the government and the voter are perfectly informed about the costs and benefits of a particular policy.

Unfortunately, the neoclassical theories are of little use in explaining two key facts of reality. First, within the same country, some reform programmes fail while others succeed. This is surprising when taking into account that the successful reform programmes are often quite similar to the unsuccessful ones in terms of the proposed policy measures (Dornbusch 1988). This points to other than purely economic factors which are crucial for success. Second, many countries follow policies which are recognized to be both unsustainable and inefficient in the long run. For example, the common agricultural policy of the European Union is generally considered as being extremely costly and distorting, both domestically and (perhaps especially) abroad. The costs of this policy are borne by three groups. First, the European taxpayer has to pay for the various subsidies given to farmers. Second, consumers in Europe pay relatively high prices for agricultural products. Third, farmers outside Europe see the (world market) price of their product fall because of the 'excess' European production. In the neoclassical framework, both the government and the voter would know when a policy becomes unsustainable and proceed to reform the policy immediately.

The combination of the similarity of failing and successful programmes, on the one hand, and the existence of policies which are known to be inefficient and unsustainable in the long run, on the other hand, can only be explained by recognizing that policy makers are not only social welfare maximizers. The political economy approach accepts that policy makers can pursue goals of their own. Hence short-run political considerations may become crucial determinants of the success of economic reforms. The exciting new theoretical opportunities provided by this approach derive from the assumption that the government consists of a group of self-interested individuals (politicians) who maximize their own utility (Funke 1993).[8] These policy makers are constantly aware of the effects of their decisions on their own popularity. This means that policy makers may only want to make unpopular decisions shortly after an election, or that they try to achieve favourable economic conditions shortly before elections in order to increase their re-election probability. In addition, the authorities may be influenced by pressure groups which try to improve or protect their current well-being. The government in turn may try to bind some of these pressure groups by the creation of political rents, even at the expense of other, less influential groups. Thus, the influence and response of pressure groups is a crucial factor determining the political sustainability of a reform programme.

Pressure groups
Roughly speaking, five different methods are used by pressure groups to influence politicians (Naert 1984). Pressure groups can try to get a grip on the decision-making process itself. They can also aim at influencing the public opinion, which may have an effect on the re-

election probability of the politician. The first way in which pressure groups can influence the government is by threatening to use their economic power. Business can set up a formidable lobby by threatening to withdraw production facilities from the country concerned. This has electoral consequences as the corresponding jobs are also lost. Labour unions also have strong positions in many OECD countries which they can exploit by using the strike weapon. Second, pressure groups may be important sources of finance for political parties. The parties in turn will be more willing to listen to the demands of their donor because of his or her financial support. Third, many pressure groups have an informational advantage *vis-à-vis* the government in the field they are operating in. Pressure groups can utilize this informational advantage in a strategic way by selectively informing the government and the public. A fourth way to influence governments is by direct affiliation with political parties. For example, environmental groups have founded Green parties, workers' movements have participated in social democratic parties and pensioners have set up parties for the elderly. In this way, pressure groups can directly take part in political decision making. Finally, pressure groups can influence politicians by (co-)deciding on specific issues. Corporatism, as this phenomenon is called, is present in all OECD countries but to differing degrees. Some countries have centralized wage negotiations, for example, during which the government, employers and trade unions negotiate agreements not only on wages, but also on employment, schooling, retirement, sickness and disability arrangements. In countries with administrative extension of wage bargains, parties which are not represented during the negotiations (non-organized employers, for example) can also be bound to the result. Similar forms of co-decision making take place in other socioeconomic areas. All in all, pressure groups can form a formidable force in society which have a strong influence on public sector decision making.

The reason why pressure groups engage in these lobbying activities is the potentially large economic rewards they may offer to them. For example, the voluntary restraint of exports to the US markets which the Japanese car producers agreed to in 1981 has resulted in a considerable transfer from US consumers to US producers, amounting to an estimated 2.6 billion dollars (OECD

1994a, p. 18). In the long run, however, this rent-seeking behaviour may have severely damaged the American automobile industry by delaying adjustments which would have been necessary anyway.

According to Mancur Olson's (1982) influential *The Rise and Decline of Nations*, the emergence of special interest groups has a negative influence both on an economy's capacity to adjust and on its innovativeness:

> The most important macroeconomic policy implication is that the best macroeconomic policy is a good microeconomic policy. There is no substitute for a more open and competitive environment. If combinations dominate markets throughout the economy and the government is always intervening on behalf of special interests, there is no macroeconomic policy that can put things right (Olson 1982, p. 233).

This is so because distributive coalitions between the government and pressure groups usually make slower decisions than the individuals who comprise the groups.[9] Coalitions must always bargain until they can agree on the joint course to be followed and how the costs of these actions are to be shared.[10] Problems arise because resources need to be reallocated from one activity or industry to another — which is a precondition for structural reform — because of changes in technology or deregulation. Vested interests in the industries concerned have an incentive to, for example, lobby for bail-outs of failing firms, thereby slowing down the attempt to improve the allocation of resources quickly and efficiently (Olson 1982, pp. 61—5).

Recent theoretical developments in the political economy of policy reform show that uncertainty about the winners and losers of reform may cause a bias against efficiency-enhancing reforms (Fernandez and Rodrik 1991). These inefficient outcomes are shown to be consistent with rational and non-myopic behaviour at the individual level. Rodrik (1993, p. 357) demonstrates how the argument works by considering an economy where a majority vote is needed before a reform can be adopted. Suppose the economy consists of 100 risk neutral voters. If the reform in question increases the incomes of 51 voters by 5 dollars each, and decreases the income of the rest by one dollar each, then a net gain of 206 dollars results for society as a whole (= $51 \times \$5 - 49 \times \$1$). Because the majority of the population benefits from the reform and the aggregate consequences of reform are assumed to be common knowledge, the reform will be adopted. Now imagine that 49 individuals know for certain that they will gain, while the remaining 51 do not know whether they will gain or lose. However, since the aggregate consequences of reform are common knowledge, the latter group will know for certain that two of them will benefit, while 49 will lose. The expected benefit of the reform of the individuals in the second group is therefore negative: ([2×$5 — 49×$1]/51 = —0.76 dollars each). Hence these 51 individuals will vote against any change in the status quo. Such a mechanism could explain why some reforms which would have been popular after implementation, because the majority of the electorate will gain, are passed up *ex ante*.[11] This may happen even when the beneficial effect of the reforms is common knowledge. The converse is also true: radical reforms in countries like Chile which are implemented under autocratic regimes have turned out to be popular, even though they received little support prior to the reforms.[12]

The above example suggests that the reform package should be sufficiently broad to let as many individuals as possible benefit from the reform. Moreover, in this example it is the uncertainty about who will benefit and who will lose which blocks the implementation of the reform. If each voter could know for certain whether he or she will lose or win, the reform would be adopted because the majority will benefit from its effects. Hence, the costs and benefits of reforms should be as transparent as possible.

Some reforms, however, are delayed even though everyone will benefit from their adoption. The reason is that the presence of pressure groups may lead to a distributional struggle about the division of the gains from reform. Each group may seek to shift the adjustment burden elsewhere. The temporary stalemate between the different pressure groups which follows is not resolved until certain groups concede. This may be the result of an electoral outcome, a formal agreement or an emerging consensus among political parties. Such delays may increase the transition costs of reforms by allowing existing modes of behaviour to entrench (OECD 1994a).

Alesina and Drazen (1991) model this distributional struggle as a 'war of attrition'. Each special interest group tries to prevent the burden of adjustment being placed on it by mobilizing resources for lobbying activities. Although the benefits of reform are distributed equally, the costs are not. The struggle ends when one party agrees to bear a disproportionate share of the adjustment costs. The reason is that delaying change is not without costs as the benefits of change will also be delayed. So because of the passage of time, one player will eventually agree on the same terms which he or she earlier found unacceptable.

The Alesina—Drazen (1991) framework can help explain why reforms are more likely to take place during crises. A crisis increases the cost of waiting, which makes political agreement more likely. It can also provide an insight into why some groups no longer resist reform although they have to bear a disproportionate share of the adjustment burden. According to Alesina and Drazen (1991), reform is not a matter of breeding consensus, but the consolidation of one group's influence over the others (which are too 'weakened' to resist any longer). The resolution of the political stalemate provides the winning group with the opportunity to impose its broader policy agenda on the temporarily weakened society. Such a resolution may be provided by an election with a clear winner, which may make it more difficult for the opponents to block the winner's reforms. Moreover, the emergence of a winning group may explain why many macroeconomic stabilizations in the 1980s have been accompanied by rather radical microeconomic reforms — the 'winner' capitalized on his or her victory by getting as many reforms as possible implemented. Finally, Alesina and Drazen (1991) show that the more uneven the expected costs of stabilization are distributed, the longer reform is delayed. Essentially, this is caused by the fact that when the burden of adjustment is less equally distributed, the gain from waiting in the hope that one's opponent will concede is larger. Reform programmes should therefore be relatively broad and as balanced as possible to stand a higher chance of gaining support.

7.5   Empirical Evidence on Policy Reform

When looking at the literature on policy reform, one thing becomes overwhelmingly clear — simple generalizations are hard to make. One reason may be that this literature largely uses the vehicle of in-depth case studies of policy reforms in particular countries.

Internationally comparable empirical evidence on policy reforms in
the OECD is available only to a limited extent.

Table 7.2 Findings on successful structural reforms

	Australia	New Zealand	Portugal	Spain	Mexico	Turkey
Start of reform	1983	1984	1985	1982	1987	1980
Political conditions						
Government	L	L	C	L	C	R
Honeymoon	(—)	+	(+)	(+)	—	(+)
Political base	+	+	—	+	+	—/+
Weak opposition	(+)	+	+	+	+	(+)
Social consensus	—/+	—	+	+	—/+	—/+
Visionary leader	+	—	+	+	+	—/+
Economic conditions						
Crisis	—	(+)	—	(—)	+	+
External aid	—	—	(—)	(—)	+	+
Nature of programme						
Broad package	+	+	+	+	+	—
Position of team						
Coherent team	+	+	+	+	+	+
Leader is economist	—	(—)	+	+	+	+

Notes: + = factor present; (+) = factor present with
qualifications; — = factor not present; (—) = factor not
present, with qualifications; R, C, L = rightist, centrist, left
of centre, respectively; +/— = present at first, subsequently
not present; —/+ = not present at first, subsequently
present.

Source: Based on Williamson and Haggard (1994), p. 563.

An exception is the seminal study by Williamson and Haggard
(1994), who also analyse the reforms in a number of non-OECD

countries. A summary of their fundings with respect to the OECD countries is presented in Table 7.2. The scarcity of empirical evidence, however, is perhaps also a symptom of the problem that countries intrinsically differ from each other, both with respect to the areas in which reforms should take place and in the actual solutions chosen.

It is important to keep in mind that the overview of policy reform in six countries provided by Table 7.2 is by no means a random sample of the countries undertaking structural reforms. The selection of countries is biased in favour of countries which had a more or less coherent programme. So economies implementing reform in a more piecemeal fashion may be underrepresented in this sample. Moreover, the sample is biased in favour of successful reforms. A great number of reform proposals never reach the implementation stage. This makes these 'reform efforts' much more difficult to analyse in an international comparison.

Keeping these reservations in mind, Table 7.2 summarizes six cases of policy reform in current OECD member countries based on the assessment of Williamson and Haggard (1994). The table reports on some of the economic and political factors which may have played a role in the successful implementation the reforms considered. These factors are grouped in four clusters: political conditions, economic conditions, the nature of the reform programme itself and the position of the team which organizes the reforms. The table serves as an illustration only, as the hypotheses are not formally tested. Moreover, inevitable ambiguities remain concerning the beginning of the reforms and the subjective reasoning needed to fill in the various cells of the table.

A glance at the table makes it obvious that only a few robust empirical conclusions can be drawn — in most cases, at least one counterexample exists. The first item in Table 7.2, so to say, tests the 'rightist hypothesis', indicating the political colour of the government. Policy reforms are often thought of as being inherently right wing. Many well-known policy reforms were propagated by right-wing politicians such as US President Ronald Reagan and the British Prime Minister Margaret Thatcher. In addition, business interests often form a powerful force in support of reforms. On the other hand, having a left-of-centre government may be advantageous in circumstances where changes need to be made which are viewed as unfavourable to labour. Reform may then be carried through causing less social tension than under a rightist government. The six cases of policy reform considered here were more often implemented by centrist or left-of-centre governments, thereby providing evidence against the 'rightist' hypothesis.

Another factor which may influence the success of reforms is whether they are undertaken early on in the term of office in the so-called honeymoon period. Immediately after a new government is formed, policy makers may enjoy greater freedom of political manoeuvre. This may be because the government was a clear winner in the elections, or because difficult decisions can be blamed on the previous government. New Zealand is the only unambiguous example in support of this hypothesis, but reforms were also carried through relatively early during the term of office in Portugal, Spain and Turkey. The Australian and Mexican governments, however, were not able to capitalize on a honeymoon period, either because there was no honeymoon or because the government was otherwise occupied during that period. Nevertheless, the honeymoon period is not the only opportunity governments have to initiate reforms — other, more suitable opportunities may also arise.

Other political factors which may help to generate support for (or undermine opposition against) structural reforms are a solid political base, a fragmented opposition, social consensus about what needs to be done and the presence of a visionary leader who points the way ahead. A solid political base is expected to be essential in the implementation phase of reforms, for obvious reasons. In the majority of the countries considered, the governments in power did have legislative backing. The Portuguese reforms form an exception to this rule as they were implemented by a minority government. In Turkey, the democratic government, which had launched its reform proposals in January 1980, was faced with an increasingly fragmented and polarized parliament. In September 1980, the military took power and provided the political backing needed to carry through the reforms.

A fragmented opposition may also help to get reforms implemented because such an opposition may not be able to challenge the proposals. Table 7.2 shows that all the governments benefited from a weak opposition. Social consensus about what needed to be done was present in only two countries. In Portugal and Spain, the desire to 'become European' played a large role in focusing this consensus. Social consensus is especially important when there is no acute crisis — in this case, visionary leadership may be a more critical success factor (Sachs 1994, p. 505). Strong leadership was important in a number of the countries considered, involving a long-term view and a willingness to take (political) risks. New Zealand is an exception in this case, as the economic vision of the reform programme was not that of Prime Minister David Lange but of the leader of the economic team, the Minister of Finance Roger Douglas.

Two economic factors which may help to get reforms implemented are the presence of an acute crisis and external aid in sustaining reforms. Crises may have the effect of 'shocking' countries out of their traditional policy patterns by creating a sense of urgency. This in turn helps to dam the influence of special interest groups which otherwise would have vetoed the reform:

> These worst of times give rise to the best of opportunities for those who understand the need for fundamental economic reform (Williamson and Haggard 1994, p. 565).

In addition, public opinion expects decisive action from politicians during crises. Crises stimulated reform in Mexico and Turkey.

External aid in the form of intellectual and financial help has played a large role especially in the less-developed economies. Mexico and Turkey, for example, received large loans and short-term credits for debt restructuring, by the World Bank and the OECD, respectively. The change in the intellectual climate in favour of policies orientated towards macroeconomic stability, and open markets may also have played a large role. These intellectual influences have been transmitted by international organizations (OECD, IMF, World Bank). In developing countries this was done by extending training to national officials and by making loans conditional on economic reform.[13] In industrialized countries, policy advice was provided, for example by conducting country studies and by publishing seminal studies. The OECD's Economic Development Review Committee, for example, annually reviews its members' economic developments, prospects and policies. The findings of these reviews are made readily available to the general public in the OECD's *Economic Surveys* series.

Most of the countries considered have enacted fairly comprehensive programmes, covering a broad array of proposals capable of rapid implementation. The exception is Turkey, where fiscal stabilization was not part of the reforms. All of the reforms were carried out by a coherent economic team, the members of which adhered to more or less the same principles. Another possibility would be to create a team where the members have conflicting views on economic policy. This may help in keeping an open mind to alternative solutions. However, none of the countries considered have chosen this option.

The final item in Table 7.2 indicates whether or not economists have had leading political positions. Having an economist as leader may be beneficial to carrying through structural reforms because economists may be able to offer more effective leadership than a minister who is completely dependent on the advice of others. In addition, economists may simply understand the process of structural reform better. However, it is not always easy to distinguish between economic and non-economic leadership. For example, Douglas in New Zealand was an accountant and not an economist, in the strict sense of the word. Moreover, the findings may simply reflect the larger role that economists in Europe play in the political sphere (Frey and Eichenberger 1993).

Notes

1. See Edwards (1989, pp. 40—47) for a theoretical discussion and some empirical examples of the interaction between (inconsistent) macroeconomic policies, credibility and structural reform.

2. We do not consider international factors, such as treaties or international aid, which can also lend credibility to reforms. See World Bank (1991b, p. 147).

3. This basically is the reason why merger and anti-trust policy become all the more important after a move towards privatization and deregulation.

4. The negative rate of protection in 1991 indicates that the import barriers against imported raw materials were higher than the import barriers against final products.

5. The New Zealand government did take several steps to liberalize the labour market before 1990. It abolished compulsory arbitration in 1984 and it encouraged decentralized wage bargaining both in private and in public sectors. Yet, according to the OECD (1993a, p. 56), many

concerns arose that the labour market was still not sufficiently flexible as businesses and employees often had only a limited ability to determine their own employment arrangements.

6. See Roland (1994) for a discussion of the issues of the speed and sequencing of privatization and restructuring in these countries.

7. On the other hand, this can also be seen as an argument against gradual restructuring, as it will make the reform more vulnerable to changes in the political climate and may undermine credibility.

8. In this section, the words 'politicians', 'policy makers', 'the authorities' and 'government' are treated as synonyms.

9. The same arguments hold for distributive coalitions (cartels) between firms.

10. This becomes less of a problem if the portion of society the pressure groups represent is relatively large. Such organizations are able to internalize a larger part of the benefits of agreeing with structural reforms: 'Thus any effort to obtain a larger share of the national income for the clients of such an organization could not make sense if it reduced the national income by an amount three or more times as great as the amount shifted to its members' (Olson 1982, p. 48).

11. The story changes when the losers receive compensation for their losses. In this case, all voters would be in favour of reform.

12. See for example Valdés (1995).

13. Conditionality may also have its disadvantages as it can weaken the domestic support for reform. International financial institutions should therefore grant borrowing countries sufficient leeway in programme design (Williamson and Haggard 1994, pp. 566—67).

8. Combating Product Market Inertia: Some Conclusions

Writing on the reality of economic policy, Tinbergen (1952, pp. 76—7) rightly drew the reader's attention to the fact that economic models and measurement do not tell us everything we need to know about economic policy. Non-economic factors are also very important. Tinbergen, for example, pointed out that the execution of rational policies was often impeded by the tendency to maintain the status quo and by personal and institutional inertia. Moreover, he added, an 'aversion of the complex' influenced economic policy wrongly:

> Many officials (...) dislike to accept somewhat more complicated reasonings or the results of calculations even if from the scientific point of view they are decidedly better than the rules of thumb often accepted before' (Tinbergen 1952, p. 77).

Tinbergen's observations suggest that structural reforms are rather difficult to implement, because policy makers both need to break new ground and to understand difficult analytical issues in evaluating proposed qualitative policies. Indeed, structural change is a very complex topic as it interacts with a large number of policy fields. At the microeconomic, macroeconomic and political levels, many conflicting issues are at stake. Moreover, privatization, deregulation and competition policy happen to be concepts that are difficult to analyse in applied economic policy models, especially where microeconomic and macroeconomic aspects need to be taken into account simultaneously. The theoretical debates on these matters have by no means been settled yet, not least because empirical evidence is scant (and if available it is often inconclusive). Paradoxically, at least from the Tinbergen point of view, qualitative policy is presently in a great state of flux. Privatization, deregulation and competition policy

197

to different degrees are important ingredients of transition economies, emerging markets, industrialized countries and the Third World, as illustrated in Chapter 2 which discussed the policy stance in the OECD, Eastern Europe and the emerging markets.

This book illustrates that no easy concepts and strategies are available. Starting from the concept of product market inertia we developed and discussed indicators that can be used to measure the extent of unresponsiveness of product markets, i.e. the 'lack' of economic dynamism. Next we have looked at ways of relating the apparent inflexibility to an economy's performance and its ability to adjust to changing circumstances. In doing so, we referred to a comprehensive strategy to tackle product market inertia which consists of three elements: privatization, deregulation and competition policy. It is extremely important that a two-tier approach is followed in evaluating these policies. One should, on the one hand, not just go ahead, as the costs of structural change can become very large if issues like sequencing, the speed of reform, etc. are ignored. On the other hand, neither should one get stuck in the quantification trap ('paralysis through analysis'). The two-tier strategy for which this book provides relevant background material suggests using different methods of quantification, making comparative analyses between countries and looking at qualitative analyses as well.

8.1   Measurement

In order to provide a comparative identification of the extent to which the market mechanism (dys)functions we discussed several methodologies that can be used at the microeconomic, the mesoeconomic and the macroeconomic level. Starting with a discussion within the framework of the structure—conduct—performance paradigm, we analysed four methods which have been applied to a sufficiently large number of countries to allow us to attempt to identify on a comparative basis the problems which OECD countries may experience with product market inertia. None of the methodologies relates to structure. Two methodologies are identified as performance indicators: the persistence of profits parameters (the long-run equilibrium level of profits and the adjustment speed of profits to this level) and the mark-up ratio on marginal costs. Two methodologies relate to conduct: the speed of price adjustment and the product market inertia coefficient, which measures hysteresis in the product market.

Although the findings do not allow us to rank countries unambiguously on the basis of the four methodologies (mainly because each indicator measures a different aspect of the concept of economic dynamism), we can list three findings that are relevant to our discussion. First, the half-life of excess profits indicates substantial persistence, with Sweden having a half-life of as much as three years; a half-life period of one year is not uncommon in major OECD economies (such as the United Kingdom, the United States and Japan). Second, the estimated product market inertia coefficients show that some hysteresis in the price mechanism exists for all economies investigated and that hysteresis on the European product markets exceeds the levels found in the United States, Canada and Taiwan. Third, in manufacturing mark-up ratios of OECD countries point out that price substantially exceeds marginal costs, as these mark-up ratios are significantly larger than 1 (the value that would prevail in the hypothetical case of perfect competition). Given the substantial amount of evidence of price hysteresis, the assumption of market clearing that is a corner stone of many economic models would seem to be rather *ad hoc*. Indeed, the sheer pervasiveness of price rigidities would seem to contradict the neoclassical objections against fix-price models.

8.2   Modelling

So the natural way of modelling industrialized economies would seem to take hysteresis and imperfect competition as starting points. We looked at the literature distinguishing two channels through which product market inertia influences the macroeconomy: the macroeconomic efficiency effect (static and dynamic efficiency) and the efficacy of policy effect (policies related to stabilization, income distribution and the balance of payments, as well as the effectiveness of fiscal policy instruments). It should be noted that theory is not yet sufficiently developed to guide economic policy unambiguously and that the available evidence in many cases is not conclusive. Moreover, it is important to recognize that the theoretical evaluation of structural changes depends on the time horizon that is being adopted. Different time horizons may account for differences in multipliers which have been reported in both the theoretical and the applied literature.

It follows from our theoretical *tour d'horizon*, that employment and per capita income are higher in the deregulated flexible economy and prices are lower provided that reallocation costs are low and that the potentially negative influence on innovation is not too strong.

These findings are *grosso modo* confirmed by the EC's partial equilibrium analysis of '1992' and the applied general equilibrium analyses of structural reform in Germany, the Netherlands and Australia, which were discussed in Chapter 6. For the medium term these calculations suggest that structural reform of product markets may yield an annual average increase in production growth of some 0.3—1 percentage points. Likewise, employment growth may increase by 0.1—1 percentage points annually (depending among other factors on whether the labour market is flexible). Inflation decreases by 0.4—1.3 percentage points. Obviously these results can only be seen as rough indications of the potential gains for comprehensive strategies that combat product market inertia.

So far, the profession has preferred the use of applied general equilibrium models to analyse these issues, mainly as this modelling strategy may offer a way out for the Lucas critique. General equilibrium modelling, however, focuses on the long run and thus neglects transition aspects and the concomitant cost of the reallocation of the factors of production. Often the costs of structural change have simply been ignored in the available calculations.[1] In addition, the country analyses that were discussed in Chapter 6 are based on the removal of rigidities and distortions which have been introduced into the general equilibrium framework in a rather *ad hoc* fashion. Thus, almost by definition, a welfare improvement is to be expected in such calculations in which suboptimality is assumed from the start (although in all cases, specific aspects of this suboptimality were based on detailed comparative empirical observations).

For the time being, given resource constraints and the need to provide transparency about the economy-wide benefits of competition, deregulation and privatization within a reasonable short time span, policy makers (and modellers) will have to resort to practical solutions like the ones which have been discussed in Chapter 6. This is so because important socioeconomic problems are involved. Structural adjustment — which for a cost-efficient solution requires flexibility of the economy — is a major policy challenge, especially for the European economies. For example, in the near future environmental policies and the completion of the internal market will require significant changes in the European production structure.[2] Clearly, insight into the costs and (especially) the benefits of market flexibility at the macroeconomic level are needed, because the policy changes which have been discussed often go against vested interests. Transparency is a prerequisite for structural change as knowledge of the costs of non-competition may help to mobilize the general public to support the necessary policy changes.

8.3 Policy

Rather than adding lessons to those provided by other authors we discuss what from the previous chapter appear to be the four main characteristics of successful structural reform programmes.

Macroeconomic stability
The best foundation for microeconomic reform is a stable macroeconomic environment. This means that preferably inflation should be low and stable, public finances should be tidy and no large imbalances should persist on the current and capital accounts of the balance of payments. Stability is first of all needed for prices to fulfil their function as signals for resource allocation, and to maintain or strengthen the incentives to save and invest. Macroeconomic stability is also a precondition for the credibility of reform, and without the latter, any reform programme would immediately be undermined.

So structural reform is easier to achieve in the presence of macroeconomic stability. However, the reverse also holds. When product and labour markets are flexible, they should be able to react more quickly to a tightening of monetary policy in the face of (expected) rises in inflation. This would reduce the adjustment costs in terms of output and employment forgone during the transitional phase to lower inflation. Thus, macroeconomic stability and structural reform can together form a virtuous circle where one strengthens the other.

Openness

The ever-increasing international integration is one of the major stimuli for structural adjustment. The need for economies to compete on the world market poses numerous challenges to both policy makers and companies:

> At its simplest, this is because international trade provides a uniquely powerful source of pressures for structural change. The constraints trade imposes are obvious: in an integrated world economy, the option of not adjusting no longer exists. But the incentives that access to global markets creates to develop new and more efficient products and processes are no less important (OECD 1987a, p. 269).

Since the beginning of the 1950s, international trade has been a powerful force to counteract the gradual rise of entry barriers due to economies of scale and product differentiation. In autarky, this would have created large incentives to take advantage of dominant positions. However, established foreign firms can penetrate or withdraw from a foreign market relatively easily by gradually varying the amount imported from the home base. Hence these barriers are a far weaker deterrent to entry by established foreign firms. Equivalently, economies of scale and product differentiation are much less an obstacle to competition from foreign direct investment, because foreign firms have already accumulated expertise and can exploit economies of scale on the home market. These effects were enhanced further by the various GATT agreements, which provided a strong impulse to the growth in world trade and international direct investment flows. As a result, many markets have become increasingly open to competition.

International economic integration ('globalization') can also be a formidable political argument to get changes adopted. Vested interests often try to avoid adjustment to foreign competition by pressuring the government to act for their cause. In the past, governments have given all kinds of financial assistance, have provided a protective regulatory environment and have tried to seal off the various channels of international exchange. Traditional industries such as agriculture, steel, shipbuilding and textiles are examples of sectors where this interventionism reached very large proportions. However, unless all channels of international exchange (trade, greenfield investment, foreign take-overs, joint ventures and even immigration) are blocked, pressures for structural change will build up over time, which eventually will make these policies unsustainable.

Transparency

Transparency about the costs and benefits of reform is what Part III of this book is all about. There are a number of aspects to transparency. First, it pays to be realistic. Painting too rosy a picture on the possible benefits of reform will foster unrealistic expectations which may slow down reforms later on during the process. Policy makers should be perfectly clear about the importance of reform, reminding people what will happen if nothing changes. Realism is also called for when preparing the financial plan which accompanies the reform programme, because insufficient financial means may also frustrate the reforms.

Second, the losers of reform should also receive attention. In every step taken towards privatization, deregulation and a more vigorous competition policy there are winners and losers. A complicating factor in this respect is that the losers of reform are often more influential than the winners. This is so because the losers are usually concentrated within a certain industry, while the beneficiaries are a much more diffuse group of people (consumers, for example).[3] Thus, special programmes of assistance are often needed to cushion the adverse effects on the losers during a transitional period.[4]

Third, the benefits of reform may only show up in the long run. The main costs of reform, however, usually become apparent rather quickly. It is important to anticipate these adjustment costs and to develop a strategy on how to deal with them. Unexpected costs can cause public support for reform to evaporate:

> the most difficult part of a reform programme is not introducing the reforms but sustaining them until they have a chance to bear fruit and thus generate political support from potential beneficiaries. How difficult this is depends on the lag between the initial reforms and the emergence of politically significant beneficiaries (Williamson 1994, pp. 20—21).

Fourth, when evaluating the costs and benefits of reform in a particular industry, the focus should not be too narrow. Although a partial equilibrium analysis provides useful information on the direct effects of removing barriers to competition, many indirect effects are neglected. More specifically, enhanced competition in one sector frees resources for use in other sectors, it improves the overall flexibility of the economic system and the capacity to innovate. In addition, a partial analysis of the benefits of deregulation may show a loss for a specific industry, while the overall effect on the economy is positive. This underlines the need for a general equilibrium assessment (or at least a macroeconomic analysis) of the benefits of structural reform. Perhaps the most important point, however, is that care should be taken not to focus too much on the production and employment effects of structural reform. The effect on (consumer) welfare is just as important.[5]

Comprehensive approach

A broad, transparent, medium-term approach is called for both from an economic and from a political viewpoint. Partial attempts of reform are often difficult to implement. The theory of second best indicates that liberalizing one market while leaving the other market untouched may aggravate the adverse effects of the remaining rigidities. An example is trade reform which is not accompanied by domestic deregulation. If both markets are heavily distorted this reform would cause investments to go to the 'wrong' sectors. A broad reform may also make it easier to compensate the losers of structural adjustment. One reason is that the gains from reform are larger and more visible, which makes it easier to redistribute some of the gains to the losers during a transitional period. In addition, some of the gains and losses of the different reforms may cancel out. Reform in one industry may erode monopoly rents, but the same sector may profit from reforms elsewhere (in upstream supplier industries, for example). There thus seems to exist a premium on simultaneously taking complementary actions.

Transparency and a clear timetable are important to foster credibility and therefore encourage a prompt response from the private sector. In addition, reforms should be framed in a medium-term context. Because private sector decision making is forward looking, the effectiveness of policies over the short term depends on their medium-term consistency and credibility.

8.4 Ways to Go

The frontiers of understanding of the consequences of product market inertia and structural reform are shifting outwards. New knowledge is being produced both at the pure scientific level of theories and theorems and in applied research. So it is to be hoped that economic policy in these fields eventually will improve as well. However, in order to achieve such progress further substantial effort must be put into theory building, evaluation and data collection.

First, it is pertinent that theories are developed which combine imperfect competition on product markets, long-run dynamics such as capacity effects of investment (both physical and in human capital) and intertemporal optimization. These theories need to provide answers to relevant policy questions, i.e. it is important that they relate to static and dynamic efficiency and investigate the effectiveness of the instruments of economic policy. It is equally important that these theories produce testable propositions.

Secondly, in addition to the applied general equilibrium models presently being used to analyse these and related qualitative policies, econometric models are needed which incorporate elements of structural change. Econometric models are needed to get a better, more complete picture of the (timing of) short-term and medium-term effects of structural change. Incorporating structural change indicators in traditional policy models may also help to get a better insight into the reallocation costs which are presently *grosso modo* neglected and may also help to prevent policy errors. Obviously, a better understanding of the determinants of the costs *and* benefits of structural reform will guide the design of better policies.

Third, rational empirical policies are only possible to the extent that the required observations are available and that (new) indicators are developed and the necessary data are collected. Data are necessary to guide theory, to assess the need for structural reform, to monitor the impact and effectiveness of implemented qualitative policies and to test models. Applied research will have to deal with national developments and analyse developments *vis-à-vis* other countries.

Indeed, it is essential that large-scale societal experiments which aim at privatization, deregulation and changes in the competition policy regime are closely monitored at the level of individual firms and consumers, at the level of sectors and industries and at the macroeconomic level. It is important that monitoring is done with different time horizons in mind. We want to know both how economic subjects are influenced with respect to their day-to-day activities, their medium-term responses and how economic activity is influenced in the long run. This is the only available solution to Tinbergen's (1952, p. 72) observation that qualitative policy is difficult to evaluate because 'our empirical quantitative knowledge of human behaviour under different structural conditions is so restricted'.

Notes

1. The Australian empirical analysis of the Hilmer report is a case in point (Industry Commission 1995).
2. In the medium term, the process of the globalization of production and the move towards a single currency pose similar challenges (Geelhoed 1994).
3. See Olson (1982, pp. 17—36) for an explanation.
4. This presumes that the identity of the winners and losers of reform can be determined *ex ante*. This may not always be the case.
5. For example, an important argument for liberalizing shop-opening hours in the Netherlands was that it would fulfil an important need in society. The Netherlands had one of the strictest regimes in the world, as shops were only allowed to be open for a maximum of 55 hours per week (Gradus 1995). Because of the increasing number of households where both partners have a full-time job, not much time is left to do shopping. The minister in charge of the shop-opening hours openly declared that he would have liberalized the opening hours even if the effects on employment had been negative.

References

Adelman, I. and J.E. Taylor, 1991, 'Multisector Models and Structural Adjustment: New Evidence from Mexico', *Journal of Development Studies* **28** (1), pp. 154—63.

Alesina, A. and A. Drazen, 1991, 'Why are stabilizations delayed?', *American Economic Review* **81** (5), pp. 1170—88.

Amsden, A. and A. Singh, 1994, 'The optimal degree of competition and dynamic efficiency in Japan and Korea', *European Economic Review* **38** (3/4), pp. 941—51.

Appelbaum, E., 1982, 'The estimation of the degree of oligopoly power', *Journal of Econometrics* **19**, pp. 187—99.

Ark, B. van, 1995, 'Manufacturing prices, productivity and labor costs in five economies', *Monthly Labor Review*, Bureau of Labor Statistics, July, pp. 56—72.

Asbeek Brusse, W. and R.T. Griffiths (1995), 'Paradise Lost or Paradise Regained? Cartel policy and cartel legislation in the Netherlands,' Paper presented to the workshop 'The interaction of Member States and EU competition policy', Center for Industrial Economics, Copenhagen.

Atesoglu, H.S., 1994, 'Balance of Payments Determined Growth in Germany', *Applied Economics Letters* **1**, pp. 89—91.

Audretsch, D.B., 1989, *The Market and the State: Government policy towards business in Europe, Japan and the USA*, New York, etc.: Harvester Wheatsheaf.

Bagwell, K. and R.W. Staiger, 1995, 'Collusion over the Business Cycle', *NBER Working Paper* 5056, Cambridge.

Bain, J.S., 1956, *Barriers to New Competition*, Cambridge, Mass.: Harvard University Press.

Barbone, L. and P. Poret, 1989, 'Structural Conditions and Macroeconomic Responses to Shocks: A Sensitivity Analysis for Four European Countries', *OECD Economic Studies* **12**, pp. 131—58.

Barro, R.J., 1991, 'Economic Growth in a Cross-Section of Countries', *Quarterly Journal of Economics* **106** (2), pp. 407—43.

Barro, R.J., 1994, 'Sources of Economic Growth', *Carnegie-Rochester Conference Series on Public Policy* **40**, pp. 1—46.

Basu, K., 'Flexibility in Economic Theory', in: T. Killick (ed.), 1995, *The Flexible Economy: Causes and consequences of the adaptability of national economies*, London and New York: Routledge, pp. 64—78.

Baumol, W.J., 1982, 'Contestable Markets: An Uprising in the Theory of Industry Structure', *American Economic Review* **72**, pp. 1—15.

Baumol, W.J., J. Panzar and R. Willig, 1982, *Contestable Markets and the Theory of Industry Structure*, San Diego: Harcourt Brace Jovanovich.

Bedrossian, A. and D. Moschos, 1988, 'Industrial structure and the speed of price adjustment', *Journal of Industrial Economics* **26** (4), pp. 459—75.

Bénassy, J.P., 1982, *The Economics of Market Disequilibrium*, New York, etc.: Academic Press.

Bénassy, J.P., 1993, 'Nonclearing Markets: Microeconomic Concepts and Macroeconomic Applications', *Journal of Economic Literature* **31** (2), pp. 732—61.

Bergeijk, P.A.G. van, 1995, 'On the Accuracy of International Economic Observations', *Bulletin of Economic Research*, **47** (1), pp. 1—20.

Bergeijk, P.A.G. van, M.A. van Dijk, R.C.G. Haffner, G.H.A. van Hagen, R.A. de Mooij and P.M. Waasdorp, 1995, 'Economic Policy, Technology and Growth', *Beleidsstudies Technologie Economie* **30**, Ministry of Economic Affairs (Directorate for Technology Policy): The Hague.

Bergeijk, P.A.G. van, C. van Gent, R.C.G. Haffner and A.J.M. Kleijweg, 1995, 'Mobiliteit en concurrentie op de kapitaalmarkt' (Mobility and competition in the capital market; in Dutch), *Economisch-Statistische Berichten* **80** (4023), pp. 780—84.

Bergeijk, P.A.G. van, R.C.G. Haffner and P.M. Waasdorp, 1993, 'Measuring the Speed of the Invisible Hand: The

Macroeconomic Costs of Price Rigidity', *Kyklos* **46** (4), pp. 529—44.

Bergeijk, P.A.G. van, C.J.W. Hiddink and P.M. Waasdorp, 1995, 'Olson Revisited: Economic Growth, Institutions and Politics in the OECD', The Hague, Ministry of Economic Affairs.

Bergeijk, P.A.G. van and D.L. Kabel, 1993, 'Strategic Trade Theories and Trade Policy', *Journal of World Trade* **27** (6), pp. 175—86.

Bergeijk, P.A.G. van and R. Lensink, 1993, 'Trade, Capital and the Transition in Central Europe', *Applied Economics* **25** (6), pp. 891—903.

Bernardt, Y., T. van Hoek and M. Koning, 1995, 'Economische effecten van liberalisering van winkeltijden in Nederland' (Economic effects of liberalizing shop-opening hours in the Netherlands; in Dutch), *CPB Working Papers* 74, The Hague: CPB.

Bertola, G., 1991, 'Factor Shares and Savings in Endogenous Growth' *CEPR Discussion Paper Series* 576, London: Centre for Economic Policy Research.

Bhaduri, A. and J. Falkinger, 1990, 'Optimal Price Adjustment Under Imperfect Information', *European Economic Review* **34**, pp. 941—52.

Bhagwati, J.N., 1991, *Political Economy and International Economics*, Cambridge, Mass.: MIT Press.

Blanchard, O.J. and N. Kiyotaki, 1987, 'Monopolistic Competition and the Effects of Aggregate Demand', *American Economic Review* **77** (4), pp. 647—66.

Blanchard, O.J. and L.H. Summers, 1986, 'Hysteresis and the European Unemployment Problem', *NBER Macro Economics Annual*, pp. 15—78.

Blinder, A.S., 1982, 'Inventories and Sticky Prices', *American Economic Review* **72** (3), pp. 334—48.

Bollard, A., 1994, 'New Zealand', in: J. Williamson (ed.), *The Political Economy of Policy Reform*, Washington D.C.: Institute for International Economics, pp. 73—110.

Borensztein, E. and J.D. Ostry, 1994, 'Economic Reform and Structural Adjustment in East European Industry', Paper presented to the American Economic Association, Boston, January 3—5.

Borges, A.M., 1986, 'Applied General Equilibrium Models: An Assessment of Their Usefulness for Policy Analysis', *OECD Economic Studies* (7), pp. 7—43.

Bos, D.I. and P.A.G. van Bergeijk, 1994, 'Structurele hervorming: Ervaringen in Nieuw-Zeeland' (Structural reform: The case of New Zealand; in Dutch), *Economisch-Statistische Berichten* **79** (3989), pp. 1134—8.

Bös, D., 1993, 'Privatization in Europe: A Comparison of Approaches', *Oxford Review of Economic Policy* **9** (1), pp. 95—111.

Bovenberg, A.L., 1985, 'The General Equilibrium Approach: Relevant for Public Policy?', in: *The Relevance of Public Finance for Policy-Making: Proceedings of the 41st Congress of the International Institute of Public Finance,* Detroit: Wayne State University Press, pp. 33—43.

Bovenberg, A.L., 1991, 'Overvloed en onbehagen; over sparen en investeren in Nederland' (Abundance and discomfort: Savings and investment in the Netherlands; in Dutch), inaugural lecture Erasmus University, Rotterdam, January 31.

Brakman, S., 1991, *International Trade Modeling: Decomposition Analyses,* Groningen: Wolters Noordhoff.

Brakman, S., R. Gigengack and C.J. Jepma, 1988, 'The Speed of Adjustment as a Measure for Competitiveness', *Austrian Economic Papers* **1** (3), pp. 161—78.

Brandsma, A., J. op de Beke, L. O'Sullivan and W. Roger, 1991, 'QUEST — A macroeconomic model of the countries of the European Community as part of the world economy', *European Economy* 47, Brussels: European Commission.

Bresnahan, T.F., 1989, 'Empirical Studies of Industries with Market Power', in: R. Schmalensee and R. Willig (eds), *Handbook of Industrial Organization,* Amsterdam: North-Holland, pp. 1011—58.

Brooks, R. and D. Gibbs, 1994, 'A model of the New Zealand economy: Reserve Bank Model XII', *Economic Modelling* **11** (1), pp. 5—86.

Brouwer, E. and A.H. Kleinknecht, 1994, 'Innovatie in de Nederlandse industrie en dienstverlening' (Innovation in Dutch manufacturing and services; in Dutch), *Beleidsstudies Technologie/Economie* 27, The Hague, The Netherlands, September.

Browning, E.K. 1994, 'The non-tax wedge', *Journal of Public Economics* 53, pp. 419—33.

Brozen, Y., 1971, 'Concentration and structural and market disequilibria', *Antitrust Bulletin* 16 (2), pp. 241—8.

Bruno, M. and J. Sachs, 1984, *Economics of Worldwide Stagflation*, Cambridge, Mass.: Harvard University Press.

Bundesministerium für Wirtschaft, 1993, 'Report on Germany's deregulation policy', *BMWi Documentation nr. 333*, Bonn.

Butter, F. den and B. Compaijen, 1991, 'Labour Market Effects of the Social Security System in the Netherlands: A Comparison of Equilibrium with Disequilibrium Simulation Models', *De Economist* 139 (1), pp. 26—42.

Button, K.J. and T.E. Keeler, 1993, 'The Regulation of Transport Markets', *Economic Journal* 103 (419), pp. 1017—27.

Campbell, B., 1993, 'Restructuring the Economy: Canada into the Free Trade Area', in: R. Grinspun and M.A. Cameron (eds), *The Political Economy of North American Free Trade*, Basingstoke and London: Macmillan, pp. 89—104.

Carlton, D.W., 1986, 'The Rigidity of Prices', *American Economic Review* 76 (4), pp. 637—58.

Carlton, D.W., 1989, 'The Theory and Facts of How Markets Clear: Is Industrial Organization Valuable for Understanding Macroeconomics?', in: R. Schmalensee and R.D. Willig (eds), *Handbook of Industrial Organization*, Volume I, Amsterdam: Elsevier Science Publishers, pp. 909—46.

Catinat, M. and A. Italianer, 1988, 'Completing the Internal Market: Primary micro-economic effects and their implementation in macro-econometric models', *Directorate General for Economic and Financial Affairs II/140/88—EN/FR*, Brussels: Commission of the European Communities.

Clarkson, S., 1993, 'Economics: The New Hemispheric Fundamentalism', in: R. Grinspun and M.A. Cameron (eds),

The Political Economy of North American Free Trade, Basingstoke and London: Macmillan, pp. 61—9.

Cohen, W.M. and R.M. Levin, 1989, 'Empirical Studies of Innovation and Market Structure', in: R. Schmalensee and R. Willig (eds), *Handbook of Industrial Organization*, Amsterdam: North-Holland, pp. 1060—107.

Commission of the European Communities, 1994, *White Paper on Growth, Competitiveness and Employment*, Brussels and Luxembourg.

Cornielje, O.J.C. and C. Zeelenberg, 1991, 'Excess Demand in the Keller Model', in: H. Don, T. van de Klundert and J. van Sinderen (eds), *Applied General Equilibrium Modelling*, Dordrecht: Kluwer, pp. 155—74.

Cottarelli, C. and A. Kourelis, 1994, 'Financial Structure, Bank Lending Rates, and the Transmission Mechanism of Monetary Policy', *IMF Staff Papers* **41** (4), pp. 587—623.

Cowling, K. and M. Waterson, 1976, 'Price—Cost Margins and Market Structure', *Economica* **43** (3), pp. 267—74.

Crafts, N., 1992, 'Productivity Growth Reconsidered', *Economic Policy* (October), pp. 387—414.

Cross, R., 1993, 'On the Foundations of Hysteresis in Economic Systems', *Economics and Philosophy* **9**, pp. 53—74.

Cubbin, J.S., 1988, *Market Structure and Performance: The Empirical Research*, London: Harwood.

Cubbin, J.S. and P.A. Geroski, 1990, 'The Persistence of Profits in the United Kingdom', in: D.C. Mueller (ed.), *The Dynamics of Company Profits: An International Comparison*, Cambridge: Cambridge University Press, pp. 147—69.

Curry, B. and K.D. George, 1983, 'Industrial Concentration: A Survey', *Journal of Industrial Economics* **31** (3), pp. 203—53.

Das, B.J., W.F. Chappell and W.F. Shughart, 1993, 'Advertising, Competition and Market Share Instability', *Applied Economics* **25**, pp. 1409—12.

Davies, S., 1988a, 'Concentration', in: S. Davies and B. Lyons (eds), *The Economics of Industrial Organisation*, London: Longman, pp. 73—126.

Davies, S., 1988b, 'Technical Change, Productivity and Market Structure', in: S. Davies and B. Lyons (eds), *The Economics of Industrial Organisation*, London: Longman, pp. 192—246.

Davies, S. and B. Lyons (eds), 1988, *The Economics of Industrial Organisation*, London: Longman.

Dee, P., 1994, 'General Equilibrium Models and Policy Advice in Australia', Paper presented at the IFAC Workshop on Computing in Economics and Finance, Amsterdam, June 8—10.

DeLong, J.B. and L.H. Summers, 1986, 'Is Increased Price Flexibility Stabilizing?', *American Economic Review* **76**, pp. 1031—44.

Dewatripont, M. and G. Roland, 1992, 'Economic reform and dynamic political constraints', *Review of Economic Studies* **59**, pp. 703—30.

Dijksterhuis, G.B., H.J. Heeres and A.J.M. Kleijweg, 1995, 'Indicatoren voor dynamiek' (Indicators of economic dynamism; in Dutch), *Economisch-Statistische Berichten* **80** (4018), pp. 652—7.

Dixit, A.K. and R.S. Pindyck, 1994, *Investment under Uncertainty*, Princeton: Princeton University Press.

Dixon, H. and N. Rankin, 1994, 'Imperfect Competition and Macroeconomics: A Survey', *Oxford Economic Papers* **46**, pp. 171—99.

Dixon, P.B., B.R. Parmenter, A.A. Powell and P.J. Wilcoxen, 1992, *Notes and Problems in Applied General Equilibrium Economics*, Amsterdam: North-Holland.

Dixon, P.B., B.R. Parmenter, J. Sutton and D.P. Vincent, 1982, *ORANI: A Multisectoral Model of the Australian Economy*, Amsterdam: North Holland.

Dixon, R., 1983, 'Industry Structure and the Speed of Price Adjustment', *Journal of Industrial Economics* **23** (1), pp. 25—37.

Domberger, S., 1979, 'Price Adjustment and Market Structure', *Economic Journal* **98** (1), pp. 96—108.

Donni, O. and F. Fecher, 1994, 'Efficiency and productivity of the insurance industry in the OECD countries', mimeo, Liège: University of Liège.

Dornbusch, R., 1988, 'Notes on credibility and stabilization', *NBER Working Paper* 2790, Cambridge.
Douglas, R., 1993, *Unfinished Business*, Glenfield: Random House.
Draper, D.A.G., 1985, 'Exports of Manufacturing Industry: An Econometric Analysis of the Significance of Capacity', *De Economist* **133** (3), pp. 285—305.
Easterly, W., 1993, 'How Much Do Distortions Affect Growth?', *Policy Research Working Paper* 1215, Washington: World Bank.
Easterly, W., R. King, R. Levine and S. Rebelo, 1991, 'How Do National Policies Affect Long Run Growth? A Research Agenda', *World Bank PRE Working Papers* 794, Washington D.C.: World Bank.
Eckard, E.W., 1995, 'A note on the profit—concentration relation', *Applied Economics* **27**, pp. 219—23.
Edwards, S., 1989, 'On the sequencing of structural reforms', *OECD Economics and Statistics Working Paper* 10, Paris: OECD.
Ees, H. van and H. Garretsen, 1990, 'The Right Answers to the Wrong Question? An Assessment of the Microfoundations Debate', *De Economist* **138** (2), pp. 123—45.
Ees, H. van, and H. Garretsen, 1993, 'How to Derive Keynesian Results from First Principles: A Survey of New-Keynesian Economics', *De Economist* **141**, pp. 323—53.
Emerson, M., M. Aujean, M. Catinat, P. Goybet and A. Jacquemin, 1988, *The Economics of 1992: The E.C. Commission's Assessment of the Economic Effects of Completing the Internal Market*, Oxford: Oxford University Press.
Encaoua, D. and P. Geroski, 1986, 'Price dynamics and competition in five OECD countries', *OECD Economic Studies* (6), Paris: OECD, pp. 47—74.
Encaoua, D., P. Geroski and R. Miller, 1983, 'Price Dynamics and Industrial Structure: A Theoretical and Econometric Analysis', *OECD Economics and Statistics Working Paper* 10, Paris: OECD.
Englander, A.S. and A. Gurney, 1994, 'Medium-term determinants of OECD productivity', *OECD Economic Studies* (22), Paris: OECD, pp. 49—109.

ENSR, 1993, *The European Observatory for SMEs: First annual report*, Zoetermeer: European Network for SME Research.

Fane, G., 1995, 'Economic Reform and Deregulation in Australia', *Centre for Economic Policy Research Discussion Paper* 319, Canberra: Australian National University.

Felder, F., 1995, 'The use of data envelopment analysis for the detection of price above the competitive level', *Empirica* 22, pp. 103—13.

Ferguson, P.R., 1988, *Industrial Economics: Issues and Perspectives*, London: Macmillan.

Fernandez, R. and D. Rodrik, 1991, 'Resistance to reform: Status quo bias in the presence of individual-specific uncertainty', *American Economic Review* 81 (5), pp. 1146—55.

Finch, C.D., 1994, 'Comment', in: J. Williamson (ed.), *The Political Economy of Policy Reform*, Washington D.C.: Institute for International Economics, pp. 114—17.

Frey, B.S. and R. Eichenberger, 1993, 'American and European Economics and Economists', *Journal of Economic Perspectives* 7 (4), pp. 185—93.

Funke, N., 1993, 'Timing and sequencing of reforms: Competing views and the role of credibility', *Kyklos* 46 (3), pp. 337—62.

Galal, A., L. Jones, P. Tandon and I. Vogelsang, 1994, *Welfare Consequences of Selling Public Enterprises: An Empirical Analysis*, Oxford: Oxford University Press.

Galbraith, J.K., 1952, *American Capitalism: The concept of countervailing power*, Boston: Houghton Mifflin.

Gali, J., 1992, 'How Well Does the IS—LM Model Fit Postwar U.S. Data?', *Quarterly Journal of Economics* 107 (2), pp. 709—38.

Gali, J., 1994, 'Monopolistic competition, endogenous markups, and growth', *European Economic Review* 38 (3/4), pp. 748—56.

Garman, D.M. and D.J. Richards, 1991, 'Monetary Shocks, Market Structure and Administered Prices', *Southern Economic Journal* 58, pp. 29—42.

Garnaut, R., 1994, 'Australia', in: J. Williamson (ed.), *The Political Economy of Policy Reform*, Washington D.C.: Institute for International Economics, pp. 51—72.

Geelhoed, L.A., 1993, 'Deregulering, herregulering en zelf-regulering' (Deregulation, reregulation and self regulation; in

Dutch), in: Ph. Eijlander, P.C. Gilhaus and J.A.F. Peters (eds), *Overheid en zelfregulering*, Amsterdam: Tjeenk Willink.

Geelhoed, L.A., 1994, 'EMU: A Challenge for National Policy', in: *Is European Monetary Union Dead?*, *PMI Discussion Paper* 3, Brussels: Philip Morris Institute for Public Policy Research, pp. 40—47.

Gelauff, G.M.M., 1992, 'Taxation, Social Security and the Labour Market: An applied general equilibrium model for the Netherlands', Ph.D. Thesis, Tilburg University.

Gelauff, G.M.M. and J.J. Graafland, 1994, *Modelling Welfare State Reform*, Amsterdam: North-Holland.

Gent, C. van, 1996, 'New Dutch Competition Policy: A revolution without revolutionaries' Paper presented at the Conference 'Economic Science: An Art or an Asset?' The Hague, January.

Geroski, P.A., 1990, 'Modeling Persistent Profitability', in: D.C. Mueller (ed.), *The Dynamics of Company Profits: An International Comparison*, Cambridge: Cambridge University Press, pp. 15—34.

Geroski, P.A., 1991, *Market Dynamics and Entry*, Cambridge: Basil Blackwell.

Geroski, P.A., 1992, 'Price Dynamics in UK Manufacturing: A Microeconomic View', *Economica* 59 (236), pp. 403—21.

Geroski, P.A. and R. Masson, 1987, 'Dynamic Market Models in Industrial Organization', *International Journal of Industrial Organization* 5, pp. 1—14.

Geroski, P.A. and D.C. Mueller, 1990, 'The Persistence of Profits in Perspective', in: D.C. Mueller (ed.), *The Dynamics of Company Profits: An International Comparison*, Cambridge: Cambridge University Press, pp. 187—211.

Geroski, P.A. and J. Schwalbach, 1991, *Entry and Market Contestability*, Cambridge: Basil Blackwell.

Gerster, H.J., 1984, *Flexibilität und Rigidität in der Preisbewegung* (Flexibility and rigidity in price changes; in German), Frankfurt am Main: Peter Lang.

Giersch, H., 1994, 'Economic Dynamism: Lessons from German experience', Paper presented at the fifth conference of the International Joseph A. Schumpeter Society, Münster, August 17—20.

Goldin, I., O. Knudsen and A.S. Brandão (eds), 1994, *Modelling Economy-wide Reforms*, Paris: OECD Development Centre.

Gordon, D.M., 1994, 'From Prosperity to Stagnation in the Post-War Economy', in: M.A. Bernstein and D.E. Adler, *Understanding American Economic Decline*, Cambridge: Cambridge University Press, pp. 34—76.

Gordon, R.J., 1990, 'What is New-Keynesian Economics?', *Journal of Economic Literature* 28 (3), pp. 1115—71.

Graafland, J.J., 1992, 'From Philips Curve to Wage Curve', *De Economist* 140, pp. 91—104.

Gradus, R.H.J.M., 1994, 'Nederlandse economie relatief rigide in Europa' (Dutch economy relatively rigid; in Dutch), *Economisch Statistische Berichten* 79 (3928), pp. 921—4.

Gradus, R.H.J.M., 1995, 'The Economic Effects of Extending Shop Opening Hours in The Netherlands', Paper presented at the 51st Congress of the International Institute of Public Finance, Lisbon, August 21—24.

Grimmond, A., 1989, 'Preliminary analysis of sectoral effects', NZIER 89/10, Wellington.

Gruen, F.H., 1986, 'How Bad is Australia's Economic Peformance and Why?' *Economic Record*, pp. 180—93.

Gual, J. and D. Neven, 1992, 'Deregulation of the European Banking Industry (1980—1991)', *CEPR Discussion Paper* 703, London: Centre for Economic Policy Research.

Haaland, J.I. and I. Wooton, 1991, 'Market Integration, Competition and Welfare', *CEPR Discussion Paper* 574, London: Centre for Economic Policy Research.

Haffner, R.C.G., 1993, 'Measuring Market Dynamics: A survey for product markets in the Netherlands', mimeo, The Hague: Ministry of Economic Affairs.

Haffner, R.C.G. and P.A.G. van Bergeijk, 1994, 'The Economic Consequences of Dutch Politics', *De Economist* 142 (4), pp. 497—505.

Hall, R.E., 1986, 'Market Structure and Macroeconomic Fluctuations', *Brookings Papers on Economic Activity* 2, pp. 285—322.

Hamilton, B., S. Mohammad and J. Whalley, 1988, 'Applied General Equilibrium Analysis and Perspective on Growth

Performance', *Journal of Policy Modeling* **10** (2), pp. 281—97.

Harrison, D.M., 1995, *The Organization of Europe: Developing a continental market order*, London and New York: Routledge.

Heijdra, B., 1995, 'Fiscal Policy in a Dynamic Model of Monopolistic Competition', mimeo, Amsterdam: Amsterdam University.

Heijdra, B. and D.P. Broer, 1993, 'Fiscal and Monetary Policy in a Dynamic Model of Imperfect Competition', mimeo, Rotterdam: Erasmus University.

Held, A., 1993, 'Deregulierung in Deutschland — Ein Erfolg?' (Deregulation in Germany — A success?; in German), *Wissenschaft für die Praxis* **4**, pp. 215—20.

Helm, D., C. Mayer and K. Mayhew, 1991, 'The Assessment: Microeconomic Policy', *Oxford Review of Economic Policy* **7** (3), pp. 1—12.

Hersough, T., 1984, 'Union wage responses to tax changes', *Oxford Economic Papers* **36**, pp. 35—51.

Hettich, W. and S.L. Winer, 1993, 'Economic Efficiency, Political Institutions and Policy Analysis', *Kyklos* **46** (1), pp. 3—26.

Hirschman, A.O., 1990, 'The Case Against "One Thing at a Time"', *World Development* **18** (8), pp. 1119—22.

Hoekman, B. and G. Pohl, 1995, 'Enterprise restructuring in Eastern Europe: How much? How fast? Where? Preliminary evidence from trade data', *Policy Research Working Paper* 1433, Washington D.C.: World Bank.

IMF, 1995, 'IMF Conditionality: Experience under stand-by and extended arrangements', *IMF Occasional Papers* 128 and 129, Washington D.C.

Independent Committee of Inquiry (Hilmer Report), 1993, *National Competition Policy*, Canberra: Australian Government Publishing Service.

Industry Commission, 1995, *The Growth and Revenue Implications of Hilmer and Related Reforms: A Report by the Industry Commission to the Council of Australian Governments*, Industry Commission: Belconnen Act.

Ito, T., 1980, 'Disequilibrium Growth Theory', *Journal of Economic Theory* **23**, pp. 380—409.

Jacquemin, A., 1995, 'Capitalism, competition, cooperation', *De Economist* **143** (1), pp. 1—14.

Jacquemin, A., 1996, 'Industrial Organisation and Competition Policy: Which Links?', Paper presented at the conference 'Economic Science: An Art or an Asset', The Hague, 18 January.

Jenny, F.Y. and A.P. Weber, 1976, 'Profit Rates and Structural Variables in French Manufacturing Industries', *European Economic Review* **7**, pp. 187—206.

Jenny, F.Y. and A.P. Weber, 1990, 'The Persistence of Profits in France', in: D.C. Mueller (ed.), *The Dynamics of Company Profits: An International Comparison*, Cambridge: Cambridge University Press, pp. 123—9.

Jong, H.W. de, 1989, *Dynamische markttheorie* (Dynamic market theory; in Dutch), Leiden: Stenfert Kroese.

Kambhampati, U.S., 1995, 'The Persistence of Profit Differentials in Indian Industry', *Applied Economics* **27**, pp. 353—61.

Keller, W.J., 1980, *Tax Incidence: A General Equilibrium Model*, Amsterdam: North-Holland.

Kelly, G.M., 1995, 'Structural change in New Zealand: Some implications for the labour market regime', *International Labour Review* **134** (3), pp. 333—59.

Kendall, M. and A. Stuart, 1977, *The Advanced Theory of Statistics*, Vol. 1, Fourth edition, London: Griffin & Company.

Kessides, I.N., 1990, 'The Persistence of Profits in US Manufacturing Industries', in: D.C. Mueller (ed.), *The Dynamics of Company Profits: An International Comparison*, Cambridge: Cambridge University Press, pp. 77—105.

Keynes, J.M., 1936, *The General Theory of Employment, Interest and Money*, Collected Writings VII, London: Macmillan.

Khan, M.S., 1990, 'The Macroeconomic Effects of Fund-Supported Adjustment Programs', *IMF Staff Papers* **37** (2), pp. 195—231.

Khemani, R.S. and D.M. Shapiro, 1990, 'The Persistence of Profits in Canada', in: D.C. Mueller (ed.), *The Dynamics of Company Profits: An International Comparison*, Cambridge: Cambridge University Press, pp. 77—105.

220   *Privatization, Deregulation and the Macroeconomy*

Killick, T. (ed.), 1995, *The Flexible Economy: Causes and consequences of the adaptability of national economies*, London and New York: Routledge.

Kleijweg, A.J.M., 1993, 'Persistence of Profits and Competitiveness in Dutch Manufacturing', *EIM/Fundamental Research* 9301/E, Zoetermeer.

Kleijweg, A.J.M. and M.H.C. Lever, 1994, 'Entry and Exit in Dutch Manufacturing Industries', *EIM/Fundamental Research* 9409/E, Zoetermeer.

Kleijweg, A.J.M. and H.R. Nieuwenhuijsen, 1995, 'Winstpersistentie in de Nederlandse Industrie 1978—91' (Persistence of profits in Dutch manufacturing 1978—91; in Dutch) *EIM Fundamental Research*, Zoetermeer.

Kornai, J., 1992, 'The Principles of Privatization in Eastern Europe', *De Economist* **140** (2), 153—76.

Kotler, P., 1980, *Principles of Marketing*, New Jersey: Englewood Cliffs.

Koutsoyiannis, A., 1979, *Modern Microeconomics*, Second edition, London: Macmillan.

Koutsoyiannis, A., 1982, *Non-Price Decisions: The firm in a modern context*, London: Macmillan.

Kremers, J.J.M., 1991, 'Naar een sterkere binnenlandse groeidynamiek' (Improving dynamism in sheltered sectors; in Dutch), *Economisch Statistische Berichten* **76**, pp. 1228—32.

Kremers, J.J.M. (ed.), 1993, *Inspelen op Europa* (The European challenge; in Dutch), Schoonhoven: Academic Service.

Krugman, P.R. (ed.), 1986, *Strategic Trade Policy and the New International Economics*, Cambridge, Mass.: MIT Press.

Kühn, K.-U., P. Seabright and A. Smith, 1992, 'Competition Policy Research: Where do we stand?', *CEPR Occasional Paper* 8, London: Centre for Economic Policy Research.

Kuipers, S.K., 1990, 'Stabilisation Policy: A Non-Market Clearing View', in: K. Groenveld, J.A.H. Maks and J. Muysken (eds) *Economic Policy and the Market Process: Austrian and Mainstream Economics*, Amsterdam: North-Holland, pp. 233—55.

Kuipers, S.K., 1991, *Marktwerking en werkloosheid in Nederland in de jaren dertig en tachtig* (The functioning of markets and unemployment in the Netherlands in the 1930s and 1980s; in Dutch), Amsterdam: Koninklijke Nederlandse Akademie van Wetenschappen.

Lang, K., 1993, 'The effects of trade liberalization on wages and employment: The case of New Zealand', mimeo, Cambridge, Mass.: NBER.

Layard, R., S. Nickell and R. Jackman, 1991, *Unemployment: Macroeconomic performance and the labour market*, Oxford: Oxford University Press.

Leamer, E.E. and R.M. Stern, 1970, *Quantitative International Economics*, Boston: Allyn & Bacon.

Levine, R. and D. Renelt, 1992, 'A Sensitivity Analysis of Cross-country Growth Regressions', *American Economic Review* **82** (4), pp. 942—64.

Levine, R. and S.J. Zervos, 1993, 'What We Have Learned About Policy and Growth from Cross-Country Regressions', *American Economic Review* **83** (2), pp. 426—30.

Lieberman, M.B., 1987, 'Excess Capacity as a Barrier to Entry: An Empirical Appraisal', *Journal of Industrial Economics* **35** (4), pp. 607—27.

Lipschitz, L., J. Kremers, T. Mayer and D. McDonald, 1989, 'The Federal Republic of Germany: Adjustment in a Surplus Country', *IMF Occasional Paper* 64, Washington D.C.

Lipsey, R.G., and K. Lancaster, 1956, 'The General Theory of Second Best', *Review of Economic Studies* **24** (1), pp. 11—32.

Love, J.H., 1995, 'The Measurement of Entry Rates: Reconsideration and Resolution, *Empirica* **22**, pp. 151—157.

Lucas, R.E., 1976, 'Econometric Policy Evaluations: A Critique', *Journal of Monetary Economics* Suppl. (April) (K. Brunner and E. Meltze (eds)), pp. 19—46.

Lyons, B., 1988, 'Barriers to entry', in: S. Davies and B. Lyons (eds), *The Economics of Industrial Organisation*, London: Longman, pp. 26—72.

MacDonald, J.M., 1994, 'Does Import Competition Force Efficient Production?', *The Review of Economics and Statistics* **76**, pp. 721—7.

Maddison, A., 1987, 'Growth and Slowdown in Advanced Capitalist Economies: Techniques of quantitative assessment', *Journal of Economic Literature* **25**, pp. 649—98.

Maddison, A., 1991, *Dynamic Forces in Capitalist Development: A Long Run Comparative View*, Oxford: Oxford University Press.

Maks, J.A.H., 1995, 'Economic Theory and Competition Policy in the Netherlands', in: G. Meijer (ed.) *New Perspectives on Austrian Economics*, London: Routledge & Kegan Paul [in print].

Malinvaud, E., 1978, *The Theory of Unemployment Reconsidered*, Oxford: Basil Blackwell.

Mankiw, N.G., 1985, 'Small Menu Costs and Large Business Cycles: A Macroeconomic Model of Monopoly', *Quarterly Journal of Economics* **100** (2), pp. 529—38.

Mankiw, N.G., 1990, 'A Quick Refresher Guide in Macroeconomics', *Journal of Economic Literature* **28**, pp. 1645—60.

Mankiw, N.G. and D. Romer, 1991, *New Keynesian Economics*, Cambridge, Mass.: MIT Press.

Marrewijk, C. van and J. Verbeek, 1993, *Disequilibrium Growth Theory: An application of the Filippov solution to economics*, Aldershot, etc.: Avebury.

Marris, R. and D.C. Mueller, 1980, 'The Corporation, Competition and the Invisible Hand', *Journal of Economic Literature* **18**, pp. 32—63.

Martin, S., 1993a, *Advanced Industrial Economics*, Cambridge: Blackwell Publishers.

Martin, S., 1993b, 'Price Adjustment and Market Structure', *Economics Letters* **41**, pp. 139—43.

Mason, E.S., 1939, 'Price and Production Policies of Large-Scale Enterprise', *American Economic Review* **29**, pp. 61—74.

Mayer, T., 1989, 'Economic Structure, the Exchange Rate, and Adjustment in the Federal Republic of Germany: A General Equilibrium Approach', *IMF Staff Papers* **36** (2), pp. 435—63.

Mayer T., 1993, *Truth versus Precision in Economics*, Aldershot: Edward Elgar.

Mayes, D., C. Harris and M. Lansbury, 1994, *Inefficiency in Industry*, New York: Harvester Wheatsheaf.

References 223

Mayes, D. and P. Hart, 1994, *The Single Market Programme as a Stimulus to Change: Comparisons between Britain and Germany*, Cambridge: Cambridge University Press.

McAuley, A., 1993, 'The Political Economy of Privatisation', in: L. Somogyi (ed.), *The Political Economy of the Transition Process in Eastern Europe*, Aldershot: Edward Elgar, pp. 189—207.

McKinsey Global Institute, 1994, *Employment Performance*, Washington D.C.

Meadows, D.H., D.L. Meadows, J. Randers and W.L. Behrens, 1972, *The Limits to Growth*, New York: Universe Books.

Ministry of Economic Affairs, 1990, *Economy with Open Frontiers*, The Hague: Ministry of Economic Affairs.

Ministry of Economic Affairs, 1994, *Adviesaanvraag aan de Sociaal-Economische Raad en de Commissie Economische Mededinging inzake een Nieuwe Mededingingswet* (Request of opinion of the Social Economic Council and the Competition Council on a new Competition Law; in Dutch), The Hague.

Morrison, J.R., 1995, 'Record of IMF-supported Adjustment Programs Assessed', *IMF Survey*, July 31, pp. 233—6.

Mueller, D.C. (ed.), 1990a, *The Dynamics of Company Profits: An International Comparison*, Cambridge: Cambridge University Press.

Mueller, D.C., 1990b, 'Profits and the Process of Competition', in: D.C. Mueller (ed.), *The Dynamics of Company Profits: An International Comparison*, Cambridge: Cambridge University Press, pp. 1—14.

Mueller, D.C., 1990c, 'The Persistence of Profits in the United States', in: D.C. Mueller (ed.), *The Dynamics of Company Profits: An International Comparison*, Cambridge: Cambridge University Press, pp. 35—59.

Mueller, D.C., 1991, 'Entry, Exit and the Competitive Process', in: P.A. Geroski and J. Schwalbach (eds), *Entry and Market Contestability*, Cambridge: Basil Blackwell, pp. 1—23.

Naert, F., 1984, 'De politieke economie van pressiegroepen' (The political economy of pressure groups; in Dutch), *Economisch-Statistische Berichten* **69**, pp. 56—61.

Neuber, A., 1995, 'Adapting the Economies of Eastern Europe: Behavioural and Institutional Aspects of Flexibility', in: T. Killick (ed.), *The Flexible Economy: Causes and consequences of the adaptability of national economies*, London and New York: Routledge, pp. 111—53.

Neumann, M., I. Böbel and A. Haid, 1985, 'Domestic Concentration, Foreign Trade and Economic Performance', *International Journal of Industrial Organization* 3, pp. 1—19.

Neven, D. and L.H. Röller, 1995, *Competition in the European Banking Industry*, Berlin: Wissenschaftszentrum Berlin.

Norman, V.D., 1990, 'Assessing Trade and Welfare Effects of Trade Liberalisation: A Comparison of Alternative Approaches to CGE Modelling with Imperfect Competition', *European Economic Review* 34, pp. 725—51.

North, D.C., 1994, 'Economic Performance Through Time', *American Economic Review* 84, pp. 359—368.

Odagiri, H. and H. Yamawaki, 1990, 'The Persistence of Profits: International Comparison', in: D.C. Mueller (ed.), *The Dynamics of Company Profits: An International Comparison*, Cambridge: Cambridge University Press, pp. 169—85.

OECD, 1983, *Positive Adjustment Policies: Managing Structural Change*, Paris: OECD.

OECD, 1987a, *Structural Adjustment and Economic Performance*, Paris: OECD.

OECD, 1987b, *Structural Adjustment and Economic Performance*, synthesis report, Paris: OECD.

OECD, 1990, *Progress in Structural Reform*, Paris: OECD.

OECD, 1992, *Progress in Structural Reform: An overview*, Paris: OECD.

OECD, 1993a, *Economic Surveys 1993/1994, New Zealand*, Paris: OECD.

OECD, 1993b, *Economic Surveys 1993/1994, The Netherlands*, Paris: OECD.

OECD, 1994a, *Assessing Structural Reform: Lessons for the Future*, Paris: OECD.

OECD, 1994b, *Economic Surveys 1993/1994, Japan*, Paris: OECD.

OECD, 1994c, *Economic Surveys 1993/1994, New Zealand*, Paris: OECD.

OECD, 1994d, *Employment Outlook*, Paris: OECD.

Okun, A.M., 1981, *Prices and Quantities: A Macroeconomic Analysis*, Oxford: Basil Blackwell.

Olson, M., 1982, *The Rise and Decline of Nations*, London: Yale University Press.

Ostry, J.D., 1993, 'Selective government interventions and economic growth: A survey of the Asian experience and its applicability to New Zealand', *IMF paper on policy analysis and assessment PPAA/93/17* October, Washington D.C.: IMF.

Paech, N., 1995, *Die Wirkung Potentieller Konkurrenz auf das Preissetzungsverhalten etablierter Firmen bei Abwesenheit Strategischer Asymmetrien* (The impact of potential competition on pricing policies of established firms in the absence of strategic asymmetries; in German), Berlin: Duncker & Humblot.

Parker, K.T., 1986, 'Global Modelling: The Techniques, the History and the Way Ahead', in C. Betton and R.M. O'Keefe (eds), *Recent Developments in OR*, Oxford, pp. 85—106.

Peeters, M., 1987, 'A Dismal Science: An Essay on New Classical Economics', *De Economist* 135 (4), pp. 442—66.

Peltzman, S., 1989, 'The Economic Theory of Regulation after a Decade of Deregulation', *Brookings Papers on Economic Activity: Microeconomics*, pp. 1—41.

Persson, T. and L.E.O. Svensson, 1983, 'Is Optimism Good in a Keynesian Economy?', *Economica* 50, pp. 291—300.

Persson, T. and G. Tabellini, 1994, 'Is Inequality Harmful for Growth?', *American Economic Review* 84 (3), pp. 600—21.

Phlips L., 1980, 'Inter-temporal Price Discrimination and Sticky Prices', *Quarterly Journal of Economics* 94 (3), pp. 525—42.

Porter, M.E., 1985, *Competitive Advantage: Creating and Sustaining Superior Performance*, New York: The Free Press.

Porter, M.E., 1990a, *The Competitive Advantage of Nations*, London and Basingstoke: Macmillan.

Porter, M.E., 1990b, 'Europe's companies after 1992: Don't collaborate, compete', *The Economist*, June 9, pp. 17—21.

Posner, R.A., 1971, 'Taxation by Regulation', *Bell Journal of Economics and Management* 2, pp. 22—50.

Powell, A.A. and T. Lawson, 1990, 'A Decade of Applied General Equilibrium Modelling for Policy Work', in: L. Bergsman, D. Jorgenson and E. Zalai (eds), *General Equilibrium Modelling and Economic Policy Analysis*, Oxford: Basil Blackwell, pp. 241—90.

Powell, A.A. and R.H. Snape, 1993, 'The Contribution of Applied General Equilibrium Analysis to Policy Reform in Australia', *Journal of Policy Modeling* **15** (4), pp. 393—414.

Rankin, N., 1994, 'Micro Foundations of International Macroeconomics', in: F. van der Ploeg (ed.), *The Handbook of International Macroeconomics*, Oxford: Basil Blackwell, pp. 1—26.

Reserve Bank of New Zealand, 1994, *Research News* **1** (1), December.

Richardson, P., 1988, 'The Structure and Simulation Properties of OECD's INTERLINK Model', *OECD Economic Studies* **10**, pp. 57—119.

Robinson, S. and L. D'Andrea Tyson, 1984, 'Modelling structural adjustment: Micro and macro elements in a general equilibrium framework', in: H.E. Scarf and J.B. Shoven (eds), *Applied General Equilibrium Analysis*, Cambridge: Cambridge University Press, pp. 243—74.

Rodrik, D., 1989, 'Promises, promises: Credible policy reform via signalling', *Economic Journal* **99**, pp. 756—72.

Rodrik, D., 1993, 'The positive economics of policy reform', *American Economic Review* **83** (2), pp. 356—61.

Roeger, W., 1995, 'Can imperfect competition explain the difference between primal and dual productivity measures? Estimates for US manufacturing', *Journal of Political Economy* **103** (2), pp. 316—30.

Roemer, J.E., 1994, *Egalitarian Perspectives: Essays in philosophical economics*, Cambridge: Cambridge University Press.

Roland, G., 1994, 'On the speed and sequencing of privatization and restructuring', *Economic Journal* **104** (426), pp. 1158—68.

Rooy, Y.C.M.T. van, 1994, 'Deregulation in The Netherlands', in: D.I. Bos (ed.), *OCFEB Papers and Proceedings* 9402, pp. 1—8.

Ross, S.A. and M.L. Wachter, 1975, 'Pricing and timing decisions in oligopoly industries', *Quarterly Journal of Economics* **89** (1), pp. 115—37.

Sachs, J., 1994, 'Life in the economic emergency room', in: J. Williamson (ed.), *The Political Economy of Policy Reform*, Washington D.C.: Institute for International Economics, pp. 503—23.

Sala-i-Martin, X., 1990, 'Lecture Notes on Economic Growth', *NBER Working Papers* 3563 and 3564, Cambridge: NBER.

Sala-i-Martin, X., 1994, 'Cross-sectional regressions and the empirics of economic growth', *European Economic Review* **38** (3/4), pp. 739—47.

Savage, J., 1990a, 'Policy issues', in: J. Savage and A. Bollard (eds), 1990, *Turning it Around: Closure and revitalization in New Zealand industry,* Melbourne: Oxford University Press, pp. 27—36.

Savage, J., 1990b, 'Summary and conclusions', in: J. Savage and A. Bollard (eds), 1990, *Turning it Around: Closure and revitalization in New Zealand industry,* Melbourne: Oxford University Press, pp. 139—45.

Savage, J. and A. Bollard (eds), 1990, *Turning it Around: Closure and revitalization in New Zealand industry,* Melbourne: Oxford University Press.

Schaik, A.B.T.M. van, 1991, *Marktruiming en inflatie* (Market clearance and inflation; in Dutch), Tilburg: Tilburg University Press.

Scherer, F.M., 1980, *Industrial Market Structure and Economic Performance*, Second edition, Chicago: Rand McNally.

Scherer, F.M., 1986, *Innovation and Growth: Schumpeterian Perspectives*, Cambridge, Mass./London: MIT Press.

Scherer, F.M. and D. Ross, 1990, *Industrial Market Structure and Economic Performance*, Third edition, Boston: Houghton Mifflin.

Schmalensee, R., 1989, 'Inter-industry Studies of Structure and Performance', in: R. Schmalensee and R. Willig (eds.), *Handbook of Industrial Organization*, Amsterdam: North-Holland, pp. 951—1009.

Schmidt-Hebbel, K. and L. Serven, 1994, 'Dynamic Response to External Shocks in Classical and Keynesian Economies', *PPR Working Paper* 1300, Washington D.C.: World Bank.

Schumpeter, J.A., (1934) 1983, *The Theory of Economic Development: An inquiry into profits, capital, credit, interest and the business cycle*, New Brunswick: Transaction Publishers.

Schumpeter, J.A., 1943, *Capitalism, Socialism and Democracy*, London: Allen & Unwin.

Schwalbach, J. and T. Mahmood, 1990, 'The Persistence of Profits in the Federal Republic of Germany', in: D.C. Mueller (ed.), *The Dynamics of Company Profits: An International Comparison*, Cambridge: Cambridge University Press, pp. 105—23.

Scott, J.T., 1993, *Purposive Diversification and Economic Performance*, Cambridge, Mass.: Cambridge University Press.

Sexton, R.L., 1995, *Microeconomics*, London: Prentice Hall.

Sheffrin, S.M., 1989, *The Making of Economic Policy: History, Theory, Politics*, Oxford: Basil Blackwell.

Shoven, J.B. and J. Whalley, 1984, 'Applied General Equilibrium Models of Taxation and International Trade', *Journal of Economic Literature* **22** (3), pp. 1007—51.

Siklos, P.L., 1995, 'The Demand for Money in New Zealand in an Era of Institutional Change: Evidence from the 1981—1994 Period', *Reserve Bank of New Zealand Discussion Paper Series G95/3*.

Silvestre, J., 1987, 'Fixprice models', in: J. Eatwell et al. (eds), *The New Palgrave: General Equilibrium*, London and Basingstoke: Macmillan, pp. 145—53.

Silvestre, J., 1993, 'The Market—Power Foundations of Macroeconomic Policy', *Journal of Economic Literature* **31** (1), pp. 105—41.

Sinderen, J. van, 1993, 'Taxation and Economic Growth', *Economic Modelling* **10** (3), pp. 285—300.

Sinderen, J. van, P.A.G. van Bergeijk, R.C.G. Haffner and P.M. Waasdorp, 1994, 'De kosten van economische verstarring op macro-niveau', (The macroeconomic costs of economic inertia;

in Dutch), *Economisch-Statistische Berichten* **79** (3954), pp. 274—9.

Smith, A. and A.J. Venables, 1988, 'Completing the Internal Market in the European Community: Some Industry Simulations', *European Economic Review* **32** (7), pp. 1501—25.

Smulders, S., 1994, 'Growth, Market Structure and the Environment: Essays on the theory of endogenous economic growth', Ph.D. Thesis, Tilburg University.

Smulders, S. and T. van de Klundert, 1995, 'Imperfect competition, concentration and growth with firm-specific R&D', *European Economic Review* **39** (1), pp. 139—60.

Snower, D.J., 1993, 'The Future of the Welfare State', *Economic Journal* **103** (418), pp. 700—17.

Solow, R.M., 1956, 'A contribution to the theory of economic growth', *The Quarterly Journal of Economics*, **70**, pp. 65—94.

Solow, R.M., 1992, 'Policies for economic growth', *De Economist* **140** (1), pp. 1—15.

Somogyi, L. and A. Török, 1993, 'Property Rights, Competition Policy, and Privatisation in the Transition from Socialism to Market Economy', in: L. Somogyi (ed.), *The Political Economy of the Transition Process in Eastern Europe*, Aldershot: Edward Elgar, pp. 208—26.

Srinivasan, T.N. and J. Whalley (eds), 1986, *General Equilibrium Trade Policy Modeling*, Cambridge, Mass. and London: MIT Press.

Stevens, B., 1992, 'Prospects for Privatization in OECD Countries', *National Westminster Bank Quarterly Review* (August), pp. 2—22.

Stigler G.J., 1978, 'The Literature of Economics: The Case of the Kinked Oligopoly Demand Curve', *Economic Inquiry* **16** (2), pp. 185—204.

Stiglitz, J.E., 1984, 'Price Rigidities and Market Structure', *American Economic Review* **74**, pp. 350—55.

Swamy, P.A.V.B. and G.S. Tavlas, 1989, 'Financial Deregulation, the Demand for Money and Monetary Policy in Australia', *IMF Staff Papers* **36** (1), pp. 63—101.

Swank, J., 1994, 'Bank Behaviour and Monetary Policy in the Netherlands', Ph.D. Thesis, Free University of Amsterdam.

Syrquin, M., 1995, 'Flexibility and Long-Term Economic Development', in: T. Killick (ed.), *The Flexible Economy: Causes and consequences of the adaptability of national economies*, London and New York: Routledge, pp. 34—63.

Thirlwall, T., 1992, 'The balance of payments and economic performance', *National Westminster Bank Quarterly Review* (May), pp. 2—11.

Thurik, A.R., 1994, 'Dynamiek en kleinschaligheid' (Small business presence and economic dynamism; in Dutch), *Economisch-Statistische Berichten* **79** (3973), pp. 732—7.

Tinbergen, J., 1936, 'An economic policy for 1936', in: L.H. Klaassen, L.M. Koyck and H.J. Witteveen (eds), 1959, *Jan Tinbergen, Selected Papers*, Amsterdam: North-Holland, pp. 37—84 (original in Dutch).

Tinbergen, J., 1952, *On the Theory of Economic Policy*, Amsterdam: North-Holland.

Tinbergen, J., 1967, *Economic Policy: Principles and Design*, Amsterdam: North-Holland.

Tobin, J., 1993, 'Price Flexibility and Output Stability: An Old Keynesian View', *Journal of Economic Perspectives* **7**, pp. 45—65.

Turner, D., P. Richardson and S. Rauffet, 1993, 'The role of real and nominal rigidities in macroeconomic adjustment: A comparative study of the G3 economies', *OECD Economic Studies* **21**, pp. 90—137.

United Nations Economic Commission for Europe (UNECE), 1993, *Economic Survey of Europe in 1992—1993*, New York: United Nations.

United Nations Economic Commission for Europe (UNECE), 1994, *Economic Survey of Europe in 1993—1994*, New York: United Nations.

Valdés, J.G., 1995, *Pinochet's Economists: The Chicago School in Chile*, Cambridge, Mass.: Cambridge University Press.

Venables, A.J., 1990, 'The Economic Integration of Oligopolistic Markets', *European Economic Review* **34**, pp. 753—73.

Vickers, J. and G.K. Yarrow, 1988, *Privatization: An Economic Analysis*, Cambridge, Mass.: MIT Press.

References   231

Vickers, J. and G.K. Yarrow, 1991, 'Economic Perspectives on Privatization', *Journal of Economic Perspectives* **5** (2), pp. 111—32.

Vincent, D.P., 1990, 'Applied General Equilibrium Modelling in the Australian Industries Assistance Commission: Perspective of a Policy Analyst', in: L. Bergman, D. Jorgenson and E. Zalai (eds), *General Equilibrium Modelling and Economic Policy Analysis*, Oxford: Basil Blackwell, pp. 291—347.

Wegberg, M. van, A. van Witteloostuijn and M. Roscam Abbing, 1994, 'Multimarket and multiproject collusion: Why European integration may reduce intra-community competition', *De Economist* **142** (3), pp. 253—85.

Weiss, C.R., 1993, *Preisrigidität und Marktstruktur: eine Theoretische und Empirische Analyse* (Price rigidity and market structure: Theoretical and empirical analyses; in German), Frankfurt/Main: Peter Lang.

Weiss, C.R., 1994a, 'Market Structure and Pricing Behaviour in Austrian Manufacturing', *Empirica* **21**, pp. 115—31.

Weiss, C.R., 1994b, 'Market Power and the Cyclical Behaviour of Labour Demand', mimeo, Harvard University.

Welfens, P.J.J., 1993, 'Privatization and foreign direct investment in the East European transformation: Theory, options and strategies', in: L. Csaba (ed.), *Privatization, Liberalization and Destruction: Recreating the Market in Central and Eastern Europe*, Aldershot etc.: Dartmouth, pp. 35—68.

Wijnbergen, S. van, 1987, 'Government Deficits, Private Investment and the Current Account: An Intertemporal Disequilibrium Analysis', *Economic Journal* **97**, pp. 596—615.

Wijnbergen, S. van, 1992, 'Intertemporal speculation, shortages and the political economy of price reform', *Economic Journal* **102**, pp. 1395—406.

Wijnstok, J.C., 1995, *De snelheid van prijsaanpassing in Nederlandse sectoren* (The speed of price adjustment in Dutch industries; in Dutch), The Netherlands: Ministry of Economic Affairs and Erasmus University Rotterdam.

Wilkinson, B.W., 1993, 'Trade Liberalization, the Market Ideology and Morality: Have We a Sustainable System?', in: R. Grinspun and M.A. Cameron (eds), *The Political Economy of*

North American Free Trade, Basingstoke and London: Macmillan, pp. 27—44.

Willenbockel, D., 1994, *Applied General Equilibrium Modelling: Imperfect competition and European integration*, Chichester, etc.: John Wiley.

Williamson, J. (ed.), 1994, *The Political Economy of Policy Reform*, Washington D.C.: Institute for International Economics.

Williamson, J. and S. Haggard, 1994, 'The political conditions for economic reform', in: J. Williamson (ed.), *The Political Economy of Policy Reform*, Washington D.C.: Institute for International Economics, pp. 525—96.

Winston, C., 1993, 'Economic Deregulation: Days of Reckoning for Microeconomists', *Journal of Economic Literature* **31**, pp. 1263—89.

World Bank, 1988, 'Techniques of Privatization of State-Owned Enterprises', *World Bank Technical Paper* 89, Washington D.C.: World Bank.

World Bank, 1991a, 'The basics of antitrust policy', *World Bank Technical Paper 160*, Washington D.C.: World Bank.

World Bank, 1991b, *World Development Report 1991*, Washington D.C.: World Bank.

World Bank, 1994, *World Development Report 1994*, Washington D.C.: World Bank.

World Commission on Environment and Development (WCED), 1987, *Our Common Future* (the so-called Brundtland report), Oxford: Oxford University Press.

Wright, V. (ed.), 1994, *Privatization in Western Europe: Pressures, Problems and Paradoxes*, London: Pinter.

Yamawaki, H., L. Sleuwaegen and L.W. Weiss, 1989, 'Industry competition and the formation of the European common market', in: L.W. Weiss (ed.), *Concentration and Price*, London: MIT Press, pp. 112—43.

Zimmerman, L.J., 1952, *The Propensity to Monopolize*, Amsterdam: North-Holland.

Author Index

233

Subject Index